A Necessary Spectacle

A
Necessary Spectacle

BILLIE JEAN KING, BOBBY RIGGS,

and the Tennis Match That Leveled the Game

SELENA ROBERTS

 CROWN PUBLISHERS NEW YORK

Grateful acknowledgment is made to Hal Leonard Corporation for permission to reprint an excerpt from the song lyric "I Am Woman" words by Helen Reddy and music by Ray Burton. Copyright © 1971 by Irving Music, Inc., and Buggerlugs Music Co. Copyright renewed. All rights administered by Irving Music, Inc. All rights reserved. Reprinted by permission of Hal Leonard Corporation.

Published in the United States by Crown Publishers, an imprint of the Crown Publishing Group, a division of Random House, Inc., New York.
www.crownpublishing.com

Crown is a trademark and the Crown colophon is a registered trademark of Random House, Inc.

Library of Congress Cataloging-in-Publication Data
Roberts, Selena.
    A necessary spectacle : Billie Jean King, Bobby Riggs, and the tennis match that leveled the game / by Selena Roberts.
    1. King, Billie Jean.   2. Riggs, Bobby, 1918–1995.   3. Tennis players—United States—Biography.   4. Tennis—Tournaments—History—20th century.   5. Sports—Sex differences.   I. Title.
    GV994.A1R63   2005
    796.342'092'2—dc22   2005006408

ISBN 1-4000-5146-0

Printed in the United States of America

DESIGN BY BARBARA STURMAN

10 9 8 7 6 5 4 3 2 1

First Edition

BoT 25.00 8/05

To Laura and Frank, Kris and Eldon,

for being an incredible transition team

CONTENTS

A Necessary Spectacle

INTRODUCTION

On September 20, 1973, the Houston Astrodome was transformed into a decadent funhouse, with dancing pig mascots in the aisles, with celebrities preening in their best threads, and with Howard Cosell spit-shined in his black tux. He was on hand to announce the event the media had dubbed "The Battle of the Sexes." Cosell described every outrageous detail as tennis star Billie Jean King arrived atop an Egyptian litter to meet Bobby Riggs, a fifty-five-year-old huckster in horn-rimmed glasses and the caricature for America's resistance to feminism.

The duel between the "Libber" and the "Lobber" would become the most-watched, best-attended tennis match in history. Though it provided a grand diversion from America's Watergate fatigue and post-Vietnam disillusionment, the uproarious production cannot be dismissed as just another farcical romp amid the turbulent seventies. The very excess of that night in the Astrodome made the Battle of the Sexes an indelible turning point in history. Without the spectacle, few would have noticed Billie's transformation into Mother Freedom. Without the spotlight, the voice of an icon would never have been heard. Without Billie using the credibility of her celebrity to speak on nearly every pressing issue of our time, a social road map for generations of women might never have been created.

Billie grasped the bigger point before the match started that evening. She understood intuitively that change had to be witnessed to be believed. In front of 90 million viewers worldwide, with Bobby serving as feminism's perfect fall guy, Billie kicked perceptions in the hotpants. She waved her wood racket to dispel myths about women as mentally weak under pressure, physically frail when pushed, and emotionally delicate when stressed.

She did all that while giving a polarized women's movement exactly what it needed: a mainstream face. Resplendent in a sequined tennis dress, with a dashing husband by her side and an entertainer's sense of the moment, Billie provided a defining image of the girl-next-door in the Astrodome. While a nation struggled alongside Archie Bunker to make sense of racism and sexism, Billie brought clarity to the debate over gender equality by matching a strong body and a fresh face to the intellect of feminism.

Her eventual triumph resonated beyond the tennis court. Immediately after the Battle of the Sexes, Billie Jean King became the most famous name in America next to Richard Nixon. She was pals with Elton John and visited backstage with the ballet star Rudolph Nureyev. She appeared in commercials, did cameo appearances on sitcoms, and, not to be forgotten, competed as a marquee star on the women's tennis tour.

But the fame she dreamed of while growing up was all at once exhilarating and debilitating. Billie was a child of 1950s McCarthyism and the daughter of conservative parents. With the burden of women's progress on her back and the image of the wholesome freedom fighter to maintain, the great liberator lived in a personal prison.

She didn't dare reveal that she was gay. Billie couldn't risk undermining the power of her voice by disclosing the truth behind her marriage to Larry King. Instead, she engaged in the life her public expected her to lead while enduring the pain and shame of a secret lesbian existence. Years later, after an ex-lover's lawsuit cost her a fortune in lost endorsements, Billie would question whether the agony of her deception had been worth it.

Millions of women could have answered that for her. Billie's sacrifice changed everything. As an integral force for feminism, she had spent her fame wisely. Politicians listened to her when Title IX — a seemingly benign bill that President Nixon had signed in 1972 to open college opportunities for women — was threatened by the college football lords in 1974. Billie put her name on the line to save the law that would transform the landscape for women athletes. Without Title IX, little girls would not have grown up to play in front of packed houses at UConn basketball games. Without it, the sports lessons of self-esteem, camaraderie, and discipline would not have reached an entire generation of women. Without it, there would not have been a summer of 1999, when the women of the U.S. soccer team swept up a nation — and David Letterman — on an unforgettable joyride through the World Cup.

More important, without Title IX, boys would not have grown up playing next to girls in an atmosphere of increasing equality and respect.

Clearly, Billie didn't just happen upon social change; she plunged into it even before her match with Bobby, honing her skills as a provocateur inside tennis. The power of her conviction gained strength with every title she won in a career that would include twelve major singles championships. She used her status to decry the sport's "shamateurism" in the late 1960s, when amateurs like herself took money under the table because the tennis majors — the Australian Championship, the French Championship, the U.S. Championship, and Wimbledon — did not permit pro players to compete. The arrival of the tennis Open Era in 1968 gave her immense satisfaction because now professionals could finally play alongside amateurs in the majors. Unfortunately for the women pros, however, the money failed to reflect the new equality; they had to settle for prize-purse crumbs, compared with the monetary awards available to their male counterparts.

Billie could not accept that inequity. In 1970 she risked her career to lead a daring group of breakaway renegades against the tennis establishment. The Original Nine, as they became known, formed the Virginia Slims circuit with the help of tennis magazine mogul Gladys Heldman and Philip Morris executive Joe Cullman. Three years later, Billie again stood out front and unionized the players to form the Women's Tennis Association. She also continued to support the women's rights movement with more than just time and words; she put her prize money into action. In 1974, Billie founded the Women's Sports Foundation, establishing a caretaker and advocate for girls' athletics, a political force that would unveil its might when the George W. Bush administration tried to undercut Title IX in 2002.

In the middle of it all, along came Bobby. To the giddy delight of all those women who had celebrated after that night in the Astrodome by screaming out of windows, by demanding raises from their bosses, by handing the frying pan to their husbands, Billie trounced every last pig squeal of chauvinism. Suddenly she was America's latest "It" gal. But she did not attain that title by herself. Three unlikely allies played critical roles in transforming her into a near-mythic figure: Larry King, her husband of nearly thirty years; Bobby Riggs, her Battle of the Sexes opponent; and Margaret Court, Billie's longtime tennis rival.

Larry King entered Billie's life in the late sixties. He was the unflappable problem solver, handsome, smart, and socially progressive. Larry adored Billie for the challenges she presented. He guided his wife's evolution as a feminist and advocate; he also supplied cover for her clandestine lesbian affairs.

Margaret Court frustrated Billie on the court, and mystified her off it. Tennis was practically all these two women had in common. Feminists and feminism made Margaret bristle. The shy Aussie enjoyed her career, but considered herself a wife and mother first. Unlike Billie and the Original Nine, Margaret resisted breaking away from the men's tour.

She just couldn't see the point. Men had always helped Margaret to advance. She could never think of them as suppressors, as obstacles to equality.

Her profound naïveté would set the course for Billie's historic moment. In the spring of 1973, while she was still the world's top-ranked woman player, Margaret accepted a lucrative invitation for a match with Bobby Riggs. She was blissfully unaware of what lay ahead.

CHAPTER 1

The Mother's Day Massacre

Margaret Court followed the money down a desolate two-lane highway. About forty miles northeast of San Diego, the road known as Wildcat Canyon slithered past orange groves and a dusty Indian reservation, and through the shadows of the Cuyamaca Mountains. It was an uncomfortable stretch, so isolated that Mexican drug smugglers favored the route for their midnight drops.

Reaching the town of Ramona, California, Margaret found a luxury housing development still in the bulldozing stage. It was May 13, 1973. A tennis has-been named Bobby Riggs and a sure $10,000 were just forty-eight hours away.

Mother's Day.

All the five-foot-ten Aussie had to do was punch a few volleys past the geezer in telescopic glasses. All the mommy of the moment had to decide was where to ace the mouthy, wrinkled runt: down the middle or out wide.

It was going to be so easy. With her husband and infant son by her side, Margaret would walk onto a court surrounded by 3,200 fans in makeshift bleachers, impose her V-8 power strokes on Bobby, and exit this lizard's paradise with the winner-take-all payday, plus an extra $10,000 in television rights fees from CBS.

Margaret often described money as an evil, but even she had to admit that the dough was the inducement that brought her here, not Bobby's sexist prattle. She entered her match with Riggs as if it were an exhibition, rather than a serious competition against a skilled and cunning opponent. And she gave no thought to its social consequences. American women were tossing bras, girdles, and nylons into trash bins, but the women's movement didn't move Margaret. She was a Mrs., not a Ms.

"I found that a difficult time," Margaret recalls. "I always felt your gift made room for you. Whether you're a man or whether you're a woman, I didn't feel you had to go over the top."

No, Margaret was never one to go over the top. She was a benevolent bystander when Billie Jean King and eight other women risked their tennis careers in daring skirmishes for prize-money equality in 1970. She was a practicing pacifist when those women—known as the Original Nine—defied the male tennis establishment to form an autonomous circuit called the Virginia Slims.

Margaret just wasn't the defiant type. She was more introverted than her vociferous peers, someone who usually minimized her presence. Margaret would almost sneak onto the court with her head tilted down, her broad shoulders slightly slumped, and her body folded inward like flower petals at night. She didn't enjoy standing out or speaking up. Sometimes she could actually feel her skin heat and redden from the neck up during interviews. To her, a bank of microphones looked about as friendly as a gang of alien invaders.

Margaret preferred to be a noncombatant amid the gender mud-slinging of the early seventies, when rational feminism was often entwined with radical lesbianism. As a devout Christian who found moral clarity in the Scriptures, she was like many alienated onlookers who couldn't separate man-bashing militants from the messengers of equality.

While activists were wearing T-shirts that read, "A woman without a man is like a fish without a bicycle," Margaret retreated into the comfort of her marriage. The hoof steps of picketing marchers, the drumbeat of feminists, the glorious music of a cause engaged, it was white noise to Margaret. She couldn't understand what all the fuss was about. Everything had changed so much, so fast, while she was away. What had she walked back into?

She had fled from fame in 1966, retiring from tennis for two years, desperate to shed her label as the Aussie wonder girl who had won thirteen majors before her twenty-fifth birthday. She searched for a pocket of solitude on the fringes of the earth — otherwise known as Perth, Australia — moving from the densely populated east coast of the country to the only dot of civilization on the other side of the great Australian desert.

In Melbourne, Margaret was a tennis legend. In Perth, she was the tall young lady with short, neatly cropped hair who owned a boutique on a quiet street.

"Nobody knew me in Perth," Margaret recalls. "I could hide away."

Barry Court found Margaret adorably gentle. Knowing little about her former tennis career, he fell in love with her kind heart and earnest disposition. It wasn't until after they were married in 1967 that he discovered who his wife had been. One day in 1968, Margaret said to her husband, "You've never traveled overseas. You don't know my background of sport. How 'bout we go for one year?"

One year spilled into the next. She hadn't touched the throat of a racket in two years, but she slipped right back into her old competitive skin. She hadn't lost a thing. With muscles as strong as tree roots carved into her arms, with lean long legs and a lumberjack's approach to the ball, Margaret was more dominant than ever. She won all four majors to capture the elusive Grand Slam in 1970. None of those victories was more remarkable than her two-and-a-half-hour epic at Wimbledon. Just before her final against Billie Jean King, Margaret received two painkiller injections into her puffy ankle left blue from a ligament she tore in an earlier round match.

She was in obvious agony. But so was her opponent. Billie grimaced through the end of the match with leg cramps and cranky knees. Her left knee had been surgically repaired years earlier, and now her right knee was buckling, too.

Somehow each woman produced spectacular shots of will, but Margaret managed her pain well enough to take a 14–12, 11–9 final. The mesmerized crowd was thrilled, if mentally exhausted, after witnessing one of the great Wimbledon championships.

They also saw one incredible leg of Margaret's journey to becoming the first player to win a Grand Slam since Maureen Connolly in 1953. She sealed it with a U.S. Open title at Forest Hills two months later.

The Slam put Margaret back on top, back in the public eye, but she declined to indulge in the popular on-tour debates over male expendability, feeling too indebted to the men in her life to diminish them. They had lifted her, not belittled her. Barry traveled the world with Margaret. He shrugged off the teases from the blokes back home and never seemed threatened by her success. She was embraced by men, not marginalized by them. She didn't realize that few women of her time could join her in saying, "I was always the leader of the gang, you know. I had eight boys in the street and I was the cowboy and never the Indian. I never felt frustrated."

She had only felt acceptance. All her life, gentlemen had routinely opened doors for Margaret, at hours as early as 5:00 a.m. That's when she used to venture into a Melbourne gym after her morning jog, passing milkmen with strides that echoed on the lonely streets as she ran to lift weights. Bulking up was as ladylike as a beer belch in the early sixties, but as a fifteen-year-old tennis prodigy, Margaret was determined to convert her angular physique into a power structure.

"A woman didn't go to gyms, but I loved that side of it," Margaret remembers. "I loved working out."

Her coach, Australian tennis legend Frank Sedgman, and the gym attendants made that possible by establishing special rules for the only woman in the weight room. They installed a curtain in the shower area just for Margaret, and kept the gym closed to men until she was gone.

"They looked after me. They supported me."

They had saved her, too. Born July 16, 1942, in the railroad junction town of Albury, New South Wales, Margaret Smith grew up in a rented home where she could measure the financial burdens on her family by the amount of alcohol her father drank. He worked as head of the dessert unit at a local butter and cheese plant, bringing home pocket change for wages and a single perk: ice cream.

"I lived on ice cream in those early years. Then, for some years, I didn't eat ice cream at all."

The Smiths didn't own a car or a television. They grew their own vegetables. With four siblings and only one bedroom, Margaret and her sister slept on the front porch, with thatched blinds pulled down from the beams to keep out the moonlight and most of the insects. In the morning, when those blinds lifted, Margaret could see inspiration across the road: twenty-four grass tennis courts that stretched out like magic carpets. Years later she would muse, "I've always wondered what would have happened if those courts hadn't been there."

Those courts became her escape. As a child, Margaret and a handful of mischievous boys routinely wiggled through a hole beneath the tennis club's fence to swipe grass-stained balls that were as flat and soggy as overripe tomatoes. They bashed them to bits, playing their own brand of tennis in the roadway, with makeshift rackets. Margaret whacked away with a thin board the length and breadth of a boat's oar.

At age eight, she got lucky. Her parents couldn't afford to buy her a real racket, but a friend of her mother's saw how gamely Margaret flailed away at a ball suspended from a string tied to a backyard tree. Next time the lady visited, she handed Margaret a dilapidated antique racket with a square head, broken strings, and no grip. It was thick, unwieldy, and perfect. Beautiful, Margaret thought.

She won her first tournament with that relic. Soon enough, she had Wal Rutter, the grumpy pro at the tennis club, turning his back while she crawled like an inchworm through the hole under the fence to practice on the most remote court, the one hidden from view by a hedge. Rutter never filled in that hole. It would become a tunnel to Margaret's new life.

She bloomed on grass, rising so fast in the local junior ranks that Sedgman whisked her away from Albury, offering her a job as a typist and a future as a player. At fifteen, she was bound for Melbourne to become a gender bender of her own design: a woman with uncommon muscle but traditional values.

In 1973, Margaret joined the successful Virginia Slims circuit, but she didn't follow Billie Jean King's formula for promotion. She didn't go door-to-door to schmooze with sponsors, or stand in traffic to hand free tickets to motorists. She didn't sign autographs at shopping centers or rise at 5:00 a.m. for interviews on every ten-watt radio station known to man.

"The other women thought I never sold myself enough," Margaret says. "I wasn't a sponsor's dream."

But she was an opponent's nightmare. Margaret swooped down and plucked up more titles than any woman in history. But she was also an unassuming wife who was happy to take career breaks for childbirth. After the first of her three children arrived in 1972, Margaret sat on the sidelines for nearly a year. She returned to the tennis mix in 1973, starting off the season with an Australian Open title.

Her priorities were family, tennis, and, especially, God, after a spiritual rebirth in the spring of 1972. Sitting in an ornate Catholic church in France, listening to Latin verses she did not understand, Margaret cried out, "If you're really real, where are you?" Weeks later, she and Barry traveled to Cincinnati for a tour event and stayed in the residence of a local family. Each day, the lady of the house handed Margaret a book on spiritual guidance.

"I think she's become a religious nut," Margaret told Barry.

She tossed the books into the rubbish — except for one: *Accepting Christ as Savior*. Margaret paid it little mind, but between tournaments she began attending religious meetings with friends who were born-again Christians. Verse by verse, she evolved into one herself.

Religion simplified Margaret's world. It eliminated political nuance and its complexities, which was perhaps one reason she never saw the social tentacles attached to the mouth of Bobby Riggs. To her, Bobby was a harmless huckster with an outdated game and a chauvinist's shtick, a threat to be taken as seriously as a haunted house. His fangs were false; his hair was dyed; his best days were cobwebbed.

"She didn't get it," Billie says. "She just didn't get it."

Bobby reveled in the perception of himself as a living, breathing punchline of the senior circuit, but there was a message in his act. In the early seventies he began speaking out against the shortchanging of senior players. He demanded more prize money for aging ex-champions like himself, while mocking Billie Jean King's own crusade for equal pay. Bobby was tired of women yakking about their independent value. He shared his stance on old-man privilege with anyone who would listen: If women are raking it in, what about us?

Bobby felt sure that any graying champ could knock the high heels off any woman anywhere. He exuded the confidence of a quizmaster, a man with all the answers, a man especially positive about one thing: A victory over a woman would mean much more than a cash infusion for the over-the-hill gang. It would mean a second lap with fame for Riggs himself.

"It was a way to come back," his son Reverend John W. Riggs explains. "He wanted to be important again."

It had been thirty years since Bobby Riggs lost his place among America's household names. In between the mighty Don Budge and the dashing Jack Kramer, there had been the sprite-sized Riggs, a player who survived against giants by exploiting their human weaknesses. He plotted his way to the Wimbledon men's singles title in 1939, and the instant attention he gained was delightfully dizzying, a feeling he never thought he'd recapture. Then came the spring of '73.

To be surrounded like a bonfire again, to be seated at the best table in the house — it all made for an intoxicating range of possibilities. But he couldn't realize any of them unless he made the match a reality. So Bobby did what came naturally for him — he put money on it. Armed with a $5,000 carrot, he sent out telegrams challenging his wish list of opponents: Billie Jean King, Chris Evert, and Margaret Smith Court.

Billie was the one he wanted, the one who really mattered. "The sex leader of the revolutionary pack," he tagged her. That was typical Riggs, a lob over the net that was meant to tease, to frustrate. To goad. Billie just let it skip out of bounds. "There was nothing in it for women's tennis," Billie says. "I kept saying, 'No, Bobby, no.'"

Margaret couldn't resist the bait. At first, hardly anyone knew that she had accepted Bobby's invitation. Then she and Billie shared a ride in an elevator at the Virginia Slims in Detroit.

"I'm going to play Bobby Riggs," Margaret mentioned as they inched down the shaft.

"What?"

"I'm getting ten thousand dollars."

"That's not enough," Billie countered, "and besides, this is not about tennis."

"What do you mean? I'm about to get ten thousand dollars."

"Margaret, I'm just going to ask one thing of you: You have to win this match."

Margaret nodded politely. Too politely.

"No, I mean it. You have to win this match. You have no idea how important this is."

Billie understood what Margaret couldn't grasp: With critics starting to assail Title IX, with companies still treating working women as credit liabilities and maternity risks, with the credibility of feminists on the line, the consequences of a loss to Bobby could be dire. However, as Billie would later point out, "Margaret didn't see the big picture."

They stepped out of the elevator and headed toward a desk that provided transportation for players to the local hotels. Before they separated, Billie turned and made her appeal one more time.

"Margaret, please win."

A large, malleable national television audience was expected to watch Margaret's match against Bobby. Billie knew this was no time for a woman to fall apart. The problem was, several early-round losses in the late sixties had earned Margaret a reputation for emotional fragility. By her own admission, she had bought into her headlining frailties until she found Christ.

"I reckon I probably would have won a lot more than what I did if I'd known how powerful the Scriptures are," Margaret explains. "I believe probably where there were some insecurities in my life, or fear of different things in my life, I wouldn't have had it if I'd known the power of the thinking mind. I mean, people go to psychologists and all sorts of people today, but it's all in the Bible."

Her religious conversion hadn't fully evolved by 1973. Heaven couldn't help her. Whether it was justified or not, nearly every player on the tour thought of Margaret as someone who collapsed under pressure — a choker.

"Our reputation is at stake, and I'm afraid Bobby will win," Billie told the press days before the match. "Here is an old jerk who dyes his hair, waddles like a duck and has trouble seeing. We have nothing to gain."

Billie had reason to be wary. She was familiar with the puckish, if not outright devilish, interior hidden behind Bobby's ham-handed persona. Born twenty-six years after Riggs, reared just a few miles from his public park haunts in Los Angeles, Billie had heard the folk tales of his crafty tactics and unquenchable taste for action. She knew he was a great competitor, an esteemed former Wimbledon champion, and an ace pool-hall hustler disguised in tennis whites.

"I just thought, here is a man who has quite a big mouth," Margaret recalls.

You almost couldn't blame Margaret. She'd never been manipulated by a man. But then she'd never met a man quite like Bobby Riggs.

Bobby would never have closed off a gym so that young Margaret could work out free from macho taunts and X-ray eyes. He wasn't in tune with women and politics.

"He was a middle-aged divorced man who knew nothing about women's liberation," John Riggs recalls. "He was rather simple-minded when it came to politics and world issues."

Bobby didn't know Gloria Steinem from a go-go girl, or Bella Abzug from a belle at the ball. But one day he opened his chops and out came a line that prompted a few giggles, and whetted his appetite for attention:

"C'mon, Billie. Let's play for some money."

Although the press took up his challenge, the players largely ig-nored Bobby—until Margaret Court said, "Yes." Privately she was an-noyed that Billie had been Bobby's target when it was Margaret who had the best record on the tour.

"I've beaten better men than Bobby in practice matches," Court announced to reporters. Hardly the taunting type, she played the good sport and went along with Bobby's schemes to hype the event. Initially, the match in the desert was, as Margaret assumed, only a publicity stunt. The out-of-the-way site was chosen because Bobby's sidekick in setting the scene—Tony Trabert—was the new tennis director at San Diego Country Estates. Any attention the match brought to the venue would put the development on the map. Bobby orchestrated a press conference in March to announce his plans to play Margaret on Mother's Day. The media lapped up the loudmouth.

"Call it the Match of the Century," Bobby spouted.

It was hyperbole with a purpose. Bobby was already applying pressure on Margaret's suspect nerves. He had too much respect for her skills not to pull every ploy he could manufacture in order to win. This was Bobby's moment, and he didn't want to squander it by taking Margaret lightly. He worked out relentlessly. Ziplocking himself in his sweats, Bobby ran at least a mile a day around a school track near his Newport Beach digs.

Training by itself, though, couldn't push back the clock fast or far enough to suit Bobby. He needed a youth potion. At fifty-five, he sought out Rheo Blair, Hollywood's top nutritional guru. Blair was the vitamin czar who had put the bubble back into Lawrence Welk, and spread an extra layer of sheen on the shine of the hardworking Liberace. Under Blair's supervision, Bobby adopted a diet of protein, dairy products, and 415 vitamins a day. NO BOOZE, NO BROADS, VOWS BOBBY, the head-lines read. He had to be strong—not just to hold the banner for seniors everywhere—but to put himself in the best position to cash in on the endorsement opportunities that were bound to pour in after his win.

Bobby's son Larry accompanied him throughout the training. Larry Riggs was a successful California stockbroker in the making, and the only one of Bobby's children who had excelled as a tennis player — even if modestly in comparison to his dad. Of all the kids, Larry was the closest to his father, the one most like Bobby — outgoing, bold, and savvy. He was the caretaker of his dad's legacy. Larry teamed with Bobby's best friend, Lornie Kuhle, to oversee his father's diligent preparation for the match with Margaret.

"For three or four months, we're talking running every day, playing six hours of tennis a day," Larry says. "Train, train, train. He was playing the best tennis of his life."

Bobby's base of operation was the Park Newport condo complex, where he was the tennis director of a swinging-singles California enclave for the Geritol set. In his bachelor pad, Bobby would relax on a black Naugahyde couch, surrounded by albums and scrapbooks, the hermetically sealed containers of his tennis glory. Outside of his door, the complex contained everything a man could ask for: a liquor store, a dry cleaner, a pastry breakfast at the club, and a choice of seven pools to plunge into on a hot California day.

He allowed the press frequent peeks at his lifestyle. To promote his match with Margaret, Bobby all but ran an open house. He worked the room day and night and never forgot to bring the odd prop, like his favorite T-shirt. Across its front ran the acronym WORMS — World Organization for the Retention of Male Supremacy.

"I think I can be as big as Mark Spitz," Bobby predicted. "I drink milk, too."

He was always full of philosophical prose, which he doled out to the media by the ladle.

"I can pitch anything . . . How about Bobby Riggs senior citizen support stockings?"

"Margaret is an even-money bet. She plays like a man, I play like a woman."

"Women who can, do. Those who can't, become feminists."

Bobby's colorful comments had reach. From tennis diehards to the man on the street, they all pounced on every outrageous sentence the flimflam man uttered. He displayed impeccable timing, and not just for comedy. In the 1970s, few sports celebrities outside of Muhammad Ali carried the pop-culture weight of tennis players. In supermarkets, women wore name-brand tennis skirts, not because they were headed to a court, but because they represented a runway fashion statement. In sporting goods stores, popular demand kept tennis rackets, balls, and shoes continually out of stock. Tennis sizzled, and Bobby was its latest walking, ever talking marquee attraction.

Wherever Bobby went, the media plundered his thoughts on the upcoming match. He had succeeded in capturing the nation's attention. Now all he had to do was win. Bobby scouted Margaret closely, taking copious notes on her style while following her around the Virginia Slims circuit. Then he candidly laid out his plan for beating her: serve her the soft stuff, throw off her power with spins, upset her rhythm with dropshots, wear down her patience with lobs.

From Lubbock to Las Vegas, the more Bobby chattered, the more folks he convinced. Jimmy the Greek, the oddsmaker of the moment, put Riggs the favorite over Court at 5–2. But the more Bobby talked up his tactics, the more pressure he felt. For months Margaret had taken Bobby's challenge casually, laughing off his jibes and quips as she continued to win on the Virginia Slims tour.

"I am not carrying the banner for women's lib," she declared.

Her indifference to the hype befuddled Bobby. Why wasn't Margaret reacting? Wasn't she worried? Then Margaret took off the week before the match to practice with her part-time coach, Dennis Van der Meer, who just happened to be Billie Jean King's coach, too.

Special workouts with Van der Meer . . . hmmm . . . she was feeling the pinch, Bobby thought. Perfect.

Two days before the match, Margaret, Barry, and their fourteen-month-old son, Danny, made the journey through the gaunt wilderness to San Diego Country Estates.

"With all the shouting and all the showbiz," Margaret says, "I guess I was shocked."

She had barely fought through the swarm of photographers that greeted her when Bobby began trying his best to crack her cool. "Do you realize, Margaret," Bobby chimed above the fray, "that this is the most important match ever played? Just think how many women are counting on you."

"Get off it, luv."

Sick of his jabbering, Margaret made a beeline for her room. She and her family were staying at the newly completed San Vicente Club along with the press. And Bobby.

Bobby's and Margaret's suites stood only a few yards apart. Late one night, after another evening of nonstop talking, Bobby stumbled through the door to his room. There, in the middle of the floor, he found Margaret playing with her night-owl son.

Wrong door.

Oops, sorry to bother you, big mistake, feel terrible. Bobby gushed every clumsy apology as he scrambled out. It was an accident, he claimed. But once word of the incident surfaced in the club dining room, many assumed the mastermind-gamer was up to his usual brinksmanship, trying out another ploy to unnerve his opponent.

Margaret, though, appeared unruffled by whatever Bobby cooked up. She treated her opponent cordially, for the most part, and even seemed to find him amusing. She got into the spirit of the event by sticking a popular button on Danny's bib: "Women's libbers speak for themselves . . . Bobby Riggs — Bleah!"

The night before the match, everyone convened in the dining area for one last supper, as Bobby called it. In a corner, encircled by reporters and well-wishers, Bobby fed off the attention, talking in his squeaky voice at the speed of an auctioneer. Surely the coyotes could hear him.

"The eyes and ears of the world are on me," Riggs howled. "I am the greatest money player in history."

The Court family dined quietly, alone on the other side of the room, removed from the carnival barker in their midst. During dinner, Danny turned his high chair into a snare drum, banging his spoon to his own beat. The rapping was so loud, so unrestrained, and so obnoxious that Margaret couldn't help but note, "You make more noise than Bobby Riggs."

There it was. Bobby was inside Margaret's head. Just where he wanted to be.

The next morning, hundreds of fans awoke early for the long drive toward intrigue. By 9:00 a.m., the hearty curiosity-seekers were camped outside the gate of the Erector-set stadium in the middle of nowhere, an arena hastily assembled for the afternoon matinee on CBS.

In his hotel suite, Bobby chatted with his nineteen-year-old daughter, Dolly, who had flown in from Florida a few days earlier for her pop's big day. "If you weren't my father," she told him, "I'd be rooting for Margaret Court."

Mother's Day morning started off inauspiciously in Margaret's suite. As soon as his parents' backs were turned, Danny had dumped his mom's only pair of tennis shoes into the toilet.

"It was the beginning of an interesting time," Margaret says.

At least her prized dress was dry. Margaret may not have possessed keen political instincts, but she did have fashion sense. For the first time in her career, she would dare to appear on-court in an outfit that wasn't strictly white. At her request, dress designer extraordinaire Ted Tinling had added some zing to her normally conservative style. He had whipped up a pastel dress trimmed in the Aussie national colors of green and gold. Margaret's name was embroidered on each side of her collar as if to introduce her at a parent-teacher conference. This counted as a bold display for her. A woman who usually sought invisibility, she was all but wearing a vanity plate.

Margaret was an unmistakable vision when she walked out on court. She loped to the net to greet Bobby before the match, towering over him as if they were dates at an eighth-grade dance. Instead of a corsage, Bobby handed her a dozen roses as they met in front of CBS commentator Pat Summerall.

"For the nicest mother in tennis," Bobby said, grinning. "Happy Mother's Day."

Nasty little man, she thought. But to the world, Margaret did not seem the least bit offended. She curtsied in front of the cameras, almost blushing submissively. All week, tales of how she had dismantled Tony Trabert's power in practice had circled the grounds. But that, Bobby believed, was the wrong preparation. She should have been practicing against a beginner.

His strategy worked, right from the start. Bobby immediately rendered the circuit's most dominating female force into a weekend hacker by dinking his serves, punching drop shots, and lobbing the ball into the afternoon sun. During the second game of the match, on a strategically placed moon ball, Margaret cracked an overhead into the net to fall behind love–30. Flummoxed in the face of Bobby's underwhelming attack, her confidence evaporated as the pressure on her built.

She was tumbling into Bobby's trap. He had made a career out of waiting for an opponent's mistake, a strategy he had learned from his first coach, a woman who continually reminded him, "Placement, Bobby, it's about placement." Connecting on just eighteen of thirty-seven first serves, and reduced to lolling through her ferocious forehand, Court's collapse happened at flashbulb speed.

Billie Jean King had nearly missed the match entirely. After stepping off a plane on a layover between Tokyo and L.A., Billie, her secretary Marilyn Barnett, and fellow tennis star Rosie Casals raced through the terminal, frantically looking for one of those coin-operated TV sets attached to the chairs in the waiting areas.

At last they found a vacant one. The women pumped quarters into the slot and flipped through the channels on the black-and-white tube. Nothing but *Gunsmoke* reruns. Finally they heard the result on Rosie's radio. In just fifty-seven minutes, Bobby had dismantled Margaret's ballyhooed power to hand her a humbling 6–2, 6–1 defeat.

Billie was beside herself. She knew Margaret's loss would not only be used to undermine the fight for equal pay on the tour, it would also provide an easy caricature for political cartoonists. She marched through the terminal, incensed and motivated. "That's it," she thought. "I've got to play him." Billie phoned her husband and told him, "Larry, now we've got something to prove."

On TV, the nation saw Bobby hop the net to embrace Margaret after a match that tennis devotees still remember as the Mother's Day Massacre. Inside, Bobby felt sympathy for his opponent. To have lost so badly, and on Mother's Day, yet. It didn't seem quite right. He had wanted a tougher fight. He had wanted a longer match. To be frank, he had wanted more television airtime.

Still unsure what had just happened to her, a bewildered Margaret accepted Bobby's hug. She looked on as John Wayne, the ultimate man's man, swaggered forward and handed Bobby checks totaling $10,000. Riggs would receive a few grand more from CBS, and who knew how much in bets he had made on himself. Margaret left with her TV guarantee of $10,000, and her pride in tatters.

After the match, she explained to the press, "I didn't expect him to mix it up like that. We girls don't play like that." The response confused Bobby. Hadn't Margaret been listening? He had blabbed his strategy to confound her with powder-puff tennis to anyone with a microphone.

"It went exactly as I thought," Bobby sung. "The whole thing was pressure."

Court's defeat was a blow to women, a tool to dismantle their crusade for validity. Bobby's instinct for timing kicked in instantly. In front of the post-match press, in an emboldened mood, he voiced his favorite male fantasy.

"Now I want King bad. I'll play her on clay, grass, wood, cement, marble, or roller skates," he declared. "We got to keep this sex thing going. I'm a woman specialist now."

He behaved as if obsessed with King. During interviews, Bobby flapped his lips again and again to issue yet another challenge to Billie: "I want her, she's the Women's Libber leader." By then, Margaret was planning her getaway, ready to take off for the French Open in Paris. But she already knew the loss to Bobby would haunt her for the rest of her life.

"It was Little Red Riding Hood walking in a poolroom to test Wolf Bobby at eight-ball," the *Boston Globe*'s Bud Collins cleverly assessed.

"It was one of my mistakes," Margaret says wistfully today.

Far too late, Margaret had recognized the magnitude of her match with Bobby. This hadn't been a tennis event, but a human saga; this hadn't been a casual Sunday hit, but a political proving ground for gender. Billie would have Margaret's political ignorance to thank for spinning her destiny into motion. In essence, Margaret was a matchmaker. Bobby had been waiting for a gal like Billie all of his life.

CHAPTER 2
Ladies' Man

Bobby Riggs always entered a room as if barging through saloon doors. He'd step foot in a place, let all eyes fall on him, and create a stir no one could ignore. Indifference crushed him. After putting poor ole Margaret Court back into her apron with his Mother's Day Massacre, Bobby happily hopped in front of every microphone in the land, eager to become America's talk-show guest.

He was in particular demand after an appearance on *The Tonight Show* in June 1973. Johnny Carson was off that evening, leaving the bombastic Don Rickles as guest host. Balding, blunt, and beloved, Rickles had a reputation for using clever insults to draw a hoot out of the crowd. But on Bobby's visit, Rickles lagged behind his guest, unable to outwit the stage hog in the chair next to him. Bobby was a riot, and he took every laugh as a sign of validation. Riggs longed to be loved, an innate neediness that his family had nurtured from the start.

On February 25, 1918, Robert Larimore Riggs came into the world in last place — the sixth and final child of the Reverend Gideon Riggs.

Half blind from cataracts, and beholden to his vision of the Lord, Gideon was a fundamentalist minister in the Church of Christ.

"I think my dad was a typical P.K. — preacher's kid — who ended up a benevolent universalist about religion," Bobby's son John explains. "He didn't take the Bible literally and thought God was about living with good character, treating people well. But he grew up with a very conservative dad in the house."

Inside their family's rambling house in the heart of L.A.'s middle-class Lincoln Heights, Gideon's sons never touched a bottle of booze or a deck of cards, never heard a curse word or a music note, never saw anyone dance or smoke. The devil's work took place in a backyard tool shack. There the boys played poker and cooked up bets in the neighborhood's unofficial headquarters of mischief. As the youngest by seven years, Bobby became his brothers' chosen ringer.

He was only four when the boys placed him in a foot race with a neighborhood kid. The Riggs brothers pointed to little Bobby's matchstick legs and demanded a handicap for the pint-sized competitor: a head start of a few yards. Bobby and his rival took their places. On your mark . . . get set . . . wait! . . . In the ear of their tiny sibling, one of Bobby's brothers delivered an incentive leavened with threat: "If you beat him, we'll take you to the ballgame today. If you lose, you'll get a kick in the ass."

Bobby scooted to victory like a windup toy off a turn of the key. The rush from earning a reward thrilled him. Soon he was hooked, a hard-core competition junkie. He loved the adrenaline rush of action, of placing a consequence on every outcome, of dismantling psyches. Gideon Riggs had been taught to pray to God for divine guidance. His son learned to prey on opponents and their aversion to pressure. With Bobby, there was never a game without a mind game. This grade-school shark pitched pennies to marked lines, played blackjack for nickels, and fanned poker hands in public parks. During the Depression, when nickels and dimes were the currency of dreams, he won entire piggybanks.

One day the twelve-year-old Bobby tagged along after his brother John to the municipal park. From a short distance he watched John smack a few balls around a tennis court. John displayed only decent form, but it was the game that immediately intrigued Bobby. He decided to give it a whack.

He borrowed a racket from a buddy and padded onto the court in his bare feet. Bobby didn't lope at the balls bounding his way, he lunged at them. He looked awkward and amateurish, but his unsteady, coltish steps attracted the eye of an interested spectator seated off to the side. Dr. Esther Bartosh was an anatomy instructor at the University of Southern California. She also happened to be the third-ranked women's tennis player in Los Angeles. Beneath the clutter of Bobby's flails and follies, the doctor saw what amounted to a lost Monet in a garage sale. On the spot, she offered to teach Bobby the game of tennis.

"Esther was a brilliant woman," recalls Gene Mako, Bobby's childhood friend and former tennis rival. "Few people know that she graduated from medical school when she was nineteen. They didn't want to give her a license because she was too young."

Good fortune had a way of finding Bobby Riggs; this time it caught him empty-handed. Bobby didn't own a racket. But he did own a bag of marbles and a trained eye for spotting a pigeon. It took only a week to find a plump bird. Clack by clack, Bobby won the last rock-hard ruble from his classmate Jimmy. Then a pivotal negotiation ensued.

"Bobby, my sister has a racket she never uses. How about me trading her racket for the marbles you just won?"

"Jimmy, you got a deal."

It was all set. A woman was about to mold Bobby Riggs into a champion. Dr. Bartosh would become the greatest influence of his life. She taught Bobby to treat the court as a dartboard, to use pinpricks over power. *Placement, Bobby, placement*, she kept reminding him. She also taught him to be a perfectionist.

"Tennis matches are won on mistakes," Bartosh told Bobby. "Let the other fellow hit the ball too hard. Let the other fellow hit the ball into the net. Let the other fellow make the mistakes. It's not how hard you hit the ball, but *where* you hit it."

She devoted hours to his instruction. Esther had married before settling in Los Angeles, but she had no child of her own. Bobby filled that role just fine.

"She loved Bobby," Mako says. "She would do anything for him. She even paid his way many times."

Three months after he started working with Dr. Bartosh, Bobby applied her formula of consistency and plucky patience in his first event. He landed in the boys' finals of a local tournament. The savvy sprite from Lincoln Heights was improving by leaps. Not everyone was impressed, though. Unmoved by the uncouth street stray on the rise, the imperial Perry T. Jones began making it his life's work to undermine Bobby Riggs.

As the longtime president of the Southern California Association, Jones selected or rejected rising talents from his posh office at the Los Angeles Tennis Club. He hand-stamped the sport's latest stars, deciding who received funds for travel, who deserved to play in national tournaments, and who was worthy of the association's special attention.

Jones preferred tall, strapping purebred prodigies, the types who called their Beverly Hills mothers "Mumsy," and lounged poolside at their Bel-Air mansions. He craved dashing, not dumpy.

"Riggs is too short," Jones growled when the subject of Bobby Riggs surfaced one day. "He doesn't hit the ball hard enough, isn't tall enough to develop a powerful serve, and will never have the reach to play a good net game."

Bobby was far from Hollywoodesque in stature — unless your version of a movie star was more Mickey Rooney than Clark Gable. He even resembled Judy Garland's sidekick, particularly in the forehead, eyes, and mouth. With his undersized frame, Bobby would never unfurl a wingspan at the net. He wouldn't have the power to blast a smoking forehand that left a vapor trail. And if you believed Perry T. Jones, Bobby wouldn't have much of a career at all.

Jones's brutal assessment of Bobby's shortcomings amused and challenged the competitive Dr. Bartosh. She would show Jones and his cast of snooty doubters. She would push Bobby harder. She believed the kid could go places.

If he could just find a way to get there.

Transportation was always an issue whenever Bobby had to travel far to events. The preacher's son couldn't afford the price of a bus ticket. Thumbing a ride, however, came cheap. When he was fourteen, Bobby hitchhiked with his brother John to Berkeley, California. Their father had arranged room and board for his two sons at a local Church of Christ. Gideon Riggs didn't fancy Bobby's tennis ambitions at first, but this was a small sign of his tacit approval. The Riggs boys had barely enough pocket change to stay around long enough for the finals. Bobby left town the next day with the California Boys State Championship.

He needed a greater challenge, though, one on a national scale. A year later his travels took him all the way to Culver, Indiana, for the National Boys Championship. Hitchhiking was out this time. Too inefficient. So Dr. Bartosh loaded Bobby in her Ford for a dusty cross-country trip that was not without its educational value. The trained instructor who knew every bone in a teen's leaden foot taught Bobby how to drive. Somehow they rolled into Culver in one piece.

Confident and calm, Bobby methodically advanced through the nationals, reaching the semifinals before losing. The unexpected blow left Bobby crestfallen. He gathered his belongings, left the court, and felt a rush of emotion. He turned his face into a corner to keep from crying — a reaction his coach would not tolerate.

"The first thing you've got to learn is to be a good loser as well as a good winner," she chided. "When you lose, you've got to smile and congratulate your opponent. That's just good manners."

Her message came with an adhesive. He would practice athletic etiquette throughout the rest of his career, no matter how humiliating the loss, no matter how big the stage. Sure, he might gloat before a match out of showmanship, but never afterward. For one thing, Bobby's heart wasn't made of stone. He never meant to crush an opponent's spirit. He simply loved a good match and a juicy challenge.

In 1935 his goal was Wimbledon, the reward dangled out for the winner of the National Boys Junior Title. A year earlier, at sixteen, Bobby had envisioned himself racing over the lawn inside the cozy Center

Court, using his racket as a divining rod to uncover winners and wowing the King and Queen on their perch in the Royal Box.

He could see it vividly, shot by incredible shot. There he was, racing to the right side of the court, swiping a forehand that kicked up the white chalk as it splashed down on the sideline. There he was again, unleashing an equally sensational shot that left the Brits dropping their crumpets on match point. Now jump the net, swim in the applause, feel the adoration of the King and Queen.

Nothing to it.

As he prepared himself for the boys' nationals, Bobby could almost feel the Wimbledon grass between his toes. He was scheduled to meet longtime rival Joe Hunt in the National Boys Junior Title finals. Hunt exemplified Perry Jones's kind of champion, a stalwart blond, with a wealthy family and Hollywood presence. But it was Riggs who was the last man standing tall when the match ended. Bobby vanquished Hunt and started working on his bows for when he met the King and Queen.

Then, out of nowhere, the offer for Wimbledon was revoked. Perry Jones again. Jones, and the rest of the tennis gods, were all in favor of allowing the junior champion to compete at Wimbledon. Unless his name was Bobby Riggs. They dismissed his talent, his accomplishment. Their decision left Bobby bereft, but he also gained a new perspective of himself: the athlete as a walking contradiction, a winner and an underdog both at the same time. To chase down his Wimbledon visions along the baseline, to plant dream shots on white chalk that lined green grass, Bobby realized that he would have to manufacture his own destiny.

He had a strategy to bypass the snobbery. A plan to circumvent the conceit. Bobby couldn't pull it off, though, without a sponsor to bankroll him.

Jack Del Valle drove into Bobby's life aboard a chrome-touched Cadillac, complete with white-wall tires. As a party-hopper at the Los Angeles Tennis Club, Del Valle was smitten with the company of celebrity, ubiquitous at every bash.

He was also an enigma.

Del Valle was a self-proclaimed manager of prizefighters, though there seemed to be no proof of it. For LATC members, the source of Del Valle's wealth was anyone's guess.

"He was an odd character," Jack Kramer, a legendary player and LATC fixture, recalls. "He hung around a lot, but no one could tell you too much about him."

Bobby knew this much: Jack shared his love of tennis and gambling. Del Valle became an investor in the ascendant tennis star, a willing accomplice to the Riggs hustle.

Amateur status to Riggs was just a polite way of saying, "Psst, pay me later." Bobby and his doubles partner Wayne Sabin barnstormed the country with Jack, cruising from town to town in high style. They rollicked through Kansas City and Chicago, more often than not screeching away on those Cadillac wheels as winners. Riggs and Sabin became a main attraction everywhere they traveled. Whenever Bobby was on the court — be it singles or doubles — Jack was in the stands, sniffing for bettors.

Bobby's following spread as quickly as gossip. Tournament directors started bidding for him to appear at their events. The payoffs violated every code of amateur ethics, but it was how the top players did business. And Bobby always did better business than most. Playing the sport's antihero earned him some colorful supporters, including Edmund C. Lynch, of Merrill Lynch, and L. B. Icely, of Wilson Sporting Goods.

Bobby sailed on Lynch's yacht, slept in its plush quarters, and spent the rich man's money. But Bobby's most inventive detour around the rules came with Icely in the driver's seat. In order to make their relationship legit in the eyes of the United States Lawn Tennis Association, Icely arranged a job for Bobby with the U.S. Advertising Corporation, the same organization that handled Wilson's business.

At $200 a week, Bobby was officially listed as part of the creative think tank in charge of the Red Heart dog food account. Bobby Riggs, kibble strategist. When the USLTA didn't buy it, Icely conjured another, far more believable, brainstorm. He arranged Bobby's transfer to a small college outside of Chicago, where Riggs toiled in the PR department and coached tennis while staying focused on his latest rival, Don Budge.

Tall, slender, and rangy, John Donald Budge was a redheaded wrecking crew who dismayed and dismantled opponents with booming backhands and blistering serves. Budge's fundamentals were considered so sound, instructors pointed to him as the model for the ideal player. Said one opponent, "Playing against him was like playing against a concrete wall. There was nothing to attack."

In 1938, Budge became the first player to capture the Grand Slam of tennis by winning the championships of France, Australia, the United States, and Wimbledon. He lost only five sets in the four tournaments. From 1937 to 1938, Budge won an astounding ninety-two consecutive matches over fourteen tournaments. It was a record that intimidated most opponents. But it didn't faze Bobby. He couldn't wait to match his finesse against Budge's force.

What a life Bobby was enjoying in the late 1930s. He dated Kay Fischer, a beautiful girl from Chicago, prowled the Lake Michigan shoreline in a convertible, and entered Wimbledon as the top seed in 1939. Bobby walked on puffy clouds through the gates of Wimbledon, sure of his invincibility. How confident was he? Before the matches began, Bobby and his British friend John Olliff approached a British bookmaker.

"What are the odds on Riggs to win the men's singles?" Bobby asked.

"Three to one," the bookmaker told him.

"And what are the odds that he'll win the men's doubles?"

"Six to one."

"Well, if I get lucky and win the singles and the doubles," Bobby pondered out loud, "I might as well put it all on the mixed doubles and go for the hat trick."

And with that, Bobby, as cool as the English mist, handed $500 to the astonished bookie: $500 when the average American wage was $1,230 a year, when a nice home cost under $1,000, when the world was on the verge of war.

"You're out of your mind," Olliff shouted at Bobby. "I've met a lot of cocky kids, but you take the cake. Nobody has ever won all three Wimbledon events on the first try."

Over the next two weeks, Bobby played with the energy of a Rockette. Fed by the adrenaline of a $500 risk, he glided across the lush Wimbledon grounds on skill and incentive. Winners kicked up chalk dust, backhands left pockmarks in the corners, just as he had envisioned. After all three titles were in hand, after drinking in the adulation of British royalty, after finishing off an unimaginable feat, Bobby paid a visit to a certain bewildered bookmaker.

Hand it over, Bobby told him. He had parlayed his foolhardy investment into a $108,000 profit.

Only twenty-one at the time, he stashed the loot in a London vault to avoid detection by the IRS or, worse, the USLTA. Bobby's newly acquired wealth bought him some of the material pleasures he craved, but the money could not purchase political worldliness. He seemed detached from the looming darkness outside his rollicking tennis world.

On Sept 1, 1939, Germany invaded Poland. A day later, France and Great Britain declared war on Germany. Bobby watched from afar as the Battle of Britain broiled an ocean away. World War II had started, and every American was following the events in Europe. Including Bobby. They had their reasons. He had his.

"I had my own special reasons — 108,000 of them — for wanting to see Hitler lose the war," Bobby wrote years later. "I sweated out the Battle of Britain from a distance, and nobody rooted harder than I did for the RAF to halt the German invasion of England."

The world was at war. Stark images of Hitler dominated the news coverage, but Bobby didn't let the depressing atmosphere infiltrate the high he was on as he careened into the latter end of 1939. He married Kay Fischer that December. The morning after their honeymoon at Chicago's plush Palmer House, Kay received her indoctrination into Bobby's self-centered existence. Swaddled in a fur coat in the frigid stands of the Chicago Armory, the new bride watched Bobby play fifteen sets in one day over the span of three matches. Ten years later, Kay would tire of being the consolation prize, of remaining home with two children while her husband fed his addiction for action. She would be the first of two wives to leave him.

Bobby's life played out on the road in the 1940s. He roamed the country, searching for challenges, using precision to blunt the power of the game's top sluggers. The under-the-table payoffs were lucrative, but he wanted to earn his keep honestly. In 1941, with his name finally big enough to draw crowds on the tour, Bobby signed his first professional contract. It was worth $25,000.

Riggs was in his prime. Many sportswriters and fans had tabbed him as the man who could topple Don Budge. But Bobby couldn't beat history. After the Japanese bombed Pearl Harbor on December 7, 1941, Bobby's career would become cloaked by war, one surging in intensity as it pushed closer to home. The draft notice arrived in 1943.

Suddenly he was on his way to a naval training station.

"To be very honest about the whole thing," Bobby later wrote, "the United States Navy did not regard me as a prized recruit."

He was an impish cutup, a self-described goofy-looking fellow in navy-issue bell-bottoms. But for two years, Bobby followed just enough orders to stay out of trouble and maintain the preferential treatment he received as an American tennis legend.

He couldn't complain about his base assignment: Aiea Barracks at Pearl Harbor in Honolulu. It was a cushy club for star jocks. His mates included New York Giants slugging first baseman Johnny Mize and Brooklyn Dodgers shortstop Pee Wee Reese, competitive athletes with big appetites for the big score.

Whether on a base or a tour through the Pacific outposts, Bobby hustled all hands on deck and land in poker games. His art of the bluff had wheels. Bobby's winnings paid for a secondhand Cadillac that he used to cruise through the swaying palms of Hawaii for the several months he was in Honolulu.

Neither his carefree nature nor his tennis skills eroded in the service. After he was relocated to a base on the island of Guam, he actually began to sharpen his strokes with the Navy's full support.

"After I'd been on Guam for a while," Bobby later recalled, "the big guns worked up a scheme for Davis Cup–style matches to be played between two-man teams representing the army and the navy."

The Army man across the net from Bobby was none other than the great Don Budge. The heated exhibition matches between them were only a prelude to a real rivalry that unfolded after Bobby was discharged in November of 1945. Amid the euphoria that was postwar America, the L.A. Tennis Club became a hopping scene, with the matches between Bobby and Budge eliciting bets from such Hollywood high rollers as Errol Flynn and Ozzie Nelson.

Bobby began turning the tide against Budge on a national pro tour. But he still had to push aside Budge one more time for a chance to face a hot young amateur about to turn pro: Jack Kramer, a handsome talent straight from the Perry T. Jones vineyard.

"Riggs had to win the right to play me," Kramer recalls. "Bobby knew what he had to do and why he had to do it."

In 1947, Budge and Bobby played for the right to sign a $100,000 contract to tour with Kramer — all the motivation Bobby needed to win the U.S. Pro Championship. The stage was set for the confrontation that tennis fans everywhere wanted to see. Jack versus Bobby made for an irresistible marquee, and Riggs knew how to exploit it.

"Bobby talked up the tour, telling everyone how he could beat me and how he wanted to play Jack Kramer every day of the week and twice on Sunday," Kramer recalls. "He was a perfect showman."

Bobby stood a sinewy five feet seven and a half inches, a cagey competitor who used speed to compensate for his short reach. Jack was a powerful, swashbuckling serve-and-volley savant, who practically growled every time he missed a shot.

Their tour opened at Madison Square Garden on December 26, 1947. Under twenty-five inches of snow, New York City's transportation was paralyzed by the blizzard. The men on the Garden marquee — Bobby, Jack, Pancho Segura, and Dinny Pails — had sunk one leg in front of the other into the snowbanks as they trudged from their hotel to the arena.

A NECESSARY SPECTACLE

They anticipated three ushers and thousands of empty seats. What greeted them instead were 15,100 spectators out of a possible 16,000 tickets sold. To most, it was a miracle. To Bobby, it meant more action for gambling. Thrilled by the fans' enthusiasm, and inspired by his courtside bets, Bobby put on a great show, confusing Jack with his surprise net attack, replete with heavy slice and lobs.

"He confounded me, to be honest," Kramer recalls. "He revealed an athletic style I didn't know he had."

But, as the months played out, Bobby wore thin — a wobbly tire balding by the mile. The grind of each tour stop and Jack's unmerciful attack-dog style, the department-store promos and the endless wave of interviews, left Bobby facing his career mortality.

"We were doing it all, sometimes carrying rolled-up canvas courts in the backs of our cars," Kramer remembers. "We did it because if we didn't, we'd be out of a job."

Jack soon grabbed an edge and stretched it into a gap. Once the record between them grew lopsided, at 69–20, Bobby had the self-awareness to find an exit. His departure from the pro tour was part of a tennis life cycle of sorts. After all, it was the young Riggs who had usurped the aging Budge.

Retirement didn't translate into more quality family time for Bobby. He didn't want to play if he was number two, but he wasn't ready to leave the scene, either. Remaining on the road with Jack, he could have been a professional best man at weddings — always equipped with a joke, a toast, and a speech, he was a perfect promoter. With his instinct for sensationalism and his penchant for hyperbole, Bobby took over the Kramer pro tour.

"It gave him something to do besides go home," Kramer says. "He liked the life."

His wife Kay worked on the tour as well, but she always traveled days ahead of Bobby to advance the next scheduled date. It made for a lonely life. Not for Bobby, though. He was never far from the whiff of a woman's perfume. Bobby made time for company in between Kramer's matches against the brooding Pancho Gonzalez. After Gonzalez went into temporary retirement, Kramer continued playing against the top newcomers, but the tour lacked a wow factor.

Bobby searched for a way to juice things up as the rock-'n'-roll fifties neared. Sex appeal, that's what the tour needed. In 1949 he had to look no further than the underwear of Gussy Moran. Gussy was the reigning sex symbol of the women's circuit. She didn't win many matches, but she fed the shutterbugs, showing up on court with panties as frilly and white as a wedding cake, just barely hidden beneath her tennis skirts.

Photographers would lie on their backs to catch a snapshot of "Gorgeous Gussy." Every few strokes, when her skirt shifted up during a sweeping backhand, a glimpse of lace triggered a machine-gun burst of flashbulbs. Which is exactly what she wanted. Gussy may have played the vixen on court, but she was no vacuous brunette.

She was the daughter of a sound technician at Universal Studios in Los Angeles. When she was seventeen, her brother was declared missing in action during World War II. Gussy dedicated herself to the war effort by working as a machinist at Douglas Aircraft. She just happened to be a court beauty who had parlayed her appeal into a contract with Bobby Riggs. He wasn't as interested in her background as in her photogenic backside.

"We gave her a $35,000 guarantee," Kramer recalls. Bobby signed the unassuming Pauline Betz as a rival for his new female attraction. Gussy may have possessed the cover-girl charms Betz lacked, but they don't give points on the tennis court for a come-hither look. Gussy couldn't beat her, and that became a problem.

"Gussy wasn't winning," Kramer recalls. "People didn't want to see her lose."

As always, Bobby had his eyes fixed on the box office, and the receipts convinced him that Pauline had to go. He visited her hotel room one evening and asked, "Can't you sprain an ankle? What will it take — a car?"

Bobby's suggestion upset and bewildered Betz, but she refused to exit the tour. Instead, she promised to make the matches closer. She played so conservatively, however, that she never made an unforced error. Gussy still couldn't win.

"Finally, one night, Gussy won," Kramer recalls. "Pauline left in tears."

"Are you happy now?" Pauline yelled at Bobby.

Actually, Bobby was miserable. The bottom line was bleeding money despite his breathless promotions. Desperate to turn the tour around, Bobby the mischief maker went into full gear. One night, unknown to poor Gussy, he cut a slit into her fancy panties with a razor blade before she changed into them for a tour event. Just before she swept onto the court, Bobby told Gussy, "When you stand in front of the press seats, bend over and that'll start some action."

As she smoothed the back of her skirt, she realized what Bobby had done. Angry, Gussy refused. Her lack of show-business savvy infuriated Bobby. Didn't she understand the art of promotion? Didn't she know that sex sold tickets? As Bobby had just discovered, even a lingerie tempt-ress had her limits.

The tour was a bust, and the failure only reinforced an opinion Bobby already held about women players: They didn't have the drawing power to merit places on the professional circuit. They were farces in comparison to their superior male counterparts.

After the tour fizzled, so did Bobby's marriage to Kay. That was hardly shocking. During their thirteen years together, he had made only cameo appearances at the dinner table. Bobby often left her in hotel rooms while he embarked on another one of his gaming binges. He showed up with the regularity of a party clown for the kids on birthdays and special occasions. He was always fun, always lovable, then out the door. There were itches to scratch. After he and Kay drifted apart, Bobby retreated to Florida to visit friends and find himself. He would discover two new loves down South.

Though wealthy, Priscilla Wheelan didn't exude the elitist snobbery Bobby loathed. She was a lovely brunette with warm eyes and a famous family. The Wheelans owned the American Photograph Corporation, a company specializing in portraits. While Bobby courted her among the palm trees, he found a fresh fix for his competitive jones: golf. God, he was a kid again, with golf balls as marbles and wins based on handicaps. Unlike the games of pure chance that he never touched—such as roulette—this gambling man's thinking game intrigued him.

Talent was a must, but so was nerve and a mind for angles. Long drives necessitated confidence at the tee box. Short chips called for a steady hand and a clutch touch. And delicate putts required immunity to pressure.

Judging a man's psyche had never been more crucial.

Bobby found golf so satisfying that he went sixteen years without touching a racket. His Wimbledon reputation as a risk-taker still followed him, though, with good reason. Bobby would flip over a good bet, but he was no con artist, unlike the ones he was associated with in a *Life* magazine article titled "Larceny on the Links."

"Riggs is a cool, calculating golfer who points like a bird dog when he scents money," author Marshall Smith wrote.

The description was fair enough, and the quote that had Bobby describing golf courses as "big, open-air pool rooms" was accurate. But he didn't consider himself a scoundrel on a par with Titanic Thompson, a towering man who would make bets with loopholes.

"I bet I can hit a ball a mile," Titanic told suckers on the course. Then, as legend had it, Titanic would drive to Pike's Peak and slam a golf ball down the side of the mountain. One mile. Pay up.

And Bobby didn't cut the same outlandish figure as John Montague did on the links. Montague was the Harlem Globetrotter of the fairway, making trick shots while playing with farm implements—rakes, shovels, and hoes. Bobby gambled on his keen ability to read a man's soul, to assess whether an opponent would weaken under pressure. Bobby could tickle a man's panic button with a wager; he made a killing fraying nerves. The action was entertaining and exciting, but Bobby was not a supreme contender at golf, not even a has-been champion. Hustling hackers was one thing, but beating his champion peers was another.

The senior division of tennis offered him the opportunity to do exactly that. In 1962, when Bobby turned forty-five, rumors started to spread that Open Era tennis was about to become a reality, with new rules that would allow amateurs to compete in the same tournaments as professionals. No more separation. Everyone's invited. Until the entry code actually changed, however, Bobby remained isolated as a pro. He couldn't play in the amateurs-only majors. He couldn't sniff the freshly cut lawns of Wimbledon until he was allowed past the gate as a returning champion — even if it was for the senior section.

B obby waited for change patiently, biding his time with preparation.

He and Priscilla were well into their marriage by the 1960s. After living in Florida for several years, Bobby packed up his family and moved to Plandome, Long Island, where he would try on a regular life as a businessman. Normalcy, for a change.

Bobby worked for his father-in-law and earned a six-figure salary as an executive with the American Photograph Corporation.

"By the time he and my mom married, he was a homebody," Bobby's son John explains. "He took the train into work. But to him, that was kind of making a silk purse out of a sow's ear. He'd still sneak off somewhere to play golf and come home late."

Bobby's wanderlust for gamesmanship didn't make for a traditional father.

"It was easier to be his son than his daughter," John recalls. "He wasn't a great dad by common standards, but he was a great guy to hang out with. He'd take me to locker rooms and to play golf. I'd drive the cart. I met all the crooks of the game. He'd introduce me to guys named the Thin Man and the Fat Man and the Fireman. And there was a hood, a guy named Tommy the Gun, who probably was packing one under his coat.

"I grew up part of his world, and for a kid, it was pretty cool stuff."

Bobby eventually built a tennis court behind the family's stately three-story home that was a breeze away from the Long Island Sound.

The court seemed more for his kids than anyone else, though. It wasn't as if Priscilla could look out the kitchen window and watch her husband play. Bobby's favorite playground was on the rooftop of a thirteen-story building in midtown Manhattan. Smoke blew in waves across the courts, turning tennis balls into candied apples rolled in coal. The culprit was a nearby Con Ed plant with its colorfully striped smokestacks popping up on the skyline like headwear from *The Cat in the Hat*.

It was the scene Bobby adored at the Manhattan Tennis Club, not the scenery. Everywhere he looked, there were Wall Street brokers hungry to make bets. But there was a problem. These men knew they lacked the skills to take the great Bobby Riggs for a ride, so how was he going to generate any serious action?

Bobby had the answer for that. He simply let the businessmen do what they did best: negotiate the odds. Bobby agreed to jump through hoops — and over chairs — to land their wagers. The challenges and props put in front of him were endless. A rooftop guy would say, "Bobby, bet you can't beat me playing with an umbrella in your left hand," and Bobby would win. Someone else would ask, "How about a full suitcase in your hand? What about a raincoat buttoned to your neck and clunky galoshes on your feet — or maybe a dog on a leash?"

"It's harder if the dog isn't housebroken," Bobby quipped.

Action hath no shame. He took on all comers and seldom lost. After six years of this improv tennis, Bobby felt ready for a rebirth. He was fifty-one when the Open era began in 1968. He still treasured the rooftop gang of old birds, but he needed to blow smoke elsewhere. He longed to compete again, to go back to Wimbledon and face the rivals from his youth on the senior circuit. But Bobby soon learned that the financial rewards for antique tennis players were meager. The senior circuit was pay-as-you-go. Playing Wimbledon meant putting down your own cash for meals, massages, and hotel rooms. For what? Piddling prize money?

At the same time, women players began asking for equal pay; Billie Jean King was the loudest voice for change. Bobby picked up the beat and formed his own one-man chorus to demand greater compensation for the senior tour. Where was the older players' share, he wanted to know. As women began picking up endorsement deals and attracting more publicity, Bobby started fighting for his ounce of attention. He hated being left out of the spotlight—and said so. He was candid about his appetite for celebrity, and resourceful in obtaining it.

This was his new cause, his new indulgence. Not surprisingly, Priscilla got lost amid his priorities. Like Kay in 1952, she wanted to know where Bobby had been all their marriage.

"My wife thought I ought to spend more time looking after my family instead of playing gin and hustling golf and tennis," Bobby once explained. "She didn't think it was dignified. Once she made me go to a psychiatrist to try to cure me of my addiction, but after a couple of sessions, I had him flicking cards into a hat. Then we spent time playing gin rummy."

In 1972 Priscilla told Bobby in loving but unambiguous terms, "I'm divorcing you, darling, because I haven't seen you in twenty years." The dissolution of a second marriage didn't leave Bobby bitter toward women. He knew Priscilla hadn't taken him for a ride; in some respects, he had taken her. With stocks and severance, Bobby exited his marriage and the American Photograph Corporation with nearly a million in the bank. He didn't need money to feel relevant, though. He needed attention.

If there was one woman who could identify with Bobby, it was Billie Jean King.

For different reasons, she shared his thirst for glory and drama. With uncanny cinematic instincts, Billie recognized how images could expedite change, how a lens could filter social transition into the mind of viewers—big and small. Billie thought in living color before there were hue buttons and tint knobs. And Bobby was the man who knew how to keep the cameras rolling.

CHAPTER 3

Tele-visionary

Even in black and white, the ornate carriage appeared gilded as it moved across the screen like a horse-drawn Fabergé egg, crawling on spoked wheels toward Westminster Abbey. The date was June 2, 1953. Queen Elizabeth II had chosen to have her coronation broadcast live to her subjects as they watched while sipping tea in parlors throughout the UK.

A day later, after film of the event had been transported by Canberra jet bombers for viewing in the United States, Billie Jean Moffitt planted herself in the Wallick family's living room. She was prepared for awe. The Wallicks owned the only TV set on 36th Street in the working-class section of Long Beach, California, a neighborhood where children dotted the lawns like ginger snaps on a cookie sheet.

Billie lived on the block in a $5,000 tract home her father had purchased on a fireman's salary. Broad-shouldered, with an affinity for sawdust, Bill Moffitt turned the porch into a dining room, built a den off the back, and squeezed the incredible shrinking backyard down into the size of a putting green.

A NECESSARY SPECTACLE

The home, all 1,000 square feet of it, contained three bedrooms, one bathroom, and a dance floor of sorts. At night the upbeat big-band tunes of Glenn Miller purred from the record player in the living room as Bill and his wife, Betty, glided over a worn carpet. Bill Moffitt went off to the firehouse each day, and treated his kids to a slide down the pole whenever they visited. Betty would stay home, often cooking up memories in her kitchen. This house didn't need Betty Crocker when it had Betty Moffitt. Billie's mom spent many an afternoon baking cookies for her two children to grab as they breezed in and out of the front door. She also made a mean pumpkin chiffon pie, and liked to paint flowers on ceramics.

"Billie Jean loved to come home; when I baked cookies she could always smell them when she got into the house," Betty recalls. "She really felt a warmth, I think, because I was always in the kitchen. Always there, I guess."

The simplicity of life in the Moffitt home provided the comfort of familiarity. Curfew was easy: dinner was at 5:30 p.m. on the dot. After running through the house on the fly from a game of stickball or football in the street, Billie and her little brother, Randy, would screech to a halt at the dinner table. Then they plopped down and competed for air time. Talking over each other, the siblings spilled every detail of their day, from school to skinned knees, reflecting a 1950s culture of sock hops, *Howdy Doody*, and social conformity.

It was Americana bliss. It was everything Bill and Betty had wanted in their own childhoods. They had both grown up in broken homes during the Depression. They worked hard to vanquish the dark images of those days, desperate to create a loving cocoon for Billie and Randy complete with good-night kisses, games of catch, and church on Sundays. There was no outward fretting about McCarthyism or the atomic bomb.

"Billie Jean came from a conservative family, especially her father," Larry King remembers. "She was cloistered in that they didn't think in terms of other people. Everything was from their point of view."

The Moffitt household mirrored the nation's mindset at a time when many white Americans felt threatened by civil rights gains, and

50

gender roles were unambiguous. As a 1953 article in *Coronet* magazine explained: "The smart woman will keep herself desirable. It is her duty to be feminine and desirable at all times in the eyes of the opposite sex."

Meticulous as well as beautiful, with her hair perfectly swept back from her porcelain face, Betty was a committed homemaker who was capable of turning yarn into a sweater, of spinning thread into shorts, skills she never passed on to her daughter.

"Oh, heavens no," Betty says. "Billie would never sit still that long."

Betty projected a feminine ideal for Billie. At night her daughter fell asleep in a room painted the soft pink of cotton candy—a product of Betty's handiwork. Today her mother admits, "She probably didn't like that color."

Billie was a tomboy, the halfback in touch football games played between the curbs on 36th Street. For a while, Betty and Bill indulged Billie's goal of becoming a Green Bay Packer. She was hard to contain, anyhow, a hopeless squirmer who hardly took a seat for anything—except TV.

When Billie knocked on the Wallicks' door, she did not ask, "Wanna play?" but "What's on TV?" On that summer day in '53 it was Her Majesty. In a satin British accent that made his words flow with the elegance of calligraphy, host Richard Dimbleby described the coronation for viewers:

"This throne—like the raised floor of the theater itself—is descended from those days, one thousand five hundred years ago, when the early kings sat for their crowning upon a mound of earth and were then lifted high upon the shoulders of their nobles so that all the peoples might see them."

"It is the moment," he added, "seated upon the throne, that she takes possession of her people."

Behold, the theater of the extravagant. Billie's blueberry eyes expanded to the size of gumballs. Every last detail of the coronation, the fantasy of jewels, velvet robes, and ornate regalia mesmerized her. It was the birth of a true-blue, first-generation TV junkie. You could get her to watch almost anything. "We would sit there," Billie says, "and watch that damn test pattern with the American Indian at the top."

That box stoked her imagination and her curiosity. She often wondered how many people were watching the same test pattern. What would happen if the curtains closed on the TV host? What if the camera light went out? Who pulled the trapdoors, and how did they hide the shadows and strings? The medium was relatively new, but the fascination wasn't. Billie had revealed a taste for showmanship and drama even before she used TV as a vehicle for dreamy escapism. Her earliest epiphanies developed as grand productions, too.

At five, Billie began daydreaming out loud one day as she washed dishes with her mother. The drudgery of drying was broken by an odd but uplifting energy that filled her body, the sensation that she was being knighted. Divinely prompted, Billie told her mother, "I'm going to do something great with my life."

Half nurturer, half serial killjoy, Betty Moffitt was equally comfortable with both roles. "That's cute, dear," she replied with her hands plunged in soapy water. "Just keep drying those dishes."

Billie didn't inherit her mother's sensible reasoning, but she did display her father's wide range of emotions. He was a rugged athlete, with a defined jaw and James Dean's pensive brow, a man whose eyes pooled when he heard "The Star-Spangled Banner," and whose temper flared on the playground basketball courts. Bill carved a bat for Billie when she was four, and swung her in circles from the waist until she outgrew games of airplane.

Billie was just like him, in spirit and in name. She was given a tweaked version of her father's name in case Bill didn't return from World War II alive. By the time Billie was two years old, her father was safe at home — at least until work put him in danger.

On a warm summer day, with wild smoke plumes rising from Signal Hill above Long Beach, Billie sat huddled with her mother on the couch, waiting for her father to stride through the door. She was six.

"We could hear all the fire engines," Betty recalls. "I don't think Bill came home that night at all. Billie was so concerned for her father. She didn't leave the sofa. She kept looking out the window. She was Daddy's girl."

She adored him. They were both passionate and intractable, a mix that invited a few battles. If Billie had one obstacle to overcome in her quest for greatness, it was stage fright. In elementary school, she would panic when oral book reports were due, frozen like a Rocket Pop with the eyes of her peers upon her. She put off a report on Peter Stuyvesant until her fifth-grade teacher, Mrs. Delph, sent a note home to her parents. Her father implored her to stop the nonsense and get on with the presentation.

"Dad, I can't do it."

The threat of a spanking by her father's swift hand did nothing to change her mind.

"You might as well kill me now."

The spanking stung, but it didn't prevent her body from turning to liquid the next day as she stumbled through her book report in front of the class. Billie was always so afraid of what others thought of her, never quite certain of where she fit in. Her self-esteem trailed behind her ambitions, and she knew it. The starlets she watched seemed so self-assured on TV, so relaxed on camera. As it turned out, all Billie needed was a different kind of stage.

She found it on the playing fields, or what passed for playing fields in Long Beach. Billie was a good athlete—all the boys on the block could attest to that. Give her the ball, and she could break every tackle and dodge every fender and mailbox as she made her way down 36th Street for a touchdown. But being a halfback wasn't exactly a ladylike career pursuit. After Billie turned ten, her parents decided it was time to end her NFL future. Her mother suggested she take up more feminine pursuits, like playing the piano or decorating cupcakes. But diversions like piano lessons could not satisfy Billie's competitive appetite. As a compromise, Bill handed his daughter a list of socially acceptable sports: golf, swimming, or tennis.

Tennis? Billie had no idea what that game was about, but if it meant running, jumping, and hitting, she was all for it. A racket was required, so she completed a dozen odd jobs around the neighborhood until she collected eight dollars. She went to a local sporting goods store and picked out a maroon racket with maroon nylon strings and a faux-velvet grip. She curled up with it on the car ride home, and put it by her pillow at night. The next day she plunged into a sport that would fill her tank with confidence.

"Hey, Billie, wanna play tennis?"

Her pal Susan Williams was the first of many to ask, and Billie never said no. Then, in June 1955, under a blue sky, with the smell of eucalyptus trees in the air, Billie stepped on the Houghton Park court for her first group lesson with Clyde Walker—a teaching pro in his sixties who preferred the hungry public-court kids over the spoiled country-club brats. Before the lesson started, Walker gave Billie her first bit of practical tennis advice.

"Close the gate, or you'll lose the whole basket of balls."

The first ball Billie smacked went over the net. She was hooked. When Betty Moffitt pulled up in the family's '47 Chevy to pick her up after practice, she asked her daughter, "How was it, dear?"

"I know what I want to do with my life," Billie declared.

"What do you mean?"

"Tennis. I'm going to be the number-one player in the world."

Betty answered her daughter's wistfulness with another "Nice, dear," another "Homework first, dear." But though her reflexive response was saturated with reality, she remained deeply supportive of Billie. Betty and Bill Moffitt encouraged both Randy and Billie to be goal-oriented, to never stop reaching for accomplishment. They had found out soon enough that Billie was never going to be a ballerina, but at least Bill and Betty could live with the sport of tennis—a game played in dresses. They rallied behind her efforts to be the best little player in Long Beach, even if their income wasn't at country-club levels.

Betty sold Tupperware and Avon products out of the house to help fund Billie's and Randy's sports ventures. Bill put up a spotlight so Billie could use the backyard fence as a nighttime hitting partner and he made do on two pairs of shoes for eight years. The sacrifices paid off. Somehow, Bill and Betty helped to create a tennis superstar and a major league pitcher on a coupon-clipper's budget.

54

Billie was one of several kids from the public courts who carried brown-bag lunches to the big tournaments held at the elite Los Angeles Tennis Club. The LATC was a posh playground for the white and wealthy. Her parents didn't say anything, but Billie could sense how uneasy they felt when they had to mix with the snooty upper classes. Unlike the socialites around them, the Moffitts couldn't afford a Coke from the counter or a two-dollar sandwich off the menu.

One day I'm going to eat at that counter and not worry about what something costs, Billie thought.

In her homemade clothes and spiffy white sneakers, Billie could see how children of modest means were received differently than the off-spring of the club members. It wasn't her peers who snubbed her, but in-crowd adults with Beverly Hills addresses. Her misfit status was underscored during her first sanctioned tournament at the LATC, held one year from the day she picked out her maroon racket. Her parents' finances were so threadbare, the Long Beach Tennis Patrons had to pick up her two-dollar entry fee.

This initial taste of real competition left Billie practically carbonated with excitement. First big event, super-duper deal, she thought. Before the matches, the tournament organizers gathered all the players together at the LATC for the traditional group photo.

"Everyone, come on out here."

"What are they doing?" Betty asked Billie.

"I don't know, Mom, but they want me out front."

Billie jumped into place, brushing any dust — real or imaginary — off her pristine blouse while straightening the snazzy white shorts her mother had made for the occasion. Billie was immaculate, picture-perfect and eager to say "Cheese."

Then a man approached Billie. He wore a bow tie on his crisp collar, a straw hat on his head, and pants belted as high as Fred Mertz's.

"Little girl?" he said.

"Yes, sir?"

A NECESSARY SPECTACLE

"You can't be in the photo."

"Why? I'm in the tournament."

Looking down at Billie's white shorts through his dark sunglasses, the man huffed, "You're not wearing a skirt or a tennis dress."

It was the same Perry T. Jones who, years earlier, had tried unsuccessfully to obstruct the career path of Bobby Riggs, another uncouth scrub without a pedigree. Billie had never thought of herself as occupying a lower rung on the social ladder; her parents never discussed their finances out loud. The grand poo-bah of Southern California tennis had just handed Billie her first lesson in class discrimination.

"In those days, in Bobby's day and my day, Perry Jones had total control over our lives," Billie says. "To play anywhere, to receive any help, and sometimes no help at all — it didn't matter — Perry Jones had to sign your entry form. He preferred a certain kind of player."

For an instant, Jones's arrogance and attitude stung Billie. Anger swept through her, but as she reluctantly stepped aside, instead of cursing, she mumbled her usual substitute: "Peanut butter!" She did ache, though, the moment she saw the wounded look on her mother's face. Betty was mortified. Billie tried to mend her heart by remaining upbeat and matter-of-fact.

"Don't worry, Mom."

"But I want you in that photo."

"Don't worry, I'll be in it next time."

Coincidentally, earlier in the day, Billie had passed a girl wearing a tennis dress. So *that's* what kids wear here, she thought. Billie loved the look. She asked her mother to sew one just like it, but loose-fitting, with room to move. Billie was never underdressed again. Her mother made sure of it.

Billie recovered from her fashion faux pas to win her first sanctioned match before losing her second. Billie's game steadily improved. She studied tennis as closely as a sleuth inspects a fingerprint. She devoured information and was determined to learn, no matter what authority planted his pear-shaped body in her way.

Jones tried to douse her spirit again, three years later, in 1958. As number two in the fifteen-and-under division of the Southern California Association, Billie had beaten the top player, Kathy Chabot. Jones allowed Billie to compete at the girls' nationals in Ohio — with one catch: She would receive no funds, and a chaperone would have to accompany her.

Thanks for nothin', Billie thought. Without money to fly, she and her mother embarked on a three-day train ride. Billie stared happily through the window while the world zipped by with all the speed of her own passing thoughts; her mother, though, spent most of the trip feeling as queasy as a pie-eating contestant.

After all those miles, Billie lost in the quarterfinals, but she did find her Ohio experience inspirational. With about a buck left in her pocket, she saw a car full of gals loading up to go east to play. Billie didn't have the money to gallivant all over the country playing tennis. The thought of her peers barnstorming the East Coast, getting better by the day, left her feeling excluded. Billie realized she had to find a way to beat the class system, to develop her gifts without seed money.

She was lucky Alice Marble still had one good lung.

In 1939, Marble had been the most celebrated name in tennis, the first female player to win the British and U.S. women's singles, doubles, and mixed doubles championships in the same year. She was also a staunch defender of women's rights. On the international lecture circuit, Marble encouraged women to participate in sports despite any obstacles they encountered. "When the day comes that a woman who is athletic will no longer be regarded as the unusual type," Marble once said, "when it will seem as natural for women as it now seems for men to be keenly interested in athletics, we'll start training girls to be active athletes. We'll not discourage them, as we do today, from taking part in tomboy play when they're six, and ten, and twelve."

Joe Bixler, an executive at Wilson who believed in Billie's potential, introduced the young player to the aging legend. Every Saturday, Betty and Bill Moffitt drove Billie the forty miles up to Tarzana so that Alice could coach her over the weekend. At night, Billie would hear Alice hacking down the hallway, coughing through her battle with pleurisy while hooked to an oxygen tank.

During practice, in between cigarettes, Alice regaled Billie with stories about Don Budge and Bobby Riggs. At times, Marble provided hints about her own amazing past as the women's number-one player throughout the 1930s. She was a hard-charging attacker disguised as a butterfly, alighting on the court with a slender frame and delicate features. An immediate connection formed between the coach and her teen pupil. Alice was an aggressor at the net, and so was Billie. Alice lived history, and Billie lapped it up. Alice knew how to be a champion, and Billie longed to become one.

Their rapport changed, though, about three months into their relationship. In a passing moment, Billie apparently overstepped her bounds by telling Alice she wanted to be the best player ever — bar none. Alice reacted as if Billie's pronouncement threatened her. She didn't care for Billie's insensitivity about her physical condition, either. Once, when Alice called to say she was too ill to coach, she overheard Billie blurt out her mock relief. Selfish, ungrateful girl, Alice remarked. Selfish, ungrateful daughter, her parents agreed. How could Billie not appreciate Alice? How could she be so spiteful? It was Billie's first lesson in the dangers of candor.

After Alice withdrew from her life, Billie slipped into a spell of self-reflection. Maybe she had been too harsh, too full of herself. After all, Alice wasn't the only person who had placed her in the brat camp. Maureen Connolly had been America's adorable firefly on the court during the 1950s, in the midst of a remarkable career, with nine majors as a teen. "Little Mo," her fans dubbed her. Then everything ended with a heartbreaking accident. Maureen was riding a horse when a truck side-swiped her and smashed her leg.

Little Mo didn't drown in her misery. She never played competitively again, but stayed in tennis as an instructor, seeing all and hearing all. A year before Alice and her prized student split up, Maureen, the most cheerful of people, had bluntly told Billie, "You'll never amount to anything with your ego." The assessment didn't faze Billie until Alice added her two cents. Was she really that self-absorbed?

Billie accepted the criticisms as lessons. She would overcome her shortcomings by applying the killer instinct Alice had instilled in her and never let overconfidence undermine her preparation. Billie's determination became transparent. Jerry Cromwell found that out. He played tennis at Long Beach Polytechnic High, too. On many days they'd walk to school together. He'd share his dreams of tennis stardom, and she'd be silly enough to share hers.

"Aw, Billie, you're just a dumb girl."

"I bet I'll change things more than you will."

But how? she had to wonder. No one listened to dumb girls. Not her teachers, who didn't even know she played tennis. Not her classmates, who hadn't even heard she was a top-ranked competitor. Fame's glass ceiling for women confined Billie, and the unfairness of that confounded her. She was convinced that the only chance for her voice to carry was from behind a platform as the number-one player in the world.

In 1961, Billie landed on Britain's misty ground for her first Wimbledon. She and Karen Hantze went as a doubles team, and the teens treated their trip like one long slumber party, dining on Mars bars and Wimpy burgers, giggling late into the night. They'd win, postpone their flight home for another day, and play again. All of a sudden, they were in the finals against Aussie stars Margaret Smith and Jan Lehane. All of a sudden, before they could even vote, they were Wimbledon doubles champs.

Cool.

It wasn't exactly a widely celebrated victory. There were no photographers at the airport and no invitations for *The Ed Sullivan Show.* In fact, no one outside of their own households seemed to care. Maybe, Billie thought, she wouldn't be famous after all. Maybe she would just plod along, play tennis in her spare time, and go to college. Just like everyone else.

A NECESSARY SPECTACLE

In the fall of 1961, Billie hopped in her 1950 Ford — a polished, standard shift, wine-colored beauty she'd bought for $310 — and began her eighteen-mile commute to Los Angeles State College. By her sophomore year, she was pulling in some side cash as a playground director and as an attendant, handing out towels during women's gym. She wasn't into exploring her tennis potential; she was into conformity.

"I was doing what everyone else was doing," she said.

In truth, Billie wasn't your natural-born freedom fighter. When young Americans began to question the fifties brand of cookie-cutter idealism, when President Kennedy urged them to join the Peace Corps and participate in democracy, Billie resisted venturing out of her conservative bubble.

Billie would acquire her taste for feminism as part of an evolution. And it was a man who pointed the way. In 1962 she was stepping out of the library elevator when her friend Marcos Carriedo stopped her. There was this guy, Larry King, up on the third floor. "Billie, he's perfect for you," Marcos told her. Larry was a bio-chem major. He didn't drink. He didn't smoke. And he loved tennis.

"Marcos, come on. Get out of here. What's with you?"

"Get in."

When they reached the library, Billie stepped out and walked toward a table in the back. All she saw were the blue eyes, the blond hair, and those red socks; they were bright enough to lead Santa's sleigh. Okay, he's a little quirky, she thought, but he's so gorgeous. Billie soon discovered that the handsome head was also brimming with ideas. Larry had so many thoughts to share. He made her think on levels she had never explored back in Long Beach.

Six months later, Billie and Larry King were dating. There had been other boyfriends — like Jimmy Dunbar who chased her in second grade, and Owen Crosby who plied her with drugstore milkshakes in the sixth — but nothing this serious. Her parents had to meet the dreamboat.

It was not a smooth encounter.

First, her father charbroiled the steaks. Larry hated charbroiled steaks. Second, her mother served salad. Larry loathed salad. As the guys stood around the grill in the backyard, Larry asked Bill about the pH levels of his soil.

"What's with this guy and his p's and h's?" Bill Moffitt wondered out loud, well after Larry was gone. "He's gotta be a real dippy-do, asking a guy a question like that in his own backyard."

Bill and Betty would warm to Larry's analytical side — eventually. In some ways, Larry shared their ethic of self-reliance. Born in Dayton, Ohio, he had grown up in a poor, dysfunctional household. Dinner was often garbanzo beans. His mother died when he was young and his father remarried, but Larry wouldn't call it an unhappy childhood — he wasn't that dramatic.

It was an enlightening childhood. Unlike Billie, Larry constantly confronted a wider picture of the world through his father's moral sense of right and wrong. At age seven, Larry saw firsthand the depth of his father's social conviction when his family pulled up to a campground at Big Bear Lake, California, for a family reunion. Everyone in the car was giddy about the upcoming get-together, with all those King cousins and relatives to see, all that playing to be done.

But then Larry's father took one look out the window and jerked the car around. After driving ninety miles to this retreat, they were heading home, with gravel spitting off the tire treads.

"We're not going in," he said flatly.

"What?" his children asked.

"They've got a sign saying 'No Blacks Allowed.'"

Mr. King was a socially conscious Quaker. He couldn't imagine being a party to racial intolerance. When he sped away from that campground, the father made a statement and set an example his son would never forget.

"He just didn't believe in treating people like they weren't human beings," Larry says. "As a kid, I was bummed. It made me really unhappy what my father did, but it was kind of a wake-up call that there are some things you can support and some that you can't support and each individual has to take action, for whatever reason, they have to take their action based on what they think is right and wrong."

61

A NECESSARY SPECTACLE

Larry grew up questioning every angle of each cultural turn, but he wasn't a vociferous radical. He was a man who processed and analyzed, who parsed ideas before acting on them. Once his opinion had been formed, he was politely unyielding to anyone who questioned it. Larry comported himself with a temperament as level and immovable as the horizon. He was calm and steady, never giving in to bad days, hardly going overboard with the good ones.

What might be a disaster to someone else was simply a problem to be solved for Larry. In fact, he seemed to revel in living on the edge so long as he could figure his way out of danger. He could choreograph plank-walkers to safety. Larry's creativity — he invented the first smoke-less ashtray — and his sincere, quiet charm left Billie rapt. She was crazy about him.

And Larry? He wouldn't go anywhere without Billie by his side. If he had to bury himself in a chemistry lab, he pulled Billie along with him — even if all she did was watch him pour fizzing liquid from one beaker into the next.

He discussed his ideas; she rehearsed her dreams. He prodded her to be ambitious; she soaked up the attention. He was infatuated by her potential; she was taken by his political passion. Gradually he taught her that gender bias wasn't just an unfair annoyance; it was legally and morally unjust.

"I'm the seventh man on a six-man team," he told her, "but why do I get the grant and you don't? I'm a boy. You're the biggest name at the school, and you can't get anything because you're a girl."

The revelation jarred her sense of justice. So much attention had centered on the racial elements of civil rights, as so elegantly illuminated in Martin Luther King's "I Have a Dream" speech in 1963, but the suppression of women's rights hadn't yet registered with Billie. She didn't huddle with Betty Friedan's *The Feminine Mystique* when it first hit the shelves in 1963 and left a nation of women wondering "Who Am I?" after they had packed the lunches, washed the laundry, and powdered their noses. Billie wasn't marching in lockstep with the burgeoning women's movement. She just wondered, Why are all these women screaming all the time?

"Billie Jean just couldn't understand why people were burning bras," Larry says. "Billie Jean was really literal. To her, you needed a bra when you played athletics.

"All I tried to do was to help her understand what was going on and not be limited by an instant reaction to people being antiwar, or burning bras, or taking positions that are really out there as being literally what they're saying. They're trying to move the whole society. They're not necessarily right or wrong; they have a point of view, and to move the center, the cows, you gotta be out there."

When Larry looked at Billie, he saw an assertive, bright woman with the courage and energy to dance on a cultural limb without fearing the height. He believed she had the potential to prod entire herds of those unengaged people who couldn't grasp the urgency for social change.

"Consider the point of view, not just the act," Larry recalls telling Billie. "That's the only way I'd helped Billie Jean, I really think. She had the intellect, she had the moral sense, and she had a huge sense of justice when she understood what the ramifications of unfairness were."

A conversion unfolded as Larry pushed Billie to consider the slights she had faced as a woman athlete as part of the larger issue of everyday gender equality. "Larry was a real feminist, and I loved it," Billie recalls. "He woke me up to that."

Here was someone who could handle her mercurial moods and support her choices. An unthreatened man.

"I guess that was the good-news-bad-news of it," Larry says. "I had such a huge ego that it wasn't on the line."

When Billie agonized over whether she should leave school to play tennis full time, when she pondered going to Australia to study under the famed coach Mervyn Rose, Larry always gave her the same advice: "Do your thing, Billie."

That kind of unquestioning support convinced Billie that she had found her match. On October 8, 1964, at precisely 2:00 p.m., Larry handed her an engagement ring over a Formica table at a coffee shop in Long Beach and popped the question. She said yes.

Bill Moffitt wasn't so sure. "How are you going to provide for her?" he wanted to know. "What if she gets pregnant right away . . . you can't live on love." The doubts Bill expressed in his stream of questions stung Larry. Bill didn't realize that, though his future son-in-law was a liberal, he was no hippie slacker. Larry had labored to get ahead all of his life.

To allay his fears, Larry took a $400-a-month job at Sealright Pacific—the proud manufacturer of ice-cream cartons. It wasn't long before Dad was won over. A wedding was held at the First Church of Brethren in Long Beach on September 17, 1965. The dashing twenty-year-old blond groom dressed in a white dinner jacket with a black bow tie and black trousers. The lovely twenty-one-year-old bride ditched her glasses for the occasion and wore a glorious white-lace gown with a veil.

The Queen would have been jealous.

For a while, Billie and Larry played Ozzie and Harriet without the kids, as downright domestic as any typical young American couple. She cooked him two meals a day, washed the clothes, and kept their modest apartment in Alhambra as tidy as a pencil box. "It was pretty plain," Larry recalls. "A kitchenette, one front room. Not much decoration unless you count my Andy Williams records in the corner." When Larry worked the graveyard shift at the factory, Billie took him lunch at 2:00 a.m.

"I was a regular wife," Billie says. "I would sleep when he slept. And get up when he got up." In essence, Billie had become her mother. Was this what she wanted? Billie wasn't sure. She still played tennis, but it was more like a part-time job, an afterthought. The edge on her game dulled, but that was the sacrifice women made for their men. Wives were supposed to trade in their dreams for their husband's ambitions. It wasn't fair, Billie thought. Sometimes her discontent spilled over into fits of sadness and anger that left Larry warding off his wife's pounding fists. That was dramatic. That was Billie.

"Everything was bigger than life with Billie Jean," Larry says. "It's got to be bigger than life."

That year, Larry graduated with a bio-chem degree. He didn't mind the claustrophobic life of the lab, because it was a place where the ultimate problem-solver could work toward long-term solutions. Billie had other career ideas for her husband.

"Billie said she wanted to be married to a lawyer," Larry says. "It was that simple."

Larry applied to law school at UC Berkeley. Naturally, he was accepted. Brainy as well as gorgeous, that's why Billie had married him. To the sound of "King of the Road" on the radio, the couple packed up the Ford and moved to Berkeley, the liberal hitching post for an entire nation.

"We had the beautiful Haight-Ashbury people around us, and it was a fun time," Larry recalls. "I can remember going across the Berkeley campus and the National Guard chasing people and some people yelling, 'The revolution is coming! The revolution is coming!' I'm thinking, 'Give me a break; that's impossible, man.' But it was great, really an amazing time."

They lived amid a culture that transmitted confusing, contradictory images. Outside their door, long-haired antiwar protesters with unruly beards debated the Vietnam War on streetcorners, with peace signs sprayed on their VW vans. On television, *The Dating Game* and *The Newlywed Game* both premiered in 1966, conveying the message that once the romance of modern courting ended, excitement in marriage boiled down to winning a washing machine on a right answer.

Where did Billie fit in all this? She wasn't a radical enveloped by any cause. Billie continued to play the role of citizen wife. Sometimes she let loose on the court, and even though her strokes suffered from underuse, Billie was still a top amateur.

With Larry sitting in the players' box at Wimbledon, Billie left the 1966 final with blades of grass imprinted on her knees from deftly fetching low volleys. She also exited with her first singles title after outlasting

A NECESSARY SPECTACLE

Maria Bueno 6–3, 3–6, 6–1. At just twenty-three years old, Billie had captured Wimbledon.

A year later she pulled off a remarkable trifecta, taking Wimbledon's singles, double, and mixed doubles titles. Somewhere, an English bookie once snookered by Bobby Riggs was thankful Billie didn't gamble. She became a star on the tournament circuit — but she still felt out of the mainstream. When her plane touched down after her three-title thrill at Wimbledon, not one photographer was on hand to greet her.

Her name had value, though. She earned decent money under the table from promoters, enough to keep the couple afloat while Larry was in law school. She saved like a junkyard dealer, hoarding the fourteen-dollars-a-day per diem that tournament organizers were allowed to give players.

But although she was the family's breadwinner, Billie still couldn't obtain a credit card — part of the male privilege that rankled Larry's sensibilities as much as his wife's. Credit card applications addressed to Mr. King stuffed the couple's mailbox. Shell, Texaco, they were all willing to invest in Mr. King's future earnings.

"Law school. Get it? He's gonna be a lawyer," Billie says. "And I'm the one getting him through school. I get zip. And Larry would get so mad."

"This is absolute discrimination," he'd say.

"No kidding," she'd return.

Her sarcasm was a good sign. To Larry, it meant she was catching on to the reality of discrimination. She may not have been a strident feminist, but she was becoming a blooming cynic about the male establishment. She didn't burn bras, but she did blow whistles when it came to exposing discrimination in her own sport. And her opinions gained clout with every win. If you've got it, she figured, use it. Larry watched from the sidelines as she fulfilled a poem he had once written to her at the beginning of their marriage.

The exact words escape Larry now, but the poem was about the power of attraction. "I was the moth and she was the light," Larry recalls. "She provided the brilliance for everybody. The rest of us were the sup-

66

porting cast. That didn't bother me. I was totally actualized, just figuring out how to solve problems and make things work for us."

He marveled as Billie whipped post-match press conferences into political roundtables. She decried the country-club mentality of tennis, and stood in favor of Open Era tennis as a way to end under-the-table "shamateurism." There were two divisions in tennis at the time. Only amateurs were allowed to play in the major tournaments, like Wimbledon and the U.S. Championships. If players wanted to be paid for their talents, there were pro circuit events run by promoters.

Billie knew all about the amateurs on the take. She was one of them.

On a long walk down a gravel path at Forest Hills during the 1967 National Championships, the USLTA president, Bob Kelleher, tried to reason with Billie. "Stop ranting so loudly about Open Era tennis, or else," was the message. He told her she was up for the prestigious Sullivan Award, which was bestowed annually on the top amateur athlete in the country. She could walk away with it if she would just pipe down about pro tennis.

"She was very spirited," Kelleher recalls today. "I wanted her to win the Sullivan Award. She had other things on her mind."

Kelleher didn't dismiss what Billie had to say; in that, he was more progressive than most of his peers. Many of the control-mongers at the USLTA liked their athletes superficially pure, believing that anything beyond their meager $196 weekly payment for expenses would sully a player's image. As an amateur in the 1930s, Bobby Riggs had thumbed his nose at the organization's oppressive system, choosing like many of his peers to make a living with payments delivered in unmarked envelopes. The world had moved on, but the USLTA was still operating out of a time capsule. Billie listened to Kelleher as he reasoned with her to wait, telling her that everything would happen in time. But "in time" sounded like too long a time; Billie had no patience for slow evolutions.

"I was getting into my twenties at that point, and it wasn't happening," Billie says. "I'd had a sense of urgency since I was born. When you can see things so clearly, it's hard on you. You see this vision and everyone looks at you like you've got three heads when it's a no-brainer."

A NECESSARY SPECTACLE

Days after her conversation with Kelleher, Billie won the U.S. Championship and kept right on talking. She felt empowered. Billie had grabbed everyone's attention, and she wasn't going to waste a moment. The noise she and others made finally triggered the most important policy change in tennis history. The tipping point arrived in late 1967 when some of the game's most celebrated players turned pro and turned their backs on the amateur establishment. John Newcombe, Tony Roche, and Roy Emerson — each a member of the barnstorming Handsome Eight — had been main attractions at the majors. Without them, tennis as the world knew it might lose its mass appeal. The International Tennis Federation blinked at the notion of a starless amateur circuit and empty stands at the majors. In 1968 the Open Era began. Suddenly, paid professionals were able to compete with amateurs at the majors. Billie was ecstatic over the prospect of earning legitimate dollars. She was ready to play on circuit dates in joint events with the men, and cash in on tennis's momentum. But then she heard Larry's wary voice.

"Watch, the women are going to get squeezed out."

She couldn't have imagined it.

CHAPTER 4

Step Right Up

A veil of rain slipped over the South of France, passed through the remote splendor of Cannes, and splashed down on 250 fans turned seals as they clapped for points in between cloudbursts. This was Billie's first match of the Open Era — and it was played with squishy tennis shoes, soggy balls, and water beading up on her cat's-eye glasses.

Her opening night as a part of the National Tennis League wasn't exactly a sensation, but it was pro tennis. The Open Era began fractiously in 1968 with everyone wanting a share. Organizers and promoters turned the available loot into taffy as new tours and events were formed to accompany the four majors: the Australian, French, Wimbledon, and U.S. championships.

A year earlier, the NTL had been the brainstorm of former Davis Cup captain George MacCall — an amiable, disorganized man with a keen talent for motivation. MacCall had collected ten luminaries of the sport for his league. The NTL's glittering marquee included Rod Laver, Ken Rosewall, Roy Emerson, Fred Stolle, Andres Gimeno, and Pancho

Gonzalez. The women on the ticket were Billie, Ann Jones, Francoise Durr, and Rosie Casals.

The players had money in their pockets. Best of all, the payoffs were finally legit. As a righteous advocate for Open tennis who had preached the gospel of checkbook transparency, Billie was thrilled to sign a two-year, $80,000 deal. MacCall even tossed in a perk: her first credit card. Of course, a man had to arrange it, but, even so, the gold American Express card carried her name embossed across the front.

"It was April 1, 1968," Billie says. "I thought, 'April Fools' Day and you get a card; lucky you.'"

Billie earned every cent of her salary as the group barnstormed through Europe on a sleepless tour of one-night stands and late-night dancing. First stop, Cannes. So this was the glamorous life, she thought, staring into raindrops that left the court grease-stain slick. It was pratfall comedy. All Billie and Frankie Durr could do was "laugh our bahoolas off" at the absurdity of it as they watched the storms gather and pass, gather and pass.

Life on the NTL road proved more enlightening than Billie ever had anticipated. She, Rosie, and Ann gradually learned to interpret the fractured English of the wonderful Frankie Durr, an education in itself. Billie also would spend hours listening to Pancho Gonzalez discuss the persecution and prejudice he had faced as a Mexican-American growing up in a blue-collar pocket of Los Angeles. His real name was Richard, but fans called him Pancho — an ethnic slur.

He eventually accepted it, and the nickname later became a term of endearment. But during the late 1950s, Pancho's deep distrust forced the handsome man with the heavenly wavy hair to seek solitude on the pro tour. Instead of traveling in the station wagons that promoters Jack Kramer and Bobby Riggs provided, he rode alone in his Ford Thunderbird. Gonzalez checked into separate hotels, sulked in locker rooms, and lost his patience everywhere. No one ever knew when Pancho might snap. Once, when a photographer dawdled too long with his lens, he lost it in the company of the Italian movie star Gina Lollobrigida.

"Would you please smile, Pancho?" the cameraman asked after a delay.

"Take the damn picture," Pancho grumbled.

Pancho and Billie soon discovered that they shared a common background, if not temperament. He, too, had his stories to tell about childhood run-ins with Perry T. Jones. He, too, often felt like a misfit in society. Each of his sagas was accompanied by a moral. When he was a child, Pancho was almost run over by a car when he darted into the street. As it passed him, the door handle of the automobile gouged Pancho's face, but he treated the scar as a character trait, not as a flaw. Billie sponged up every word. Pancho wasn't a brooding bore to Billie. He was emotional, sensitive, and accessible.

The NTL that Pancho and Billie were helping to create consisted of an endless stream of matches, with eighteen stops in twenty days. Players traveled in vans that teetered on winding roads, and slept in hotel rooms no bigger than couch cushions. In some cities they had to lay down their own portable courts. In others, they wished they had.

In the Po Valley in Italy, they stepped onto a court still wet from the freshly poured asphalt. The surface covered the exact dimensions of the fair territory. Playing on the baseline meant standing on dirt an inch below the court. By the time the event ended, the balls were the color of charcoal briquettes.

Sometimes the locker-room showers leaked and hot water was just a memory. Some nights the exhausted players plopped down on thin mattresses covered with threadbare sheets. In spite of the spare conditions, the NTL was a blast. The women picked up tips from the men, and the men discovered the women had talent. The guys and gals got along famously on the court — and off. The local juke joints were hoppin' when members of the NTL troupe arrived after a long night on the court. They were still high off the adrenaline kick of playing, still loaded with a reservoir of vigor they refused to squander by going to bed before 2:00 a.m.

"We were crazy," Billie recalls. "We had so much energy."

Billie danced with Rod Laver until Roy Emerson cut in. They all sang along when the Beatles blasted through the speakers, and tapped their feet to every other tune. Jazz, country, pop or rock, foreign or domestic. So what if their next flight left at 7:00 a.m.? It didn't matter. Caught in the thick of the 1960s, this rollicking group was as close and snug as a group of college freshmen on a road trip.

Unfortunately, a tidal wave of Texas tea submerged the NTL before its first season ended. Oil baron Lamar Hunt had bankrolled World Championship Tennis, a rival alliance that lured many of the game's top players by offering generous contracts the underfinanced NTL could never match. If your name carried enough wattage to light up a tennis marquee, Hunt wanted you in his league. Unless you were a woman. Because his was a males-only bastion.

At first it wasn't clear to Billie how the ascendance of this new league might disrupt whatever tennis equality the Open Era was supposed to supply. She had a lot on her mind. Just out of law school in 1969, Larry had accepted a job with a legal firm in, of all places, Hawaii. It was an eleven-hour flight from the East Coast to an island state completely disconnected from tennis civilization. Larry didn't mind; he didn't have to make the commute. But Billie often did. Suddenly she was a lawyer's wife, loathing every ounce of small talk that tumbled from her mouth. Every time she visited her husband, she smiled, nodded her head, and clenched her teeth in a kill-me-now sort of way.

"She wasn't there a lot," Larry says. "In and out."

The experiment only lasted a year or so, and then the couple returned to San Francisco, where Larry began exploring a field perfectly suited to his talents: tennis promotion. In law school he had dabbled in marketing activities with some buddies who shared his goal of taking tennis out of the country clubs and bringing it to the urban stadiums. Larry netted $5,000 on his first main event. It was all too easy.

"The mistake of making money on your first promotion is you think you were somehow responsible for it," Larry says. "Well, the next time we learned. We did a much better job on a promotion, but we lost $10,000 because it rained and the highway patrol was telling everybody not to go out if you didn't have to. Here we had an indoor event, yet we were rained out. We didn't have a single person walk up that hadn't bought a ticket in advance."

The downpour failed to dampen his enthusiasm for promotion. Larry believed that the marketplace needed more events starring women. He saw them as assets rather than liabilities. But not too many other men shared his view. By the end of 1969, women had been completely pushed aside by the WCT, all but shut out of the tennis mix, exactly as Larry had predicted. The big purses and regular gigs belonged to the men, who retreated into a "Spanky and Our Gang" mentality, all but hammering a "No Girlz" sign on their club door.

Hardly any of them stood up for the ladies, not even Rod Laver or any of the guys with whom Billie had blithely toured in the defunct NTL. From every direction . . . nothing but arrows. Billie didn't foresee the betrayal, and the hurt was overwhelming.

" 'We don't want you,' that's what they told us," Billie recalls. "That was a profound wake-up call. I was crushed; I was devastated. I could not believe they didn't want us."

Table scraps were left as one event after another for the women dried up. In 1970, Billie asked the USLTA what the women's schedule for the next year looked like. To her amazement, one hardly existed. The International Federation of Tennis had assembled a Grand Prix list of events, but there were thirty-four tournaments for men and only nineteen for women. The discrepancy confounded Billie. In her progressive mind, players were genderless entertainers, not male or female. She had seen how women as well as men could prompt fans to cheer and applaud madly, or silently sit on their hands. Both sexes played good matches and bad matches. Gender was irrelevant.

It sounded rational, but her reasoning wasn't shared by the men who wrote the checks. The imbalance in the prize money remained mind-boggling. Riches for the men; rations for the ladies. Men would leave some events carrying winners' checks worth $3,500, while the female champion would take home only $600. Women often couldn't stuff one dime into their bank accounts unless they advanced past the quarterfinals.

Shrinking opportunity, shrinking purses. Professional tennis was phasing out women. At first they silently suffered the establishment's indifference, going along submissively, as happy as Dust Bowl survivors with the few drops they were receiving.

"Empowerment was not easy for everybody," Billie says. "There was a transition going on, but not everyone was ready."

Pop culture and politics were primed to inspire the reluctant. On television, Mary Tyler Moore was making it after all as a single gal in the big city. Her character, Mary Richards, was plowing ahead as a TV producer, tackling a profession outside of nursing, teaching, or homemaking, without a single male by her side. Yet she remained unthreatening, the gentlest of gender benders, the most feminine of feminists.

Things were a bit more raucous in the nation's streets. Women marched, protested, and boycotted for the New Feminism. "This is not a bedroom war," author Betty Friedan declared. "This is a political movement." Somewhere between Mary Richards and Betty Friedan, Billie lurked, wondering when the women of tennis would finally demand change. They needed a rallying point to reverse their passivity.

Enter the impresario of ego, Bobby Riggs's old nemesis, Jack Kramer. As the promoter for the Pacific Southwest Open in Los Angeles, Kramer was about to toss a match on a gas leak. The spreadsheet for his 1970 tournament listed two distinct levels of prize money, one from Neiman Marcus, the other from a garage sale. First place for men: $12,500. First place for the women: $1,500.

"The reason Jack Kramer was offering a $12,500 first prize to the men and a $1,500 first prize to the women was that he actually believed that was overpaying the women," Larry King says. "I think it was Manuel Santana who said he'd rather watch cattle graze than women play tennis."

The bias was so egregious, so out of line, the enraged women enlisted the powerful Gladys Heldman — founder and publisher of *World Tennis* magazine — to reason with Jack. Gladys returned from the meeting with this blunt assessment: "Kramer's an ass."

The women weren't demanding absolute equality — they knew better than to ask for overnight progress — but they believed in a bigger pot, or at least a good-faith effort at baby steps toward equity. But reasoning with the intractable Kramer was useless.

"The girls are talking about boycotting your tournament because of the low prize money," Heldman told Kramer.

"Fine with me," Kramer replied. "I'll take the $1,500 and throw it in the men's singles."

Besides, Kramer believed crowds came to see the men and were little more than amused by the female sideshows.

"They knew how it was going to be," Kramer recalls. "It wasn't going to change. The men were the big draws back then."

In the locker room at Forest Hills, only weeks before the Pacific Southwest Open, the women were beside themselves. What were their options? A boycott would be self-defeating. Creaming Kramer would result in police action. Then Gladys whisked into the locker room with improbable delight in her voice. She had the answer: The only way to equality was through autonomy. As savvy and shrewd as any tycoon, Gladys had made a few well-placed phone calls and was prepared to announce a tournament for women in Houston. Better yet, they would hold it the same week as Kramer's man-fest. The event offered $7,500 in prize money, thanks to Joseph Cullman, a Philip Morris heavy hitter who had agreed to sponsor the tournament through the tobacco company's Virginia Slims brand. Bleachers were already being erected; tickets were already being sold.

On the spot, Kramer was snubbed by Billie and eight brave comrades: Rosie Casals, Nancy Richey, Val Ziegenfuss, Kristy Pigeon, Peaches Bartkowicz, Kerry Melville, Judy Tegart Dalton, and Gladys's daughter, Julie Heldman. They would become known as the Original Nine.

As soon as the players made their stand, the USLTA's seersucker suits went into a wad. Don't you dare, they warned. The organization refused to sanction the tournament and threatened to suspend anyone in the field. The women tried to circumvent the USLTA decree by signing symbolic one-dollar pro contracts in Houston.

"We felt we had no choice," Richey says. "What was there to lose? The money wasn't there."

The USLTA wasn't amused. In September of 1970, flaunting their might, oozing hypocrisy, the officials suspended the ladies anyway, banning them from the Federation Cup and the Wrightman Cup and stripping them of their national ranking. The careers of Billie, Rosie, and company might have ended right then if not for their gumption as risk-takers. With immeasurable help from the deep-pocketed executives at Virginia Slims, they started their own breakaway circuit.

"We were fighting for our livelihood," Casals says. "We wanted to earn a living; we wanted to play sports, be accepted. People looked at us and said, 'Why aren't you in the kitchen? Why aren't you raising children, getting married, etcetera, etcetera?' We said, 'Why should we?'"

Other women — Margaret Court, for one — fell in line with the USLTA and continued playing in the traditional events. Some of them feared that retribution would snuff out their careers; others were fundamentally opposed to feminism. By 1970, that word conjured dramatically different images for different people. Many women, even some self-described feminists, were turned off by the increased volume from lesbians who were ratcheting up the radicalism.

The vociferous gay movement had begun to blend in with the women's movement after the 1969 Stonewall Rebellion. In the midst of the New York City mayoral race, and a day after the funeral of Judy Garland, police raided the Stonewall Inn, a gay bar in Greenwich Village. As three drag queens in sequins, and a butch lesbian were led to a paddy wagon, hundreds of gays began pelting authorities with rocks and pennies, triggering two nights of rioting.

Gay empowerment was born. And so was fear among a public turned off by the startling images they had witnessed — men in drag, women in combat boots? They were alienated by the militancy of some lesbians within the women's movement. Suddenly, feminists were linked to lesbians and lesbianism was linked to feminism.

This view was captured in one particularly vile response from a reader shortly after the 1971 launch of *Ms.* magazine: "Now that I have

read your magazine, I know for sure you are a witch . . . long-haired com-
mie dyke slut who dates negroids." Though they refrained from using
such vulgarity, many women felt similarly unsettled by the women's
movement.

Margaret Court was one of them. In her mind, a separate tennis circuit for women would create a petri-dish environment. If left to live and
travel together without the company of men, she reasoned, women
would be more likely to experiment with their sexuality.

"I thought it represented a moral slide," Court says. "I thought it was
much healthier for the men and the women to be together."

Court remained with the other USLTA members, including Virginia Wade, Evonne Goolagong, and Chris Evert, the intriguing sweet-
sixteen ingenue from Florida, who, in her first year, was already a darling
in tennis.

"It was an uneasy time," Evert recalls. "I think my father just
thought it was more secure for me to be with the USLTA, but it was difficult for everyone involved on both sides."

Evert, Wade, Goolagong, and Court gave the USLTA enough stars
to form a rival circuit to the Slims. Eager to pit their group against the
renegades, the USLTA ended its two-month ban on the Original Nine.

"Virginia, Chris, and Margaret, they had the support of the USLTA
and the entrée of being the good guys," Casals says. "We were the
bad guys."

How would the brazen few survive? The women themselves weren't
sure at first. Before the Slims circuit began, the Original Nine had to negotiate tournament prize money. But they had no promoters to negotiate
with, and none of them had any idea how to determine the size of each
purse. Sitting in a semicircle on Gladys's bedroom floor, several of the
women tried to calculate their worth.

"We have to disclose how much we've each been getting under the
table to figure out what the marketplace is," Billie reasoned as she looked
around the room. "I'm going to reveal what I get. . . . Okay, it's about
$2,000 per week." Billie then told the group she believed Rod Laver and
Margaret Court received about the same amount. "I'm lucky I get my

way paid," one of them quipped. The players burst into laughter. The levity provided a much-needed respite from all the fears. Everyone in the room understood: It was success or bust.

Making financial demands — even in polite discourse — was a brand-new experience for these women. To flout authority, to gamble on the public's interest, to slap a dollar figure on their talent, these were necessary steps if they wanted to achieve independence from the men and inclusion in the mainstream.

Strange how one step led to another. This took courage. This took feminism.

The *Ms.* crowd applauded the group's audacity, but they disdained the logo that marketeers had developed for the Virginia Slims tour: "You've come a long way, baby." As if smoking a cigarette were a symbol of progress for women, as if "baby" weren't as demeaning as a slap on the behind. Billie wrestled with it, too. But she decided the financial benefits of a sponsorship outweighed the politics of brand identity.

After adding a half-dozen players to their ranks, the Original Nine were ready to start an eight-event circuit together. But they could not live off the goodwill of Tobacco Road alone. They needed more sponsors. They needed wheels for their movement.

With all the persuasive powers of revival-tent ministers, Larry and Billie asked Kjell Qvale, an executive with British Motor Cars in San Francisco, to help them secure a presenting sponsor for a local event. This was Billie's first one-on-one schmoozing of a sponsor, her first marketing pitch of a dream. It was her innocent foray into the underworld of money.

So she met a thug. Well, he seemed like a thug, anyway. A slick guy with a slicker name — Jerry Diamond. He was Qvale's PR man, the hard-case who handled all of his boss's negotiations. Qvale agreed to back the event, provided Jerry Diamond ran it.

Diamond was a classic New Yorker with the works. He'd grown up over a jewelry store, and spoke in a street-tough accent.

We don't have a chance, Billie thought after she had her first taste of Diamond's shtick.

Diamond listened to Larry and Billie's plans. He didn't say yes. He didn't say no. He said he wanted to think it over. What he really wanted was advice. Diamond hit the phone lines to his tennis pals, and soaked in their feedback. Meanwhile, on their way home, Billie and Larry debated whether they had closed the sale with Jerry. They had their doubts even without knowing that one of Diamond's advisers was Jack Kramer.

Kramer, of course, cackled over the idea of anyone sponsoring a tennis event without men. He convinced Diamond that the women had no chance of capturing the public imagination; but when Diamond relayed Kramer's warning to Kjell Qvale, the car dealer ignored his right-hand man.

"Jerry was putting on the auto show for Kjell and the other dealers," Larry King says. "So, when his number-one supporter of the auto show said, 'Jerry, you're going to do this for me,' Jerry had to do it. But he hated it."

Diamond had his principles; he loathed anything that lost money. Qvale dropped $13,000 in the first year, but he loved all the publicity the event generated and proudly told Billie, "We're going to do it again."

"You couldn't have made Jerry unhappier if you'd have driven a nail through his heart," Larry says. "The second year, we lost like $7,000."

By the third year, business was looking up. In 1973 the USLTA realized the self-sabotage of two competing circuits in tennis. The Virginia Slims black sheep were not going away. In fact, their prize money and popularity were on the way up, so much so that Margaret Court joined the renegades when she returned from giving birth to her son.

The USLTA brass soon surrendered to fiscal reality, asking, "Why not one circuit and one prize pot for all?" Promising an equal purse at the U.S. Open — the first major to make such a gesture — the USLTA merged with the Virginia Slims to form one tour.

Now everyone was together, playing anywhere of her choosing. It so happened Evert signed up to play in a certain Bay Area event.

"Chris Evert played, and that Friday night, when the audience was lined up around the arena block," Larry recalled, "Jerry had this shit-eating grin. All of a sudden he loved women's tennis."

A NECESSARY SPECTACLE

Before there was peace on the tour, before Chrissie and Co. joined the Slims crowd, the Original Nine and their converts spent three unsteady years grasping Billie's star-studded coattails for survival. She practically needed a crowbar to extricate herself from the pressure of being the official torch-bearer, standard-bearer, bearer of all burdens.

Anything Billie mumbled or whispered morphed into a symbol. "Whatever I said or did, it was magnified, scrutinized," Billie recalls. "It was, 'Billie, what do you think?' 'Billie, what does this mean?' And it was all the time." The inordinate attention and ridiculous demands stretched the elastic of her sanity, and strained her marriage. She was traveling to events, isolated among her tour friends. While she was earning prize money, her husband was excavating a money pit.

"In '71, '72, '73, I didn't make a nickel promoting these tournaments, and the prize money she won made it so we could afford to survive, but she just thought I was a total playboy because I ran these tournaments," Larry says. "You know what? I was just doing what I wanted to do, which I thought was helpful to her career."

The events he promoted provided a stage for women's tennis — and, eventually, prize money for everyone, including Billie. It was an odd and conflicting cycle: Larry promoted in one city, Billie played in another.

Whether the event was a Larry King production, Billie and the Slims players knew it was their job to keep the turnstiles spinning. There was nothing glamorous about their grassroots campaign. The players worked the crowds in between matches, stumping for themselves. They crawled into the stands to grip and grin; they stood at street intersections waving free tickets for circuit events. The stress was enormous.

"You name it, we did it," Nancy Richey recalls. "We talked to anyone who would listen."

Billie was consumed with promotions, attendance figures, and newspaper coverage. She didn't need any more distractions. In February 1971, she felt a queasiness sneak up on her while on the court. She knew it right away. She was pregnant. Larry and Billie discussed having the baby, but, deep inside, she knew her marriage was in a tenuous state, too fragile to inflict it upon a child.

They hardly ever saw each other. They were living separate lives.

But, according to social mores, she was supposed to have the baby. She was supposed to be a mother. She was supposed to drop everything for her maternal instincts. Her mother did it; every woman did it.

Other players walked away for nine months, returned to the tour, and played on. Margaret Court, for one. Abortion was taboo in 1971, even as the pro-choice activists were gaining the momentum that would result in the *Roe v. Wade* Supreme Court decision of 1973. With her life always, it seemed, perched on the cusp of social transition, Billie refused to follow the cultural signposts or listen to political rhetoric. Instead, she followed her heavy heart.

"It was my body and, as difficult as it was, my choice."

A month later, she and Larry paid a doctor $580 for an abortion. After two hours in the recovery room, Larry helped Billie slip into a car for the drive home. Three days later, keeping another commitment, she played a tournament in St. Petersburg, Florida. She promptly suffered dehydration on her way to a loss.

It was one of her few defeats that year. Throughout 1971, Billie ticked off title after title with her attacking serve-and-volley style, picking up prize money in every city on the circuit, in each major on the calendar. She became the first female player to inch past $100,000 in earnings for an entire season. Male stars were tallying $200,000 and more, but breaking the six-figure barrier for women signaled progress. Money meant empowerment, influence, and independence.

And the more Billie spoke out against inequality, the more the press described her as an ogre. The more attention she received, the less privacy she enjoyed.

"I felt like everyone was grabbing at me."

She bristled when strangers touched her. When Billie dined out, she might as well have been penned in a petting zoo. Men, women, and children, they all approached her for an embrace, a handshake, a pat on the back, or an air-kiss on the cheek.

"It was tough for Billie Jean," Larry King says. "For years she couldn't eat out at a restaurant. She gave up her life. But that's part of what she wanted, you know? She wanted tennis to be a big deal, and that's the price she paid."

Most of the overzealous fans meant to be supportive, but Billie found them invasive. They pulled chairs up to her table. They asked for autographs in the bathroom. They begged for pictures in the grocery store — and her fame was just beginning.

She was the "It" woman, the player earning most of the ink. Some of Billie's more insecure peers coveted the attention she received. Suddenly the inside jokes didn't include her. Invitations got lost on their way to her mailbox. Jealousy was rampant on the women's tour in 1971, and it wasn't just directed at Billie. As the money and glory escalated, the newcomers — particularly the sixteen-year-old Noxzema girls with their honey-brown ponytails and their mass appeal — posed a threat to the pioneers and they resented it.

Chris Evert's coy allure attracted a new audience to the tennis arenas. It did not, however, please her older peers — except for Billie. To her, Chris Evert was a welcome relief. Here was a kid to diffuse the glare, a starlet to share the celebrity duties. With her fluid two-fisted backhand and tanned petite features, Evert became the wholesome teen who helped with the heavy lifting.

The press adored Chrissie. From the covers of magazines, at the center of the sports pages, she left everyone smitten. She was uncommonly poised for an adolescent, and her cool demeanor only made her more mysterious — and more resented.

"Well, the women treated me like shit," Evert recalls with her typical candor. "They were not nice. I was the first one. I was the guinea pig."

She became the object of their bitterness. To many of the women, Evert was a golden girl who had sashayed into the tennis world on the back of their hard work, collected the prize money they had sacrificed to amass, and retreated into her happy nuclear family.

"The women made it blatantly clear that I was not their favorite, and that I was intrusive," Evert recalls. "It was, 'How dare you come in, take all our money and get on the cover of *Newsweek?*'"

What's more, not a lick of sweat appeared on her incandescent skin.

As Chris would later explain to *Time* magazine, "No point is worth falling down over." What a piece of work. Bye-bye, Miss American Pie. If only they could have wished her away.

The catty attitudes incensed Billie. Whatever they thought of Chris, Billie was not going to let them alienate a star in the making. At Forest Hills in the summer of 1971, at a table outside the club, Billie gathered players for a lecture on Evert Envy.

"You guys, she is our next star," Billie scolded. "She's a good person. You guys say hi to her."

"Chris doesn't say hello to us," the women snipped.

"She's not supposed to say hi to you. God, you're older than she is. Look her in the eye and say hello. It's the right thing to do. She's going to be a superstar. She's it, okay? She's exactly what we need. Plus, she's a nice person. So get over it. If you don't like that she beats you, tough, beat her."

The kind words hid Billie's own state of mind over Chrissie's emergence. Evert unnerved her. Heading toward twenty-nine, Billie couldn't help but wonder how many miles were left on her disintegrating knees, how much resistance she could muster against the charge of this wunderkind.

Throughout the 1971 U.S. Open, Chrissie had introduced herself to America with oiled groundstrokes as she set up on the baseline like a bodyguard — immovable, impenetrable, and intimidating. The crowds practically cooed over Chrissie's sun-splashed presence. Her opponents could withstand neither her unflappable strokes nor her partisan backing. Unglued by both, Frankie Durr exited the 1971 U.S. Open in tears after losing to Evert, another victim along the tenacious teen's twenty-two-match winning streak.

By the U.S. Open semifinals, it was Chris versus Billie; new versus used; prodigy versus history. Or that's how the press played it, in one version or another. Billie couldn't decide what it was. Just the thought of the match forced her to consider her tennis lifespan. If Chris dispatched her, it would signal a slippage from the pedestal. If she became the crowd's darling, what would that make Billie? The jilted flame?

Negative energy swirled like a dust devil in Billie's head. After warming up on an outside court before the semis, she ducked into the locker-room shower and tried to rinse away the anxiety. The steam rose, and soon she couldn't tell the difference between the water trickling on her face and the teardrops running down her cheeks. She cried, aching and panicking at the same time.

God, get hold of yourself, she thought. *It can't end here.*

She slapped her thigh, pumped her fist, and pulled herself together. Then she joined Chrissie for that stroll through the tunnel.

"It was a long walk," Evert recalls, "and I'll never forget this — Billie just starts chatting at me. I'd never heard of anything like that; you didn't talk to your opponent before a match."

As they neared the stadium, Billie offered Chrissie some advice.

"You're riding the crest of a wave," Billie told her. "Enjoy it."

Chris was perplexed. What had she just said?

"I didn't know what the hell she was talking about," Chris says. "I was sixteen. I was stupid."

Was Billie trying to compliment her, or to undermine her confidence? Chris had no idea. Billie stopped talking as they warmed up. Once the match began, she quickly shut out the crowd's raves for Chrissie, and began delivering a variety of weapons that confounded her glistening opponent.

"She proceeded to just chop up my game," Chris says. "She gave me a lot of junk and beat me."

Using the fast grass court to her advantage, Billie ended Chris's vaunted winning streak. As the fans greeted Billie's feat with a rousing ovation, and ushered her off the court to whistles and cheers, she filled with pride. They still appreciated her after all. Billie wasn't done, not just yet. She could still shake the young players on tour, still rev up her competitive pistons.

"When I came across Billie Jean, I was a bit scared and overwhelmed by her," Aussie great Evonne Goolagong once admitted. "I was a young girl from the country, playing against this woman who was ranting and raving at the umpires as well as herself. I am sure that I lost big matches to Billie Jean because I was too busy looking at her instead of concentrating on my own game."

Billie's outsized presence could be distracting—even to her closest friends. After unnerving her pal Rosie Casals in the finals for the 1971 U.S. Open title, Billie finished the year ranked number two. The number-one position belonged to the sunny, if daunted, Goolagong, but Billie felt the season would go down as one of her best.

But by 1972 the momentum of the U.S. Open had evaporated. The season started dreadfully. In the middle of a two-month slump, Billie had yet another encounter with self-doubt. She contemplated an escape from the incessant pressure to be the outspoken leader, from the daily grind of practice and play, from the pain in knees that one day would resemble baseballs from all the seams sewn during countless surgeries. She thought about pulling the ripcord on her public life. Disappear; vanish. It sounded enticing even before her abortion became a headline.

The story wasn't meant to get out, but suddenly Billie found herself in the hostile arena of national politics. A petition from *Ms.* magazine had arrived at her home, requesting a signature from anyone who had ever sought an abortion. Billie never saw the letter, but Larry did. He scribbled in her name without telling her.

The *Ms.* story ran, accompanied by the petition. Eventually the item worked its way through the press until the *Washington Post* published a piece implying that Billie's abortion had resulted in one of her best seasons. To make the revelation more excruciating, the source for the *Post* story was someone close to her. Larry.

"I was so upset with him," Billie says. "He told Gladys, and Gladys told everyone. He thought it was the right thing to do. I'm not saying I wouldn't have signed the petition, but I would've wanted to make that decision. He didn't ask my permission."

It was too late for apologies. Billie confronted the ensuing hoopla with candor, admitting the truth even as she seethed inside. The story eventually landed in the *Los Angeles Times*—the paper that landed on the doorstep of her childhood home in Long Beach every morning. Her parents read all about it. Billie had never said a word to them about the procedure. She didn't dare. She received hate mail in bundles, and tearful confessionals, but she couldn't broach the subject with her mother and father.

They had a certain image of Billie, certain expectations. A few weeks after the story broke, Billie retreated home, knowing her parents had read the coverage. The subject was the elephant sitting in the living room. It was Mother's Day.

The family settled in to watch a *60 Minutes* segment featuring Billie; the piece made no mention of the latest controversy. Billie exhaled for a moment, but after a commercial break, and another tick-tick-tick, the show aired another story. On abortions.

The awkward silence snapped. I cried for three days, her mother told her. Billie, don't you love children, don't you love Larry? The questions were understandable, but Billie didn't give anything more than vague reasons for her decision. She was sorry she hadn't told her parents, and was devastated by the way they'd found out.

"She hated paying the price with her parents," Larry says. "Really, she felt free being able to join the other women and support what was right, that women have a choice with their own decisions, well before *Roe v. Wade*."

Was that Billie's feeling, or Larry's? Whichever it was, in the end, Billie's core instincts took over, lending her the voice to speak out on a volatile issue. To the applause of many feminists, she became an advocate for abortion rights. She may have arrived at activism by accident, but she was determined to wear the cause well.

"It had to do with ethics," Larry claims with conviction. "How do you lead people if you're not honest? You have to lead by moral choices, not by telling people what they want to hear. I would never be a politician. But she had the right gumption. I'll tell ya, she was, well, she was a great wife."

But it was exhausting being everything to everyone. Everyone was a critic. Everyone had an opinion of her. One day, in a car ride from San Francisco to Los Angeles, Mona Schallau decided to take on the role of backseat driver to Billie's career. Mona couldn't ignore all the focus the fans and the media placed on Billie's every utterance, and she bitterly resented how much attention they lavished on the celebrity. Mona decided that Billie's motivations were completely self-centered, that the stars made too much money, that they received too much adulation.

And who was Mona Schallau to say such things? She was a decent but unspectacular player on the circuit who, only three years earlier, had played for a pittance. Now she was sharing a ride with the great Billie Jean King, and she couldn't resist the chance to give the legend an earful.

Billie listened to every word in disbelief. Too much attention on her? After so many years of nothing? After so much sacrifice? This was too much. Right then, Billie decided she needed a break from the cacophony of judgment. Find some space, Billie thought. Get some air. For ten days in the spring of 1972, Billie didn't even grip the throat of a racket until she and Larry took a leisurely hit on a court near their San Francisco apartment.

"I'm retiring," she told him.

That was it. She was sure, absolute, as firm as a handshake.

"Every emotion Billie shared was on a big scale," Larry recalls. "She lurched from one to the next."

On the walk back to their apartment, after crossing two debris-strewn parking lots in pensive silence, Billie changed her mind. "Forget what I said," she told Larry.

Rejuvenated by her brief hiatus, Billie rediscovered her love for the game. She soared over the $100,000 mark in winnings again in 1972, and regained her number-one ranking for the first time since 1968. Another gender barrier snapped when Billie appeared on the cover of *Sports Illustrated* as the 1972 Sportswoman of the Year — a place historically reserved for the Sportsman of the Year.

Actually, there was one of those, too. She shared the spread with UCLA basketball coach John Wooden. She was not in the least upset with this game of gender halvesies. She knew it was a step, a start. Hell, it was history.

Some fans may have found her strident. Some journalists may have described her as blustery. But on that *SI* cover she was a living, breathing, smiling, unthreatening symbol of change. Despite her stance on abortion and on other political causes, she was still the active body and congenial face of the women's movement.

"She wasn't over the top," Gloria Steinem says today. "She was just brave. She just saw a need and filled it."

Billie enjoyed widespread popularity. For years her drawing power fueled the Slims' success. In 1971 the tour hit nineteen cities and paid $309,000 in prize money. A year later it passed through twenty, with $501,275 at stake. Even the USLTA couldn't ignore those numbers. That's when the organization finally reached an accord with the Slims group in 1973.

"Once I got onto the Slims tour, I saw what it was doing for women's tennis," Court recalls. "I think, at one stage, you could see down the line how it was getting even larger than the men's tennis. You could see how women's tennis was going to come to the forefront because in those early years it was very hard for the women to get that recognition unless there was a King-Court final. We'd always be pushed to the background."

Margaret was a reluctant convert. She was still leery of a women's tour divided from the men, convinced that such a cocoon fostered homosexuality.

"You know, I praise God I was on tour with my husband at that time," Court declares.

The public never knew about the whispers of lesbianism on tour. They only saw a group of women who wowed them with their work ethic at every stop on a schedule that included twenty-two cities and a total of $775,000 in prize money by 1973. Somehow Billie, once the chubby teen in the rhinestone-studded glasses, had grown into the fit woman who used her stardom to foment change.

She experienced the rewards and enjoyed the prosperity, all without having to follow the circuit's success from the grave. Posthumous benefits—that was the damn luck of most pioneers. Billie was alive to hear praise—even from her critics. By the end of the 1972 season, even Mona Schallau had come around. After watching Billie's life scoured by the public and press, after watching her maintain focus on the court despite every distraction, Mona decided, "Billie, you don't make enough."

Stinson Beach was a tiny wormhole from the chaos just north of San Francisco. Billie's journey took her up the Pacific Coast Highway and through a few hills until the road crossed the peninsula. She drove along the stunning, jagged coastline, past a restaurant with four tables and a lunch counter, and took the dirt road on the left. After steering past a few hippie houses, she parked her car at the beach.

This was her nirvana. At the end of the 1972 season, Billie spent several weeks vegging at Stinson Beach, sitting against a tree trunk, gazing at the ocean. She wrote letters and processed her life. At night she did all the normal things, hitting the movie premieres, doing the laundry, while trying to wrap her mind around the question *Why?*

Why did she need the limelight? Why was she camera starved?

Part of it was ego, she concluded. But part of it was passion. The mix left her with an insatiable desire to matter, a craving that had begun when she'd stood chin-high to that kitchen sink and told her mother she wanted to do something great with her life. She returned to tennis with a perspective on what she had accomplished, and what loose ends she still needed to tie up. The goals were beyond men by then. The Slims tour was on the go, and needed organizing. It needed benefits, a plan, a structure. Almost by force of habit, women didn't unionize; they capitulated. But in 1973, Billie invited sixty-three women to a conference room inside a London hotel. Betty Stove locked the door. No one, it seemed, was getting out until the players agreed to form the Women's Tennis Association.

"It was tense," Billie recalls.

Some women still worried about the establishment, concerned they'd be ostracized for organizing. They wondered whether Billie knew what she was doing. Hours passed. Discussions were followed by silence, followed by more discussions. Larry King had already drawn up the bylaws. It was up to Billie to sell them. By the end of the session, the women agreed to unite. They became an entity operating on their own circuit, attracting their own crowds, inching closer to the men in prize-money equality. They acquired access.

With mounting incredulity, Bobby Riggs watched their progress from afar. Why were these women worth all that loot, he wanted to know. Why were they the centers of attention? Any talk of economic equality grated on Bobby. In his estimation, the women's tour would end up being just another Gussy Moran experiment gone sour. He still viewed women as arm-candy accessories in a male domain.

"Women belong in the bedroom and kitchen, in that order," Bobby rattled out loud. He had his own cause, economic equality for senior players. Any one of them was more than a match for the best female player, and, to prove it, while providing himself with the media platform he craved, Bobby waved a red towel in Billie's face. "How can you not play me?" he continually asked her. He believed his inflammatory rhetoric and matador tactics would eventually incite Billie to charge toward the proving ground of his choice — the tennis court. Billie didn't bite.

"Billie Jean kept turning him down because there was nothing in it for women's tennis to beat the 1939 champion of Wimbledon," Larry King recalls. "So she refused, and she was consistent in refusing; and Bobby, through default, set up what became the Mother's Day Massacre with Margaret Court, because he couldn't get Billie Jean to play."

The blood had barely dried on Bobby's racket when his people started phoning Billie once again. After Margaret lost, Billie's instincts told her to play Bobby. But this reflex collided with the reality of a potential failure. There could be dire consequences for taking Bobby's dare.

"Larry, wait a minute, I don't know if I want to do this," she told her husband. She wondered if she was up to the challenge. She knew what was coming, the scrutiny, the responsibility. The pressure.

"I knew how scared I would be," Billie admits. "My stomach would be going into knots. Just to think about it, it was like, whoa, in the bottom pit of your stomach. Oh my God. I can't lose. I've got to win."

Billie realized that a good deal more than just her standing and pride would be at stake. The humiliation a loss might inflict on her was the least of it. "This is about history," she pointed out. "The tour could go away, Title IX could be damaged. Everything is so tenuous."

She and Larry had to think this through for other reasons, as well. It was a pivotal time in the couple's plans to create spin-off enterprises, using the steam from the women's movement and Billie's celebrity.

"Billie Jean and I were driving across the Bay Bridge and she was reading *Sports Illustrated* and they had no coverage of women," Larry recalls. "She was railing on why doesn't *Sports Illustrated* give some coverage to women? I said, 'Billie Jean, that's not their market; their market is men. If you want to have a women's sports publication, you're going to have to do it yourself.' She said, 'Then let's do it.' That's why we started womenSports publications."

At the time, Billie was also preparing to launch the Women's Sports Foundation as a nonprofit watchdog for girls' athletics. A lot of synergy could be derailed if she lost the Riggs match.

"We had all this stuff going on, and we knew it could be a powerful adjunct," Larry says. "But the only way Billie Jean was going to do it was if she was going to prove something."

In late June, just before Wimbledon, she answered Bobby's bravado with a firm "yes" and slipped into the role of womankind's avenger. The contract called for a best-of-five-sets match — at Billie's request, and at ABC's need to fill time — with a $100,000 winner-take-all purse plus $150,000 in ancillary rights. With such lucrative stakes, Billie and Larry knew that announcing the match would produce a media frenzy. They held off for a few weeks, allowing time for Billie to concentrate without Riggs or the press disturbing her. She knew how Bobby had dogged Margaret at events before the Mother's Day Massacre. She didn't want to hear from him until after Wimbledon. Free from distraction, Billie won her fifth Wimbledon title. Days later, peace came to an abrupt end.

On July 11, 1973, Billie and Bobby sat side by side during a packed press conference at Manhattan's Town Tennis Club. "The Ali-Frazier fight was 'The Fight,'" promoter Jerry Perenchio proclaimed to the full house. "This is 'The Match.'"

All but scripted by Perenchio, the sex-charged squabbling began.

"I'll tell you why I'll win," Bobby piped. "She's a woman and they don't have the emotional stability. She'll choke just like Margaret did."

Billie listened to Bobby's blather with amusement, weaving back and forth as he filibustered his way through the press conference. Nasty little man, that's what Court thought of Bobby's antics. Margaret had suppressed her desire to say so out loud. But Billie had never been much good at keeping her opinions to herself. She could only hear so much. After one too many crackpot remarks about women, she countered with venom.

"That creep runs down women. That's why my feeling is like — hate. I like him for many things, but I hate him putting down women, not giving us credit as competitors."

Bobby was crestfallen, pained by how personally she took his canned jabs. It was in fun, in the spirit of promotion, in jest. Didn't she get it?

Bobby looked at Billie, and pleaded, "Please don't call me a creep. You don't mean it."

"Creep," Billie confirmed. "That stands."

The circus of the surreal had begun.

CHAPTER 5

Blue Suede Shoes

Billie was sitting in a Houston toilet stall.

For two weeks she had been in solitude, hunkered down in a coastal sanctuary in South Carolina. Her return to the tour the week before her match with Bobby was head-spinning. Privacy was a lost hope — even in the bathroom.

A handful of players strolled into the locker room of the Net-Set Complex, gathering their equipment in preparation for a Virginia Slims tournament in Houston, an event unmercifully scheduled as a lead-in to Billie's duel with Bobby. Chatting it up, unaware of Billie in the nearby stall, these women revealed just how much faith they had in her. Publicly, the tour players had patted her on the back for stepping up to repair the damage Margaret Court's loss had inflicted on women and women's tennis. But in front of that bathroom mirror, they formed a line of Doubting Thomasinas — except for one player whose loyalty to Billie could never waver.

"I don't think Billie can beat him," someone said.

"What do you mean?"

A NECESSARY SPECTACLE

The question was raised in a voice as soft and gentle as a cocked fist. Rosie Casals couldn't hide her anger or disbelief. She had been at Billie's side through the rise and fall of the NTL and the ups and downs of the circuit's evolution. Now she stepped forward as her friend's truculent defender.

Her parents had named her Rosemary, but that had always seemed a bit long-winded, given her compact, abbreviated frame. Rosie or Rosebud made for a better fit. Though she was only five feet two, no one would call her short on moxie. Rosie would march in quick steps onto the court, acting the role of undaunted gladiator against bigger, more powerful opponents. She was a top-five player in her own right — only her mental "Billie block" in singles kept her from advancing to the number-one spot.

Rosie was also one of the few women on the tour who truly possessed what was known in the 1970s as va-va-va-voom. The crowds adored this feisty merrymaker. She was bold enough to play her matches wearing spangles and sequins. Never a conformist, she colored outside the lines. If Billie was the high-profile ringleader of the Original Nine, Rosie was the spirited core of its inner circle.

She believed in Billie. But in the days before the showdown, here was the unbearable truth: Many of the players were using their prize money — the very same dough they had earned courtesy of Billie's fight for equality — to place bets on Bobby.

"The players crushed me," Billie says. "Here I am, in the toilet, hearing this. I couldn't believe it."

The turncoats had been caught up in the thrall of the nationwide gambling frenzy Bobby had whipped up, action that ribboned through every beauty parlor and barbershop from America to Europe. Who do you like, the Libber or the Lobber? With betting slips flying, bookies were as busy as short-order cooks. At press dinners, dollar bills were stacked under salt shakers. Even politicians got into the act; in the U.S. House of Representatives, congresswoman Bella Abzug placed a bet with a half-dozen of her fellow pols. But at least Bella plopped her money down on Billie Jean.

Billie understood the lure of fast cash — hey, she loved money, too — but she felt ambushed by those gals lined up in front of the sinks. She slid back the door latch, stepped out of the stall, and approached the bathroom mirror.

"Just silence," Billie recalls. "They didn't know what to say."

She washed her hands, glanced at the women, and walked out, leaving the awkward dead air to speak for itself. Part of Billie understood how Margaret's loss had thinned her peers' confidence. After all, from the moment she'd agreed to play Bobby, she'd felt the dread circulating through her own blood. She felt absolutely petrified — right down to her fingertips.

"My job in the match, and I remember this being very clear, was to change the hearts and minds of people to match the legislation of Title IX and what we were trying to do with the women's movement," Billie recalls. "It was to validate it, to celebrate it, and to get going toward changing a world where we had equality for both genders.

"I was terrified."

Fear of disgrace kept Billie awake at night in the months before the match with Bobby. Anxiety made her twitchy. Her speech became as fast and high-pitched as Minnie Mouse on helium.

By the time Billie reached Houston the week of the match, her panic had begun to dissipate. Preparation was her peacemaker.

In isolation at the Shipyard Plantation in Hilton Head, South Carolina, residing at her buddy Dick Butera's condominium hideaway amid the sea oats, she pulled herself together two weeks before the match.

"She was like a prize fighter preparing for a bout," Larry King recalls. "She was intensely focused, with a select few around her."

Butera was one of them. He was a fast friend, the president of the Philadelphia Freedom, a team in the WTT league that Billie and Larry had developed. World Team Tennis was their dream, a way to bring the best players into a team atmosphere during events between the majors, designed as a grassroots venture to stir up interest in the game on the local level.

Butera was not only a disciple of Billie's vision, but he was married to one of Billie's closest friends, Julie Anthony, the cerebral center of the tour, who was working toward a Ph.D. in psychology. Along with Larry and Billie's secretary, Marilyn, they formed a protective alliance for Billie before the match. In their company, she was free to funnel all of her energy into training. They screened Billie's calls and answered reporters' questions.

Within days, Billie's confidence began a recovery process. It helped that her health rebounded, too. Much to her dismay, the press had assigned Billie a mystery illness when she went underground.

Had she slipped into hiding to default to Bobby? No one knew.

The whispers had begun a month earlier, when Billie had failed to defend her U.S. Open title; she'd been forced to retire during the third round against Julie Heldman.

Punch-drunk with a fever, slogging through shots as if striking the ball under water, Billie fizzled out in the heat and humidity on Court No. 22, a popular spot located in front of the terrace at Forest Hills, a place where patrons could go tipsy for tennis.

Cheers to Billie. That's what fans expected to say. Then Billie shuffled out of the locker room and onto the court three shades of pale. Understanding her name value to the draw, knowing ticket sales depended on her presence, she refused to deliver a no-show.

"Those first two years, we didn't have a tournament if I didn't play," Billie recalled. "That's what they told me, 'You can't miss it.'"

The U.S. Open was too much, though, especially against an opponent whose compassion for Billie's predicament stood mud-puddle deep. This was Julie's chance to conquer Billie, to poke a little hole in the aura of tennis's freedom fighter.

As the match dragged on, her body filled with quit, but it couldn't touch her heart. Billie wanted to finish, if only to give Julie's win credibility. Defaulting was not an option. She was going to finish on her feet.

Throughout the afternoon, Billie labored in between points and squeezed out extra time on the changeovers. The tactic rankled Heldman, who repeatedly screamed at the umpire, "She's taking too long!"

"You know what, Julie?" Billie finally called out over her latest opponent's rant. "If you want it that bad, I'll default."

Billie's dramatic exit, down 1–4 in the final set of her fourth-round match, became a springboard for suspicion. When she retreated to South Carolina, the press wondered if she'd slipped into hiding as a prelude to pulling out. No matter how often her camp tried to refute the rumors with updates on her improving condition, doubts remained. *Newsweek* played it safe and peeled Billie's image off their cover before its press run. ABC executives called meetings to discuss alternate programming in case Billie turned out the lights on the Battle of the Sexes.

The nervous reactions infuriated Billie. This was not some chronic illness that would hamper her play, or a convenient alibi for cancellation, or a psychosomatic reaction to pressure. It was a virus, for crying out loud. After a few days of rest — and a bagful of Three Musketeers bars — the illness had been flushed out of her system.

She was fine, better than fine. Each morning in Hilton Head she awoke in a condo on a golf course, ambled out to the driving range, and slapped a few balls into the blue sky. It was a nice warm-up to each day, with practice and strategy sessions to follow. As preparation for Bobby's junk-ball attack, Billie fielded hundreds of weak lobs every afternoon, each hoisted high into the sun in an attempt to replicate the Astrodome's court lighting.

Though she remained beyond the reach of the media frenzy, there were plenty of TVs on the premises. Billie followed the swirl of attention surrounding the match. She heard the sexist quips flapping like bats from Bobby's mouth. Once in a while she would flip on ABC and there she was, feeling Bobby's bottle-cap muscles in one of those ubiquitous match promos that seemed to run every five minutes.

One Saturday afternoon, Billie strolled in from the courts and found Dick Butera lying on the floor, watching a college football game between Stanford and Penn State. It was halftime. The Stanford band began playing Helen Reddy's "I Am Woman." She watched as the tuba players, drummers, and flutists started to swirl and curl across the field until they formed a set of initials.

BJK.

The measure of her transcendence had just unfolded on the fifty-yard line. As Billie listened to the music, the last lines of the lyrics swam through her head: "Yes, I've paid the price . . . But look how much I gained . . . If I have to I can face anything — anything."

This tribute wasn't an ego trip for Billie; it was more a moment of self-discovery. This is it, she thought, this is why I'm putting my credibility on the line, why I'm willing to risk humiliation. She and Dick turned to each other with tears in their eyes.

At age five, Billie had told her mom, "I'm going to do something great with my life." Now she knew. Now she got it. Her match with Bobby would define her clairvoyance.

At that moment her happiness was galvanizing. She was going to win. The Helen Reddy song told her so. Her mind confirmed it.

Nothing could ruin her inner peace but Bobby Riggs. It was Marilyn who carried the rumor from L.A. to Hilton Head. She had caught word of a side deal between Bobby and promoter Jerry Perenchio: Win or lose, Bobby would be taking home a slice of the gate receipts.

"That's it," Billie fumed. "The match is off. Bad vibes. Call Perenchio. I want to tell him."

Dick tried reasoning with her. Maybe it's bad information, he said. He called Perenchio and urged him to soothe his show's angry leading lady. The promoter caught the first flight to the East Coast. As soon as he and Billie had settled into a car at the airport, she was in Jerry's face. By the time they left a restaurant in Sea Pines, she was in his wallet for an extra $40,000.

Negotiating through rage worked for Billie. Now she could concentrate solely on Riggs. The more she analyzed him, the more flaws she uncovered. His lobs were shallow. His waddling strides were slow. His body had the elasticity of balsa wood. His harmless drop shots, spins, and slices were designed to fall safely in the court. Gradually she formulated a strategy. Extend the rally. Apply pressure without force. Wait for the error. It was all there to see as she noted every move, every quirk, every opening. She immersed herself in Riggs.

And Bobby? He was immersing himself in women.

Steve Powers owned the hottest pad in Beverly Hills—the former digs of the movie star Betty Grable. He was a wealthy businessman with enough dough to provide an all-night lust garden for his buddies' macho fantasies. Lovely ladies drifted on floats in the pool. Cigars were passed out like pamphlets. Glasses clinked endlessly.

Hugh Hefner admired Steve's taste in the tawdry. Often the Peter Pan in silk pajamas visited Steve while on scouting trips. He would look over the gaggle of beauties with their cups overflowing, and select a few lucky gals to join him at the Playboy Mansion.

Another frequent overnight guest of Steve's was Larry Riggs, Bobby's stockbroker son. "Come on over," Larry told his father one night on the phone. Larry glanced around and detailed the scene, making sure to enumerate all the poolside assets. Not too long after, Bobby and his best buddy, Lornie Kuhle, popped in for a look.

Their jaws dropped. Freshly minted as the Court conqueror, having just signed up for the Riggs-King circus, Bobby immediately felt the power of his newfound celebrity with every young lady that nuzzled up to his wrinkled neck.

"Hey, Steve, what do you think about me taking over your guesthouse between now and the end of the match with Billie?" Bobby asked. "We do all our promotions, best we can, right out of your house."

It was a deal. Bobby moved right in, duffel bag at his side, vitamins in his pockets, ready for action. This was the life, basking in the sun, indulging in his stardom, hanging out at a pleasure palace in the months before the match.

"Bobby lived there, and let's just say a good time was had seven days a week, all hours of the night," Larry recalls.

There was one more mansion amenity. In Steve's backyard, the tennis court remained a vacant status symbol—even with Bobby as a guest. For two months he only set foot on the court for photo shoots.

Bobby loved the lens. There was a lot of ham in this chauvinist pig. During the buildup to Billie, he assembled a slapstick photo gallery:

Bobby serving a ball in a Little Bo Peep bonnet; Bobby dressed as King Henry with a drumstick in his hand; and Bobby swinging as Tarzan with Jane. He was a willing participant at a costume party that never ended.

Clearly, Bobby's brisk dispatch of Margaret Court had given birth to hubris. Slowly but surely, lady by lady, the hustler was on the verge of being snookered by fool's gold. He believed his win against Court meant he could best any woman. If those soft spins made Margaret dizzy, Billie would fall victim to his garbage-pail tactics, too.

"You may ask me if I need a game plan for Billie Jean," Bobby told a *Time* reporter. "I don't need a game plan. I'll let her start something and I'll finish it. I have such a vast assortment of tennis weapons in my arsenal that I can handle anything she can throw at me. I'll psych her out a little bit. I'm psyching her out already. She won't admit it, but I can see her coming apart at the seams already."

In fact, it was Bobby who was disintegrating. Most days and nights, he sat poolside, mixing drinks in his mouth as a party trick. He'd sip bourbon, take a swig of Coke, and slosh it around his gums. See? Mixed drink. Pleased with himself, he took long drags off a stogie that was as thick as a roll of quarters. Cigars and bourbon, the breakfast of champions.

Larry tried to save his father from self-destruction, all but henpecking him, repeatedly asking the same questions: Why don't we practice a little, Dad? Why don't we get into shape?

"I'm the player," Bobby told him. "You aren't."

The more his son persisted, the greater Bobby resisted. He was almost belligerent.

"I beat Margaret Court, and she can kill Billie Jean King anytime she wants," Bobby crowed. "I'll hammer her. I don't need to practice for Billie Jean King. She's terrible. She's got no forehand. She slices the ball, and comes to the net; I'll lob over her head. No problem."

Bobby had it all figured out. All he had to do was show up on September 20. In the meantime he would continue jabbering, enchanted by the power of his own words. "Women should keep their biscuits in the oven, and their buns in bed," he intoned.

The daffiness of his delivery somehow insulated Bobby from audience hecklers on every soundstage he visited. He traveled from stage to studio like a bespectacled stand-up comic on tour, resuscitating his celebrity with each quip. The whistle stops were pure déjà vu, a rekindling of the mid-1930s, when Bobby and good old Jack Del Valle had hit the road in their Cadillac, owning the audiences wherever they went.

"It's like being reincarnated," Bobby told sportswriter Will Grimsley. "This is the greatest thing I've ever done, bigger than Wimbledon or Forest Hills, bigger than winning the pro tour. This is the highlight of my career."

The proof was on the Los Angeles freeways. Inside his Lincoln Continental, with a license tag that spelled out his name, motorists honked if they loved Bobby — and even if they didn't. Bobby was in demand. On NBC's *Monday Night Baseball*, he joined Curt Gowdy and Tony Kubek as a guest announcer at Shea Stadium. In the stands, as a salute to Bobby's indomitable spirit — or his prowess as a stud — he saw a sign that read, RIGGS VERSUS SECRETARIAT: TWO TO FIVE.

From the initial press conference announcing the match in July, to the pre-match introductions in Houston, Bobby barnstormed the media. Promoter Jerry Perenchio was often on hand to prod Bobby's more outrageous tendencies. "Stroke of brilliance, Bobby," Jerry would quip after another one of Bobby's zingers.

Bobby appeared on *Today* and *60 Minutes*, and breezed past all the local reporters in between, infiltrating the national consciousness with his irrepressible image. He became the artist of his own caricature. "If I can't play for big money, I play for little money," he told Mike Wallace. "And if I can't play for a little money, I stay in bed that day."

Every line had a hook at the end. He reeled in mainstream Americans one curious onlooker at a time. Bobby was a great diversion for average folks stuck in the gas lines during the OPEC embargo, for the viewers watching a PBS series on the disintegration of the family, and for the readers who followed the depressing daily headlines from the Watergate scandal. If Americans were turning to Pet Rocks for comfort, why couldn't Riggs become a sex symbol amid the chaos?

Bobby's fame wasn't reasonable, but it was real. *Time* magazine confirmed it. Drawn with a cartoonist's pen, his rabbit teeth and thick glasses, male-pig button and mussed hair, jumped off the magazine's glossy cover. This was America's new heartthrob — he was fifty-five and far out.

"He loved it," Lornie Kuhle remembers. "It was a second childhood. When he was Wimbledon champion he got all the attention, and here he was getting it again — fifty-five years old. He was reborn."

Bobby was the darling of the damsels once again. Women fawned over his scrawny frame in a testament to the aphrodisiac powers of celebrity.

"Instant fame has done a lot to improve my social life," Bobby wrote after his second divorce. "As a divorced man, constantly on the go, I have been getting the red-carpet treatment, especially from the opposite sex. But if a girl gets serious, wants the lifetime franchise, an exclusive deal, I can't go for that. I'm not ready to block out all the other action."

He flashed a sly grin as Playboy Bunny types surrounded him in an after-shave commercial for Hai Karate cologne. Women would slip Bobby their phone numbers in restaurants. "Yoo-hoo, Bobby." He heard it everywhere he went, a siren's song for the senior. Bobby responded, occasionally to his regret.

One night at Steve Powers's fantasy nest, a femme fatale fleeced Bobby after he fell asleep drunk. He awoke $1,800 lighter. "There wasn't even any sex," he complained to the press.

How could women be so smitten by this Mr. Magoo of philanderers? How could they be so taken by his truculent rants and raves? Outside the women's movement, beyond those who understood how damaging Bobby's act could be to their liberation efforts, ladies cuddled the harmless charmer. And he cuddled right back.

"He was like a number of guys I've seen in these big-time powerful positions," Kuhle recalls. "Which is, they're so strong with males and they're so strong in business and they're so strong in sports, but when they're around women, they're actually pushovers. He was that way, too. Bobby was an absolute pushover. He couldn't be more respectful,

Blue Suede Shoes

more nice, to women. He'd do anything. He'd bend over backwards for women."

The respect he had for women didn't sell. Objectifying them, however, provided him with the folklore status that translated into the best seats in the house.

"Why wouldn't he do what he did?" Billie remembers. "It made him money."

His endorsement opportunities were exponential. He was working deals for toiletries, clothing lines, and tennis equipment. The legend of Bobby Riggs grew with every reporter who visited him at the Powers manse.

"For six hilarious, mind-boggling days, I followed him around as he wallowed in the limelight and hustled games on the Beverly Hills tennis circuit," Roland Flamini wrote in *Time*. "During that time, he was so blatantly chauvinistic that I began to suspect that he was really the Women's Liberation movement's secret weapon."

The more visible Bobby became, the more Billie withdrew. Naturally, all predictions led back to that convincing loudmouth hogging the headlines.

"Riggs will outclass Billie Jean King in their match at the Astrodome," Flamini predicted, "but I would be more confident if he had gone into training earlier instead of living it up in Beverly Hills."

Bobby was in the lap of luxury. Billie was on the outskirts of nowhere.

In a remote section of Texas identified as a part of Houston on the map, though it hardly touched the perimeter of downtown, Billie arrived to compete in the Virginia Slims of Houston event on September 16. Spectators would plop down three dollars to watch her play in this prelude to Bobby. Having survived the cattiness in the bathroom and with Marilyn Barnett by her side, Billie declared herself fit. She said she felt wonderful, and she dismissed all the imaginary maladies reported in her absence. She did not have hepatitis. She did not have hypoglycemia. She did not need life support. Her radiance was proof.

As if her thoughts had been kept in a packed closet for weeks, they

107

all came tumbling out once the door opened. She talked nonstop to a throng of reporters about progress. In this very city, she reminded them, the women's circuit had started with few reporters on site.

She couldn't escape them now. She played through the Slims event, revealing her vigor in every win. Between matches, she resumed concentrating on Bobby. One evening in a back room at the Astrodome, Billie and her coach, Dennis Van der Meer, popped in a videotape of Bobby's match with Margaret.

Until then, Billie had only caught the highlights, not the complete match. And yet all she really needed to see was a single, telling moment during the intro: Margaret accepting Bobby's roses with a curtsy.

"That's where she lost it," Billie said. "Dennis, rewind it."

She pointed to the screen. "See where he gave her the roses and she curtsied? It was over. Dennis, she shouldn't have curtsied. She should have smacked him over the head with them. She didn't get it."

But Billie got it. Bobby had dismantled Margaret's psyche before the first serve. And now he flaunted his genius for gamesmanship from the instant he touched down in Texas, where everything was bigger, including the bets, the boobs, and the bourbon shots. Bobby had arrived in Houston two weeks before the match. Accompanied by Lornie Kuhle and Rheo Blair — plus Rheo's collection of vitamins — he checked into his Astroworld Hotel suite across the street from the dome. The location was convenient for Perenchio.

He had Riggs hoppin'. One hour, Bobby was hitting balls in a bank parking lot. The next hour, he was mugging with one of Bobby's "Bosom Buddies" — a host of chesty women whom Perenchio had hired to play ornaments on Bobby's arm. Each night he jived his way through exhibition matches against celebrities and notable locals under a bubble-covered court erected in the Astrodome parking lot.

The court jester was at it again — the rooftop days revisited. He maneuvered around folding chairs and orange cones, sidestepping his way through his fans, conning them one after another.

Poor Bill Archer, the congressman. Poor Denton Cooley, the heart surgeon.

He hustled fans in the stands for $100, but gave them an "I Got Hustled by Bobby Riggs" T-shirt as a sucker's souvenir. He gave his enemies on the sidelines a chance to hoodwink him, but out-hustled even the most cunning.

The day before his match with Billie, Bobby offered an ex–chemistry major an enticing formula: He would spot weekend hacker Larry King a 4–0 lead to play him. Larry had volleyed with Bobby many times for fun in the past, but never in such a loaded setting, or under such bizarre circumstances.

"He had chairs on the court, and wore galoshes," Larry recalls. "I was sweating bullets! Here I am in front of a thousand people, there are six television cameras rolling, and I can't win a point. All the times I had hit with Bobby, it was no big deal, but I wasn't ready for the moment."

Larry wilted while Bobby ticked off six straight games. One King down, one to go.

Bobby's mind raced with the delight. He had everyone scammed — even Billie's husband. I'm the King of the Kings, he thought. Trouble was, this royal partyer didn't retire to the throne room at night. At 1:00 a.m., in the middle of his Astroworld suite, Bobby tossed back vitamins like popcorn while he flirted on the threshold between good humor and bad taste.

In front of reporters, he slipped on a T-shirt with cutouts over his nipples, bearing his breasts. His older brother John stared. "Take that off, Bobby," he ordered. "It's nauseous in the extreme." Then he scolded Bobby into going to bed.

Billie had rest down to a science. She stayed up late, too, but always slept in, a routine that trained her body to reach its energy peak by 8:00 p.m. — match time with Bobby. While Bobby focused on his sideshow calendar and promotional stunts, Billie attended to details. In the weeks before the match, she had overseen everything from her haircut to her footwear. She wanted to face Bobby in comfort.

She knew exactly whom to call. As even Margaret Court understood, no special occasion was complete without a dress by the British designer Ted Tinling. On cue, Tinling worked his imagination overtime to satisfy Billie's wishes for movement and style. It was a night match, a formal occasion, so there had to be sequins. It was on television, in front of the world, so there had to be color.

He conjured up Billie's dream tennis dress away from the eyes of the press. About a week before the match, Tinling flew into New York's Kennedy Airport from England on his way to Houston. Guarding the secrets of couture, he refused to open his bags at first for customs officers. Tinling planned to unveil the dress like a fall fashion line, with the court as a catwalk, with Billie as the model.

There were other accessories that required Billie's attention, too. As if straight from an Elvis catalog, Billie selected blue suede shoes with white soles and white stripes. At first the designers at Adidas resisted, acting as if Billie had been smoking Crayolas.

"I had to fight with Adidas to get those blue shoes," she recalls. "I said, 'We have color TV now; we've got to do it.'"

Billie's childhood fascination with television came into play here. She wanted to capture everyone with her Technicolor dream, even those viewers who turned on the tube for nothing more than a look at her dress. If they didn't change the channel, she had a chance to change their minds. To get the most bang out of the ratings, to reach people from Nebraskan outposts to island nations, she had to put on a show. "It was lights, showtime, and glitter," Billie says. "I loved that stuff."

She awoke on Thursday, September 20, 1973, at noon. She ate a little breakfast, capped off by the first of many candy hits. Marilyn Barnett, Dick Butera, her parents, and a string of other folks stuck their heads into her hotel room. Hyped to the point of combustion, Billie walked down to the grocery store and stunned every shopper on the produce aisle. She bought cheese, apples, and more candy.

"I was absolutely focused on whatever I was doing. I was on automatic pilot, moving from one thing to another, without being distracted. If I was in the store, I was fixed on that, reading the labels on the boxes."

The day was dragging. Billie retreated to her luxury room at the Houston Oaks hotel, about a dozen miles removed from the Astrodome.

She spent her time lying on the floor with her feet propped on her bed, listening to the radio, humming along with "Jesus Christ Superstar."

She was ready. Nothing had been overlooked, not so much as a hair was out of place. Long, wispy bangs were trendy during the era of Lauren Hutton, but that cut could also be distracting. Billie's 20/400 vision was enough of an impediment. She didn't need hair strands cluttering her view, so she got a sensible trim before the match.

"I just tried to visualize 'How will I be comfortable?'" Billie says. "I wanted my hair short. In front, I had my hair back and shorter than usual. That was functional, but I thought it looked nice, too. I didn't think it was quite dressy enough. But for this match, and because sometimes my bangs would hit on my forehead or my glasses, I did it this way."

She was that curious child again, the one who squinted at the television screen, looking for the strings that held up the puppets, who wondered what would happen if the curtain fell or the actors stumbled or a spotlight blew. Every detail mattered when you staged a spectacle. She had learned that much from Queen Elizabeth's coronation.

CHAPTER 6

A Perfect Match

J ust beyond the Astrodome marquee, the largest crowd to ever watch a tennis match entered the doors; 30,492 fans had come to catch it live, to say they were there, to take part in history.

Socialites and celebrities scooted into their metal folding chairs, sitting as tight as broom straws on each side of a green acrylic court rolled over a patch of concrete, a space usually reserved for the Houston Astros' infield.

From the six-dollar seats, high above the floor, the court resembled a grass divot.

A $100 ticket bought a courtside seat — a place to see and be seen. Ken Howard and Blythe Danner, TV stars of *Adam's Rib*, were there, as was singer Glen Campbell, who shuffled through the masses, sporting a red rhinestone blazer that could have been snipped from a whorehouse curtain. The moon-faced boxer George Foreman arrived in a navy blue suit with a polka-dot shirt, taking a seat next to the scowling football legend Jim Brown.

"I'm looking at Billie Jean King; I think she's going to win this," Foreman predicted. "She's too strong, has too much stamina for that man."

"I'm going with Bobby Riggs," Brown grumbled.

Brown's pick was remarkable in its isolation along racial lines. Before a single camera panned the Astrodome, ABC had taken its microphone on the road to ask movie stars, sports icons, and players for a favorite.

Out of Rafer Johnson, Rosie Greer, and Foreman, Brown was the only African-American to pick against Billie—an unscientific poll for sure, but it reflected black empathy for a woman's pursuit of equality.

"You could just see the reflection of the culture," Gloria Steinem recalls. "Just as the feminist and civil rights movements were alive, just as the abolitionists' and suffragists' movements were alive, the understanding of the parallels between sex and race goes very deep."

The other taped responses were just as illuminating. The rising young star on the circuit, Chris Evert, doubted Billie's chances. The nineteen-year-old teen with the swinging ponytail softly provided her insight: "I saw Bobby beat Margaret, and I think he's a really tough player."

From author George Plimpton to playboy designer Oleg Cassini, the men placed themselves in Bobby's camp. Actor Cliff Robertson deviated from the pro-Bobby trend, but justified his selection of Billie this way: "She plays, some people say, very much like a man."

This was exactly the sort of ear-grabbing banter ABC execs had hoped to hear. Their network had paid $750,000 for exclusive broadcast rights, and they were getting their money's worth. And it wasn't just Americans who were adjusting their antennas to witness the drama. Worldwide, an estimated 90 million people were staying up at all hours to follow the action.

The cameras started rolling at 8:00 p.m. A pre-match montage of still shots—including a promo photo of Bobby and Billie arm-wrestling—flashed as the lead-in, accompanied by a bastardized version of "Anything You Can Do, I Can Do Better." On cue, Howard Cosell stepped into the ABC broadcast booth in his ruffled shirt and tux, and surveyed an Astrodome that was saturated in an excess of excess. The University of Houston marching band stutter-stepped across the field while a pig-headed mascot danced in the aisles to the blaring strains of "Conqueror." Bobby's Bosom Buddies trotted around in outfits so form-fitting, they looked like wet-T-shirt contestants.

In the stands, some spectators wore signs around their necks that read LIBBER VS. LOBBER. Others declared I LOVE BOBBY or I LOVE BILLIE JEAN with campaign-style buttons as big as pie tins pinned to their blouses or jackets. There were men in denim leisure suits and cowboy boots, blue jeans, checkered flannels and John Deere caps, khakis and shirtsleeves and rented tuxedos. There were women in bell-bottomed trousers and T-shirts, homespun skirts and cotton blouses, rayon pantsuits and clogs, and red-carpet evening gowns complete with sky-high heels. Business overflowed at the portable bars as bubbles raced to the top of champagne glasses.

But this decadent scene — something hatched from the brain of a Roman party planner — needed a final, garish touch. Jerry Perenchio had already proven himself a genius at exploiting American taste, whether he was pitching bouts between Muhammad Ali and Joe Frazier or partnering with Norman Lear to produce *All in the Family* and *Maude*.

After one production meeting, Roone Arledge turned to one of ABC's most charismatic and popular talents, America's Olympic darling Donna de Varona.

"Are we really going to do this?" Arledge asked her, pondering the vast scope of the upcoming broadcast. "What do you think?"

De Varona found the idea exhilarating, on target.

"His instincts were right," de Varona recalled. "He didn't need me to confirm them."

Perenchio validated Arledge's *cojones*. He was a visionary "say-when" promoter who wouldn't stop pushing his product until someone said no and really, truly meant it.

The perfect accessories for his chicanery were Billie and Bobby. If Billie would oblige, Perenchio was about to test the bounds of showmanship — officially escalating the event to gone-bonkers level — to produce a stunt almost as memorable as the match itself.

Again, if Billie would oblige.

Billie had arrived at the Astrodome at 4:00 p.m. to take the measure of the massive dome, to drink in its towering heights and vast expanse. "This is it, man," she thought. "Gotta get used to this place." She hit a few balls on the Sportface carpet, took a shower, drank some Gatorade, and ate more candy.

Wearing glasses that looked as if they had been cut from jelly jars, with a bracelet dangling from one wrist and a sweatband wrapped around the other, Billie waited inside the visitors' clubhouse. It was a stark room, buried like a bunker under the arena floor, a place completely isolated from the stadium buzz. She sat before the locker that her brother, the San Francisco Giants relief pitcher Randy Moffitt, had used whenever he pitched for the Giants against the Astros.

All that preparation for Bobby had been a source of peace; she had been drawing on her natural cool throughout the day. The pressure she had felt since July had dissolved, and so had her fear of failure. But now, with the match less than an hour away, the serenity gave way to jitters as Billie again contemplated the impact a loss could have on her career. Her Wimbledon victories, her U.S. Open titles — none of them would be remembered if she blew this match.

Billie couldn't just sit there indulging those thoughts; she knew the power of negative thinking. There was only one thing to do.

"Where's the party?" she asked Dick Butera. They left the locker room and jumped into an elevator with about a dozen disbelieving fans. Upstairs, Billie milled around a party for players on the Virginia Slims tour. It didn't help.

"Billie Jean looked into the eyes of the players and she could see they all thought she was going to lose," Larry recalls. "They had no real faith, and Bobby had promoted this aura of 'any male can beat any woman.' That's what made the whole thing so great, that Bobby pushed a myth — like the myth that the world was flat for Columbus. The myth was there and everybody believed it, because it hadn't been proven

▲ *As a traditional woman, Margaret Court always put her husband, Barry, and her children over tennis.* © *Bettmann/CORBIS*

▲ *The diminutive Bobby Riggs ascended to Wimbledon glory in 1939 by using guile against his Goliath opponents.* © *Hulton-Deutsch Collection/CORBIS*

▶ *Bobby's first wife, Kay, would discover the obsession her husband had with tennis and action.*

© *Hulton-Deutsch Collection/CORBIS*

► *Billie Jean Moffitt married Larry King in a wedding that was reflective of the traditional values Billie grew up with as a child of conservative parents in the 1950s.*
© *Bettmann/CORBIS*

◄ *Billie and Larry capitalized on Billie's fame from her match with Bobby by launching a magazine for women in sports and establishing the Women's Sports Foundation, a nonprofit organization to support athletics for girls.*
© *Bettmann/CORBIS*

▲ *There was nothing Bobby wouldn't do for the attention he craved, including dressing in drag on the court.* © Owen Franken/CORBIS

▶ *Billie and Bobby played to the cameras, but they genuinely liked each other, too. Their friendship lasted a lifetime.*

© Bettmann/CORBIS

▲ *Understanding the value of the press, Billie and Bobby were a promoter's dream as they willingly hammed it up before their match.* © *Bettmann/CORBIS*

◄ *Billie was constantly surrounded as her match with Bobby neared. After the match, her fame would grow to the point where it suffocated her personal life.*

© *Bettmann/CORBIS*

▲ *Billie disclosed her lesbian affair with Marilyn Barnett to the press with her husband by her side. Although he was often lonely during their twenty-year marriage, Larry loved Billie unconditionally.* © *Bettmann/CORBIS*

▶ *Billie's ex-lover Marilyn Barnett lost her attempt to win a palimony suit when the judge ruled her claim was an attempt at revenge.*
© *Bettmann/CORBIS*

▲ *Members of the 1999 U.S. women's soccer team were the children of Title IX, which Billie stood up to save in the 1970s and again thirty years later. The soccer team's vocal leader, Julie Foudy, reminded many of Billie as she fought to keep Title IX alive after the George W. Bush administration attacked it.* © Reuters/CORBIS

▲ *When Billie coached Venus Williams in Fed Cup, it was an appropriate pairing. Venus along with her younger sister, Serena, grew up to be the millionaire beneficiaries of Billie's vision of women earning equal pay and equal endorsement value.* © Reuters/CORBIS

▶ *Billie and Elton John have been the best of friends since 1974, a relationship formed when he was the bold rebel of rock and she was the outspoken voice of the women's movement. They had both fame and personal struggles in common.*

© Lucy Nicholson/
Reuters/CORBIS

wrong, yet. But Billie knew what everyone was thinking: She had no chance."

Billie might as well have been in the toilet stall again. As soon as she heard the snippets of cocktail conversations, she wondered whether she had any real support beyond her inner circle. Minutes after arriving at the party, she thanked Ted Tinling for the gorgeous dress, said hello to her few true-blue friends, and made her escape.

Back to the clubhouse. Back to her sanctuary.

That was where she remained until Jerry Perenchio walked in, nervous as a prom date, only a half hour before showtime.

"Are you ready?" he asked.

"I was born ready."

A few feet behind Jerry, a half-dozen college hunks from the Rice University track team stood wearing scanty togas. They flanked a makeshift Egyptian litter with orange and red feathers as big as palmettos pluming from a gold lamé throne — a tinfoil knockoff of Cleopatra's favorite mode of transportation. This wasn't some float the marching band had left behind. It was the last item sitting in the Promoter from Oz's toy chest.

"Um, Billie, this is probably something you wouldn't want to do," Perenchio asked gently, "but would you want to be on that litter? We'd love to take you out on it."

"God, that would be great."

"Oh my God," he said. "It's okay?"

"Okay? It's fantastic!"

Perenchio had expected Billie to turn him down flat, to reject the litter as too gaudy, too outlandish, too everything. He still didn't realize that she was more than his match in media savvy; Billie understood how a grand entrance could turn a single moment into a lifetime memory. The relieved promoter filled her in on the rest of the script. Once they reached the court, Bobby would present her with a two-foot Sugar Daddy and make a tongue-in-cheek reference to suckers. Then Billie would hand Bobby a gift of her own, a squealing baby pig. Jerry's wife had masterminded that particular touch.

"A pig? Perfect," Billie said. "I'm going to name it Robert Larimore Riggs."

"What?"

"That's Bobby's formal name."

"God, you know that?"

"Yeah, I know that. This will be so cute, but you gotta promise me one thing: The pig does not get eaten like bacon. You can take it to a farm, but do not have that little baby eaten. I don't want him hurt."

They agreed, even though that scrubby brown piglet would end up squirming from its handlers, squealing for its freedom.

It was about ten minutes before the match when Perenchio exited the locker room. Moments later, Billie was lounging atop an Egyptian litter, carried through a tunnel on buffed legs until she was lofted out into the arena floor opening.

The crowd reacted with awe, escorting Billie's short ride with flash-bulbs and applause.

Billie waved with a parade queen's touch at no one in particular, while fearing her litter might flip like a hammock.

Focused on balance, she didn't see the giddy couples getting married in the stands, or the men dressed in aprons to mock women, or the women raising their fists to defy men. And, just as well, she couldn't hear Cosell's nasal repartee during her televised intro.

Here was the controversial media figure who had stood up for Muhammad Ali's draft resistance and Muslim faith. Here was the celebrated broadcaster with the floppy ears and sloping nose, his head topped with a shiny black hairpiece he kept stored in a shoebox.

Here was Cosell, portraying the arrival of Billie as if she were auditioning for Homecoming Queen, telling America, "Sometimes you get the feeling that if she ever let down her hair to her shoulders and took off her glasses, you'd have someone vying for a Hollywood screen test."

Years later, Billie would hear Cosell's description of her for the first time and say, "'If she'd grow her hair . . . get rid of her glasses . . . she could be a movie star.' And I'm like, 'I don't want to be a movie star! I'm a jock; I'm an athlete! I love and have passion for what I do.' It's just horrible. He was talking about my looks! He didn't talk about one of my accomplishments."

Billie's accomplishments were not part of the script. Cosell and the other commentators were supposed to be, by Perenchio's design, an opinionated, polarizing bunch. Jerry wanted pyrotechnics in the booth, and he got them the moment the broadcast began. Naturally it was Cosell who lit the fuse when he explained how Billie had refused to play Bobby if Jack Kramer — the Hall of Fame tennis player and Riggs's good pal — had been part of the telecast.

At first, ABC executives thought Billie's stand was a ruse, "part of a psych-out procedure." But she was in earnest. Kramer had tried to obstruct her fight for financial equality, and though she'd paid him back by leading a boycott of his precious event, his attitude toward women still rankled. For three weeks she had demanded that Roone Arledge dump Kramer from the broadcast booth.

Arledge finally acquiesced, but Billie felt compelled to make a public statement regarding her stand. She enlisted her husband to make her feelings known. Just before the match started, Larry appeared on television to tell viewers, "Billie Jean does not feel she will be able to perform adequately and would be adversely affected by having Jack Kramer share this forum with her today."

In a taped reply, dapper Jack explained that he had voluntarily stepped aside because he didn't want Billie "to use me as an excuse for losing to Bobby Riggs." He not only stayed out of the booth that night, he stayed well clear of Texas, opting instead to watch the broadcast with Arthur Ashe on a television in the lobby of the L.A. Tennis Club.

"Roone was a friend of mine, and I understood what was going on," Kramer recalls today. "He was a good man. I was supposed to get $2,500 to do the match, and he paid me anyway. So I ended up like everyone else in America that night: I watched it on TV."

The sniping between Kramer and Billie fit right into the evening's charged atmosphere as the match took on a surrealistic feel. To the TV viewers, the camera hovering high in the Astrodome rafters made the court appear squat and misshapen — a reflection off a fun-house mirror.

To Billie, the view seemed oddly appropriate given the warped social mood of the early 1970s.

"It mirrored how we thought. I'm like, 'Jeez, here we are, right on schedule.'"

A gum-smacking lineswoman wearing bell-bottoms took her place on the baseline after a chair umpire in a purple tux took his position. A bleary-eyed man with a construction-board sign that read KING WEARS JOCKEY SHORTS sipped on a drink in the stands.

Bobby made his arena entrance Perenchio-style, on a glittering red rickshaw with gold wheels, surrounded by Bobby's Bosom Buddies. He was in heaven, an attention junkie receiving his fix. He stood against a cinderblock wall and gave an interview to ABC's roving reporter, Frank Gifford, and explained, "I'm going to try to win for all the guys around the world who feel, as I do, that the male is king and the male is supreme."

Billie's conversation with Gifford was more subdued. In a measured and confident voice, she noted the differences between her preparation and Bobby's: "He's been living a pretty fast life."

That Beverly Hills bingeing was obvious to her before a single ball was struck. During the warm-up, sweat formed under Bobby's jigsaw bangs and trickled down his forehead. But it wasn't Bobby's faltering nerves that induced all that perspiration. It was his commercial sense of duty. In an air-conditioned but terribly humid Astrodome, Riggs played the first three games wearing a yellow jacket with a red Sugar Daddy logo emblazoned across its back. It was ludicrous playing attire. But what was his coach and loyal sidekick supposed to do? Lornie Kuhle wasn't about to peel it off Bobby's soaked shoulders—he knew that there was too much at stake. And he was right.

"He put Sugar Daddy on the map right there," Kuhle points out. "There were almost a hundred million people watching. Their sales went way up because of that. What do you think they did after the match? He went ten years and made $50,000 a year from them as a spokesman, showing up doing stuff for them every year. He picked up a half-million just from wearing that jacket. Bobby's theory was, whenever you make a deal with somebody, give them more than what they ask for. He always did that. If they asked, 'Would you do *x* for *x* amount?', he'd do two times *x*."

Advertising for the Astrodome match ran about $50,000 a minute, and Sugar Daddy reaped enormous benefits from Bobby's marketing instincts. But Riggs was practically tripping over the middle-aged pudge spilling over his beltless white shorts. And the jacket had nothing to do with that.

Before she crawled off the gold litter, Billie had decided that, win or lose, she was going to be the steady aggressor, forcing the hustler to hustle until his limbs were as heavy as lead pipes and his lungs burnt like the cigars he adored.

She knew her temper could pose an even bigger threat to her than Bobby's game. Stay physically relentless, Billie cautioned herself, but emotionally reserved. Bobby could unveil any of his usual antics on the court. He could taunt her with one-liners, he could pull a donkey out as a doubles partner on a changeover. Billie was determined to stay placid throughout.

In her blue Adidas shoes, with sequins dancing under her lapels, she walked onto the court a tad nervous but uncommonly stoic. Betty and Bill Moffitt sat in the stands waiting for the event to begin. The Moffitts had never been meddlesome stage parents. It had been five years since they'd last attended one of Billie's matches. But she wanted them in Houston. She knew this was special. She knew this was about history.

Since their arrival three days earlier, they had barely mentioned the match to their daughter. They didn't want to pile onto the pressure.

Betty and Bill sat behind the three-foot curtain that formed a flimsy barrier between the court and the premium seats. Betty's gray hair was coiffed to perfection, and Bill was handsome in his striped dress shirt. All around them, couples were making friendly wagers: Who was going to do dishes for the year? Who was going to fly back first class?

The TV camera focused on Cosell up in the booth. He draped his arm around guest analyst Rosie Casals, caressing her neck as she spoke.

He did not do the same for Jack Kramer's stand-in, Gene Scott, a top American player with impeccable tennis knowledge, who stood firmly on the side of on-court male superiority.

Cosell would play mediator between his two colleagues throughout the night. Rosie kept him amused with her pointed, rapid-fire comments, beginning with the grand entrance. When Riggs held up the pink-bowed pig Billie gave him before the match, she said, "That's too cute for him. He doesn't resemble that kind of pig."

"Rosie, telling it like it is," Cosell chortled. But whenever Casals's remarks became too harsh, Howard would gently chastise her. Unbeknownst to the audience, little of this byplay was improvised. In her earpiece, Rosie was continually receiving instructions to hit Bobby hard and often. Years later she would confess that "the producers told me exactly what to say. I think I was a sideshow. They wanted me to play a certain role."

Rosie considered Bobby so loathsome, she happily obliged. But she would pay for the acidic commentary, even though the words hadn't all been hers. Viewers sent her hate mail excoriating her performance as biased and downright rude. She would be virtually blackballed from TV for years for following the ABC producers' instructions. Cosell and other male broadcasters were allowed to assail athletes. America was not, however, ready for a strong female voice in the booth.

Many Americans weren't ready for Billie, either. She turned bias on its head from the very start of the match. Billie held her serve, and took the first game by extending her body to its last inch and slapping a backhand volley for a winner. The breathtaking shot sent a message throughout the stadium. Here was a grinding, grunting, graceful athlete, ready to show that fierceness and femininity weren't mutually exclusive.

In the fourth game of the first set, Billie allowed the audience to see the adrenaline that was pumping through her veins. She pulled back her wooden Wilson to unfurl a backhand passing shot down the line that ricocheted off Bobby's metal Head racket. While Bobby looked at his racket in disbelief, Billie clenched her fist by her side, pursed her lips, and walked defiantly back to the baseline.

"She's walking more like a male than a female," Cosell remarked.

The Bobby lobs that had diluted Margaret Court's power, and the slick Riggs spins that had crossed up her rhythms, weren't fazing Billie. The more Bobby tossed up flares, the more deadly Billie's overhead smash became.

"Bobby kills you with unspectacular stuff," Gene Scott remarked. But Riggs's inability to unveil a dangerous weapon — a huge serve, a deep volley, a running forehand — crippled his efforts to keep up with Billie. It was 4–all in the first set, and Bobby was uncharacteristically subdued — as if his sense of humor had been hit by a tranquilizer dart. Stunned by Billie's attacking net game, the huckster was worried and increasingly weary.

"Comedy has gone out of Bobby Riggs," Cosell intoned.

Billie was gaining momentum. Although the score was close, she was dominating Bobby. By the eighth game of the first set, Bobby was in a panting panic, moving like a rusted tin man, soaked to his rib cage. He walked in cat circles to catch his breath. At 15–love, Billie airbrushed a forehand drop volley that arched over the net and landed softer than a toe-tap. Bobby raced to retrieve the surprise shot — a clever tactic he thought he owned the patent on. He wielded his racket to flick the ball on an extreme angle cross-court.

A magnificent shot, one that summoned a rowdy *"Yee-haw!"* from some members of the crowd. But Billie sprinted to the ball, and as her momentum whisked her into the doubles alley, she snapped a backhand winner into the open court.

The camera shutters crackled and the crowd noise rattled the steel girders. The excitement gave the Astrodome the feel of a Jiffy-Pop bag that was about to burst open. But Bobby was nowhere to be found. During the point, after his dashing retrieval, the exhausted Riggs had taken a seat on the sideline. Billie's obvious athletic superiority had unnerved him. He had envisioned a nervous slug, not a resilient slugger.

The programmers at CBS were just as surprised and disappointed as Bobby was. Their network had broadcast the Mother's Day Massacre the previous May. To counter ABC, CBS had scheduled the hit movie

Bonnie and Clyde to start at 9:00 p.m., on the assumption that Billie would reprise Margaret Court's quick fade.

But Billie wasn't fading; she was arriving. One witness to the revolution was Claudine Longet, the ethereal French actress and singer. Wearing Ray Nitschke's Green Bay Packers jersey — number 66 — and braided pigtails, Longet summed up the myths Billie was smashing with every overhead. Her comments to Frank Gifford were ditsy but dead on.

"She's playing so well, so hard, she's the aggressor," Longet said. "It's fantastic."

Gifford asked Longet if she resented Riggs and his chauvinistic antics. "Oh no," she replied, "it's just that he's been bragging so much. I really like him. He's a nice man." Then she curled two fingers on the side of her head to make a pair of bunny ears and said, "He looks like a rabbit and all that, but it's fun to see a lady with a lot of dignity playing so well."

That lady was starting to look like a ringer to Mr. Riggs. On golf courses and tennis courts, in games of backgammon and cards, he had always had a discerning eye for cons. However, this was a con of his own making. He had bought into his own rhetoric, his theory that all women were equal in the classic Riggsian way: Margaret had collapsed, therefore so would Billie.

But it was Bobby's nerves that frayed first. With the first set on the line, he double-faulted on set point. That was unthinkable. Bobby had made his career capitalizing on others' mistakes. He couldn't double-fault. But the score said otherwise. The first set belonged to Billie, 6–4.

"And the women in this arena are standing and cheering for Billie Jean King!" Cosell exclaimed.

During the four-minute break between sets, Bobby plopped down next to Lornie Kuhle and combed his fingers through his chop-shop hair. Billie calmly sat in her sideline chair, with Dennis Van der Meer on her right and Marilyn Barnett on her left. Larry King sat two chairs away. Bobby was flummoxed, but not about to fold. In fact, he wasn't discussing strategy with Kuhle, he was talking action. Down one set, Bobby intended to turn a comeback into cash. With the Vegas odds in his favor all week, it had been difficult to find a big strike, but now he could sell himself as an underdog.

He sent Lornie into the stands to find Dick Butera. Before the match, Bobby had offered to wager $5,000 on himself at 8 to 5; Dick had insisted on 2 to 1. Bobby backed off, but after the first set, Lornie popped up to Dick's seat with a proposition.

"Bobby says he'll take it at 2 to 1."

Dick and Lornie haggled back and forth. Finally, Dick looked down at Billie and asked, "What do I do?"

Billie sat there fuming. "Dick," she said, "I'm trying to play the match." She wondered whether the wager was just another Riggs gambit, one more distraction meant to take her out of her game. She decided to remain above the ruckus, and told Dick and Lornie, "You guys can discuss whatever you want."

But the betting byplay had pushed her buttons. She stalked back onto the court more juiced than ever. Maybe too hyped, in fact. The energy rush generated a false high. At the start of the second set, Billie snapped a backhand half-volley long, a shot she had delivered upon silken strings for the entire first set, when she had earned 28 of 34 points with winners.

The lapse cost Billie a break of serve. This is what Bobby needed, something to rebuild his confidence, his hope. He already knew the truth: He was woefully unprepared for Billie, horribly out of shape. But maybe, just maybe, the pixie dust on Billie's net angles had finally vanished.

A flicker of resolve registered in Bobby's body language. He squared his shoulders and put everything he had into his serve. Billie didn't flinch. Before Bobby could pounce, she broke back after sprinting toward the baseline for a deep volley. Turning into the shot for torque, she whip-snapped a backhand winner that curled like a comma as it cut across the court. Bobby hung his head, a man out of answers and out of gas.

It was a sad, lonesome sight. Even feminists felt for him. Most of them realized that Bobby wasn't really a villain, just a screwball lug who reminded folks of an obnoxious, crass favorite uncle. Suddenly the struggling fifty-five-year-old became the sentimental favorite. The Astrodome crowd tried to encourage him with peppy cheers. Someone cried out, "We love you, Bobby." All that love couldn't fill his lungs, though. And sentiment couldn't save his legs.

The swaying crowd couldn't move or soften Billie. She refused to treat Bobby as a vulnerable butterfly caught in the wipers. She stayed on the attack. She didn't deviate from her increasingly aggressive plan: serve and volley, pull Bobby in with a half-volley or a drop-shot, then punch a winner past his stiff and aging body.

"I'll tell you," said Howard Cosell to himself as well as to the viewers at home. "She's tough."

Billie gained a break of serve when Bobby mindlessly pushed a forehand volley into the net. Without yielding a single point on her own serve, she emphatically closed out the second set, 6–3. This had all the makings of a blowout, but Billie wasn't banking her prize money yet. During the changeover, she told Frank Gifford, "I never think I've won until it's over."

"Good luck," Gifford told her. "You're a helluva gal."

Bobby opened the third set drier. He had peeled off his sopping blue polo and slipped into a yellow shirt. The look was all that changed. Billie immediately bullied Riggs with an unforgiving backhand return down the line. She wasn't giving an inch.

Hangdog and helpless, Bobby stopped waiting for Billie's patience to wear thin. He was beaten and he knew it. There was no way to save face. He wasn't going to entice any unforced errors with his dinks and spins, as he had against Margaret. Billie was mentally tougher than the demure Aussie; she couldn't be flimflammed or gulled. And he wasn't going to try to regain the edge with anything underhanded. Instead, Bobby remained true to his code as an honest hustler. He unraveled like a perfect gentleman, taking his medicine squarely in his jabbering jaw. No complaints, no commotion.

"It's been a night I think not expected by most, a night Billie Jean King has thus far dominated," Cosell told his audience, and his commentary continued as Riggs served, down 0–2 in the third.

"Funny, going into this telecast, one couldn't be sure how to treat it. Would it be high good humor? Well, of course it couldn't be all that because too many women in this country were taking this match seriously in the wake of all of Bobby's talk and in the way he victimized Margaret Court. But it would seem there would be a mixture, some antics on the court by Bobby. None of this has thus far eventuated. It has not been a comic night for Bobby."

No, it was an excruciating night for Bobby, validating for women and self-affirming for the California girl who grew up with the kind of hopes reserved for wishing wells. Inside Houston's Astrodome, deep in Marlboro country, a woman was about to blow smoke in the face of the status quo.

Bobby had been reduced to the role of fall guy. A fall as painful as it was hard. After Riggs dumped a half-volley into the net that allowed Billie to hold serve for a 4–2 edge in the third set, he flexed his bony hands and tugged at his fingers. Cramps.

"That surprised me," Kuhle says. "He'd never had hand cramps before. I think it was a sign of nerves. The pressure and strain had gotten to him."

Bobby winced and walked to the sideline. He fell into his chair like a prizefighter in the losing corner. Kuhle vigorously massaged his hand and arm, shoved a cup of Gatorade in his face, and shouted encouragement into his ear.

C'mon, Bobby. Fight through it, Bobby.

Billie sat with her feet in Marilyn Barnett's lap. Billie wasn't letting on, but her legs had started cramping. Let this match end, she thought. Marilyn rubbed down Billie's calves to keep the muscles warm while everyone waited to see if Bobby could continue.

The fans hissed during the delay, not sure whether the hustler was hustling or hurting. A few minutes later, after popping a vitamin, Bobby returned to endure the rest of his comeuppance. His diminishing presence was giving a lift to progress. Yet, somehow, not everyone in attendance got the message.

The colorful quick-draw artist Leroy Neiman had his mind on other

dimensions of the match as he worked with a flurry from his perch behind the baseline. Instead of capturing a cultural turning point with his
brush, he chose to paint a lovely lineswoman from an angle that exaggerated the view of her derriere. A butt shot, to be blunt.

"This is an angle I've had all night," Neiman told Frank Gifford.
"And it's a little distracting for me."

"I've seen," laughed Gifford. "Very distracting."

So even Bobby's looming demise couldn't quite stifle the frat-boy
guffaws. But Riggs wasn't in on the joke. Trailing 3–5, he stepped forward and tried to delay the inevitable with his serve. Billie decided to silence Bobby's bravado, right then, right there.

"I hope Jack Kramer is watching this," Rosie Casals announced over
the air, and she could barely hide the smirk in her voice. The match
wasn't over, but she could already taste her friend's victory. At 30–all, Billie wielded her racket like a cue stick to poke a backhand cross-court
winner into the corner pocket of the court, setting her up for a first
match point. On that prompt, Rosie yelled, "Right on, baby! What's
Bobby going to do now?" Billie blew the closeout, though. She crushed
an overeager forehand into the net. "That's as close to being a choke as
we've had tonight," crowed Gene Scott.

"The only choking there will be on the court is Billie Jean choking
Riggs," Casals snapped back.

At deuce, Bobby dumped a forehand into the net. Gene Scott could
not believe it. How careless, he said, how nonchalant. Howard Cosell
disagreed. "I don't think he's nonchalant, Gene. I think he's dog-tired."

Billie earned her second match point, but blocked a return into the
net. Bobby took a deep breath. His legs had turned to Jell-O and his
hand had cramped into a claw. His body no longer moved, it slurred.
Clean out of resolve, he served a double fault to give Billie her third
match point. Bobby's deep fatigue revealed itself when he flubbed a
shoulder-high backhand volley — one of the easiest of all volleys — into
the bottom of the net.

That was it: 6–4, 6–3, 6–3. The match was over. Billie closed her eyes and tilted her head to the rafters. Her smile radiated joy and relief. The child of television tossed her wood racket high into the air in a made-it-after-all Mary Tyler Moore moment. Then she jogged to the net and danced lightly in her blue suede shoes.

Bobby met her there. Springing on the last worn coils in his knees, he had jumped the net to greet her, barely clearing the cord. This was Bobby at his best, showing class beneath the caricature. He placed his hand on the small of Billie's back. The gambler leaned in to pay homage.

"I underestimated you," he said in her ear.

She smiled, patted Bobby on the shoulder, and hugged Dennis Van der Meer. Then she searched out Larry. For weeks, Billie had kept all the pressure she was under in its place so she could play. She had held up under intense scrutiny with a mixture of elegance and might. Now, with the match finally over, it hit her. She had done it. She had dismantled female stereotypes, vindicated Title IX, and rallied a movement. Her eyes pooled with tears as she slipped into her husband's embrace.

"On Bobby's side, it was a huge promotion, and on Billie Jean's side, it had huge meaning," Larry King says. "The marriage of the two made for great theater. They have all this reality TV nowadays, but that was reality TV."

No, this was beyond reality TV. Though awash in hype, the unscripted Billie and Bobby Show didn't cheapen social values, but profoundly affected them in a positive way.

As Donna de Varona points out today, "The guy was older and was this and that, but the truth is, it was a worldwide movement that needed a finishing sentence. And Billie Jean King gave it to us."

She had submerged herself in the hype and pressure, not for tennis, but for the cause of gender equality. Billie understood that she had to beat Bobby to win credibility, but she also knew that the accomplishment had to be seen to be heard. Its outlandishness served a purpose. It was a necessary spectacle.

"You felt this was a symbolic match that was going to be used against women and to humiliate them if Billie Jean lost," Gloria Steinem explains. "And for her to take that on, to put herself under that pressure, is the true meaning of heroism."

Around the country, feminists celebrated Billie's bravery with toasts in bars, with cheers from their sofas, with delighted screams out dorm windows. There were tales of women who asked their bosses for raises the very next day.

Just as important, little boys went to sleep on the night of her triumph with a fresh, enlightened view of women. These were boys who would grow up to become fathers of female soccer players, basketball stars, and tennis prodigies.

Howard Cosell had started the evening as one of Billie's doubters. Evidence of how the match influenced men can be found in the way his commentary evolved throughout the event. Before the first serve, he had patronized Billie while belittling her accomplishments and her cause. By the end, he was complimenting her emotional strength and conceding her social importance.

"It began to become a cause célèbre — equality for women," Cosell concluded in an impromptu monologue. "It was Billie Jean who fought for equal pay at the U.S. Open and got it. All of the women in America — or at least most of them — seemed caught up with the anticipation of this match. Billie Jean went into virtual seclusion. There was talk before the match about her health, whether or not she'd be able to go ahead with the match as scheduled or postpone it. It turned out, instead, that Billie Jean King was perfectly ready, not only ready, but willing and able. She played her own game."

ABC ended its telecast that night earlier than scheduled. Billie had closed out the show on her own terms and in her own time. *The Streets of San Francisco* would be seen in its entirety.

The post-match jostling around Billie was relentless. After the TV cameras faded to black, Larry King lifted Billie onto a courtside table to hold up the trophy. He could have been placing her on top of the world.

A minute later, George Foreman bulled his way through the crowd to present her with the $100,000 check. Billie blew kisses to everyone, playfully stuck out her tongue at Dennis Van der Meer, and stretched out her arms like a sunbather in the arena lights above.

But there was no relaxing for Billie. Her mind and body hummed. She was so revved up, she had to grab a cold beer near the clubhouse in the belly of the Astrodome. While waiting for Bobby to comb his hair, she kicked off her shoes and strolled around the dais barefoot. Then she finally sat down for questions.

"How did Bobby play?" someone wanted to know.

"He played like a woman — like a lot of women I've beaten on tour."

Bobby was a gracious loser. He didn't blame his lack of fitness or preparation. He didn't diminish Billie or make excuses. The stand-up comic turned out to be a stand-up guy. Esther Bartosh would have been proud.

"She was too good," Bobby said. "She played too well. She was playing well within herself, and I couldn't get the most out of my game. It was over too quickly."

Right after Billie had captured the first set, an invitation circulated through the Astrodome press box. It read, "You are cordially invited to the Bobby Riggs Bridge Jump." The poke at the pig was the brainchild of Stella Lachowicz, the public relations maven for the Virginia Slims circuit.

Bobby had indeed promised to jump off a bridge if Billie beat him, and had there been a bridge handy, he might have taken the plunge. He left the Astrodome depressed, angry with himself for taking his opponent so lightly. He didn't say a word to Lornie as the two men went back to the Astroworld Hotel.

They were soon joined by Bobby's son. Larry Riggs had refused to attend the match. He had witnessed his father's cavalier approach to training. He had known what was coming. But this was hardly the time for

I-told-you-so's. Neither Larry nor Lornie had ever seen Bobby this despondent. He left them to soak in a tub of ice, to plunge his old bones into the cold, numbing water. He didn't want to feel anything.

For the first time in months, Bobby was alone. No distractions, no girls, no booze, no autograph seekers. Only his gnawing thoughts to keep him company: How could he have been so foolish? He was the smart, witty, charming Bobby Riggs. He was the studied gambler — the hoodwinker, not the hoodwinked.

More than an hour went by. At one point he wondered if he should submerge his misery beneath the surface of the water forever. Outside the bathroom door, his best friend and son worried. But Bobby finally crawled out of the tub, toweled off, and slipped into his trademark persona: life of the party.

He had agreed to attend a cocktail fête at Perenchio's Astroworld penthouse and there was no way to escape it. A business bigwig had paid Bobby $10,000 to put his face on medallion coins, funny money to be distributed at the party. On one side was Bobby's image as an emperor, and on the other was a cartoon of a male-chauvinist pig. Its value had diminished considerably by the end of the match.

The same pig that had escaped in the Astrodome was in the arms of a partygoer. Robert Larimore Riggs — as Billie had named him — had his snout stuck in hog heaven as he gobbled down roast beef, cocktail shrimp, and carrots.

The indignities of losing. With a drink in his hand and a Bosom Buddy stroking his back, Bobby wondered out loud, "Think anybody will want to take me on, now that I'm a loser?"

"I love you," cooed a blond babe nearby.

One by one, the gleeful and gloating filed into the room to collect their bets and flaunt their windfalls. Dick Butera waved a $10,000 check with Bobby's signature on it; writers Nora Ephron and Grace Lichtenstein also showed off the swag they had collected after Billie's triumph.

Bobby had lost more than just a few wagers. It wasn't widely known, but Jerry Perenchio had been working to line up Chris Evert as Bobby's next opponent in a winner-take-all match worth an incredible $1 million. With Bobby's loss to Billie, his dream date with Chrissie was off.

That alone should have made any talk of a fixed match ridiculous. Yet many thought Riggs had engineered his own defeat. Years later, he even took a lie detector test on attorney F. Lee Bailey's television talk show to prove his match with Billie was not a scam.

"Fable . . . Bobby Riggs's mythology," Larry Riggs says. "That kind of stuff, it's for people who would say, 'Oh, I know he could play better. He wasn't running and trying.' But, you know, let's see anyone not play for three months and go out and play.

"Bobby was perfect, perfect for Billie Jean King as it turned out for her. The guy was a bigmouth and put his foot in it. He did it more and more. Wouldn't train. Wouldn't work out. Overconfident. Played her in her backyard with her own balls, her own court. The idiot just stepped right into her trap."

Billie made a cameo at Perenchio's post-match bash, too, and offered a quick thank-you to all her supporters. How about a rematch, she was asked. "No amount of money," she replied.

She headed back to her hotel on Post Oak Road, immensely satisfied. She had known right away how important the match was for women, for their empowerment, their self-confidence, and their pride. The event would transform Billie into a legend. In the three decades since the match, women still thank her for the inspiration her victory provided. Or they share a laugh over the absurd theater that made the moment and its lessons memorable. But immediately after the event, all Billie wanted was some anonymity, some peace. She loathed parties—all the hugs from strangers, all the meaningless chitchat. She yearned for intimate moments.

Back at her hotel room, with her parents, her husband, and a couple of friends, Billie could finally lie on the floor, prop up her feet, and relax. There was one sweet surprise awaiting her return: The hotel management had arranged for ten parfait glasses filled with ice cream to be delivered to her room the second she walked through the lobby. Billie had given up the stuff to train for Bobby, and everyone knew it.

She had entered the hotel with her small entourage, including her young secretary, Marilyn Barnett, who was still dressed in the brown and blue halter dress she had worn to the match.

"In yoga," Marilyn had explained at the Astrodome, "brown stands for money and blue stands for spirit."

That was Marilyn. She was different, so light and effervescent, so delicate. She didn't look as though she could ever pose a threat to anyone.

CHAPTER 7

Hiding in Public

On September 21, 1973, Billie Jean King made page one of the *New York Times*. A headline describing "Mrs. King" as the victor over Bobby Riggs "amid a circus atmosphere" sat just beneath the banner news of the day: NIXON AIDES AND COX FAIL TO GET ACCORD ON TAPES.

"I think I was the second-most-recognized person in the country after Nixon in the seventies, going by the Q-ratings," Billie says.

She wasn't just a tennis player anymore. She was an A-list star. The glitzy stage presence and cinematic savvy she had displayed at the Astrodome now defined her image. People the world over suddenly recognized her as the spirited gal who had climbed off that Egyptian litter in a sequined tennis dress to dismantle sexist perceptions with her sliced backhand. But, deep inside, she was still Billie from Long Beach, a fireman's daughter struggling to find people of substance amid the superficial trappings.

In the spring of 1974 a message at the front desk of her London hotel led her to a special and enduring relationship. There were always stacks of messages for Billie — fame's paper trail. Who didn't want a piece of her? But this was different.

> *Billie:*
> *Call me.*
> *Elton*

The note stunned her. Billie and Elton John had met months earlier at a pre-Bobby bash. Elton had already gained celebrity as a rockin' and rollin' Liberace, an audacious crowd pleaser who strutted across concert stages like a syncopated runway model dressed in outfits rolled in glitter. He sang his songs from high atop a pair of striped platform shoes and wore white-rimmed glasses as big and round as bicycle mirrors. When he first met Billie, Elton had the taste of big-time fame on his lips; he had just scored another major splash with the song "Rocket Man." She was about to turn Bobby Riggs's name into a feminist anthem.

Billie had once pulled over on the side of a hilly San Francisco street when Elton's "Your Song" came on the radio. Unknown to her, Elton, a rabid tennis fan, always checked the scores to see how Billie was doing. But the two members of this mutual admiration society had stood on opposite sides of the room at that Houston party, neither knowing how to approach the other. Then Elton John's manager, Tony King, intervened.

"Hi," he purred to Billie in his deep, sexy voice. "I'm Tony, and I work with Elton John, and he's dying to meet you, but he's too shy."

"Guess what? I'm too shy, too," Billie replied.

Still, no one made a move. A few minutes later, as the party began to break up, Tony shouted, "This is ridiculous," and he tugged Elton over until the rocker was standing in front of the tennis star he idolized.

"Hi," was all that Elton could think to say.

"Hi."

"Coming to England anytime soon?"

"Yeah, in a few months, you know, for Wimbledon."

"Call me, let's get together."

And then they parted. Billie assumed she'd never see him again.

Call me. Sure. Doesn't everyone you meet at a party use that line? But there it was, on hotel stationery, a message from Elton asking her to get back to him.

"He came right over," Billie recalls. The two sat in a booth at the hotel restaurant and bonded immediately.

They talked about his music and her matches. They talked on and on.

"I got my Rolls Royce," he told her. "I've got twenty-eight speakers in it. You wanna come listen to music? Let's go sit in the backseat and just listen to music."

A driver sat behind the wheel while Elton and Billie slipped into the backseat of a cavernous luxury carriage for an eight-track jam session. Billie could hardly feel the earth beneath her. How cool was this?

"That was it," Billie says. "I knew it was forever."

Elton understood Billie. He had experienced the same angst she felt as a shy person leading a public life that was as frightening as it was gratifying. They were both grand personalities, blessed with theatrical instincts, but very simple in the things that brought them joy. Music, tennis, uncomplicated stuff.

"They hit it off so fast," Larry King recalls. "I'd been to Wimbledon many times with Billie and spent most of the time in the hotel room. It was completely out of character for Billie to do anything else but tennis during Wimbledon. She was so focused. But in the first week they met, Elton took Billie and me out nightclubbing during Wimbledon. Next thing you know, we're at a club with Mick Jagger."

The fast life wasn't Billie, but there was something magnetic about Elton.

"He loved what Billie Jean represented," Larry adds. "She was sort of the bad girl of tennis for shaking up the establishment. He had the same impact on rock. I think they also had a real feel for what each other went through with fame."

Early on, they were also bound by an internal struggle: They were both under scrutiny and in the closet.

Billie had difficulty confronting her sexuality crisis. So she internalized the issue along with all the stress she faced in her post-Bobby life. Sometimes the pressure made her ill.

At a table near the blue-tiled bar at Celia's, in San Mateo, the salsa had all the kick of a mariachi band and the tart margaritas could snap your head back, but, flopped on Billie's plate, as bland as chalk, sat a double order of flour tortillas. The afterglow of Billie's win against Bobby had combusted, leaving her stomach filled with embers. A doctor who said that she was courting ulcers had eliminated just about anything flavorful from her diet. The emotional relief Billie found after beating Bobby had dissolved into unease, the price she paid for living under the world's spyglass. Stress often doubled her over.

"What she cared about and worried about, what brought on attention," Larry King says, "I think it made her sick."

Billie not only felt ill at times, she also felt imprisoned. As the scrutiny of her private life accelerated and deepened, she felt compelled to lie, to contradict, and, eventually, to surrender. Few people noticed the self-loathing that was eroding her self-esteem. Billie hid that behind a variety of roles. She was the ultimate poised athlete. She was the perfect daughter. She was the spunky wife. She was Mother Freedom for women everywhere.

All those labels. But Billie had no idea which description, if any, fit her best. She didn't feel like a radical feminist or a housewife or a superstar. There was a reason Billie found it so difficult to define herself. She wouldn't dissect her sexual identity crisis — one that continually plunged her into fear and shame.

"I had very soft boundaries when it came to sexuality," Billie says.

Billie certainly didn't see herself as a lesbian; she couldn't even say the word. She didn't identify with the militant images still resonating from the 1969 Stonewall Rebellion. In that sense, Billie felt as put off by lesbians as Margaret Court had been. She often rationalized her sexual confusion, telling herself, *I like men's bodies; I love men; I love Larry.*

"I was struggling. There was so much shame."

For years, Billie threw herself into her tennis career and her mission to make things better for women. Those were her passions. But they also served as diversions. There was no time or incentive for self-discovery or soul-searching when, Lord knows, she couldn't get lost in a crowd.

"When you're playing tennis and you're busy every day," Billie admits, "it's a great way to put everything on the back burner."

Any hint of her sexual confusion would have belied her image and would have injured the tour and her pocketbook.

"I really wanted to talk about it," Billie says, "but I was nervous because if I failed the tour, I couldn't live with that fact at all. I was trying to confront it, but I also had people around me who knew I was trying, you know, trying to figure out who I was, telling me that we would never have a tour if I started talking about it.

"That's a huge responsibility, but that's what I was told by certain people. So, when you hear that, you think, 'Shit, I can't put my sexual preference on the front burner when it means the whole bloody tour and the future of women's tennis.'"

Any public revelations would have also outed Billie to her parents. She couldn't do that to them. They had only recently come to terms with her abortion. Bill and Betty Moffitt were conservative churchgoers who found comfort in the 1950s code of social conformity.

Larry King was not so easily shocked, however. As he recalls, "Billie Jean, in our first two years of marriage, let me know she had problems. I was young and naïve, but I was her husband, good, bad, or indifferent, you know, I'd help her with her problems.

"The bottom line was, I didn't see any reason to get divorced because Billie Jean had identity problems. I felt that even when it all got sorted out, if Billie Jean was going to grow old and gray, she would be much better off growing old and gray with me than with any other person on the planet."

His unconditional love was noble, if suffocating, to Billie. His love enabled her. Billie didn't have to decide between him and a woman because Larry never forced the issue. Instead, she pushed forward: Don't think, she told herself, keep moving.

In 1974, Billie's image as Lady Liberty became the linchpin for King Enterprises. Her signature emblazoned the wood handles of Wilson rackets; she wore her own BJK Adidas shoes, and endorsed Carnation Instant Breakfast for those busy souls on the go. She smiled for Colgate toothpaste and slathered for Aztec suntan lotion.

Between takes, Billie stayed busy with her *womenSports* magazine and founded the Women's Sports Foundation with former Olympian Donna de Varona. They launched the WSF as a nonprofit advocacy group for female athletes with a $5,000 check Billie had received at an awards banquet. The foundation would eventually become the big fist in the fight to defend Title IX against assaults by the male athletic and political establishments.

"It was established as a grassroots effort," Billie says. "It was like, 'Let's not just sit here, let's do something for girls.'"

Throughout the 1970s, Billie seemed ubiquitous and in the background of every scene. She was one part player, one part celebrity, one part *Norma Rae*. She was everywhere. Everywhere but with Larry. He was the tireless pitchman of the Billie empire, hopscotching from city to city, displaying his wares like carpet samples. It's called World Team Tennis, he'd tell any potential sponsor. Imagine, the top players on teams located in America's thriving cities, barnstorming through the summer, with stars like Billie coaching and playing. He sounded ingenious. He sounded passionate. He sounded sincere. If anyone doubted him, Billie's name lent his presentations credibility.

Larry wasn't threatened by the arrangement. He reveled in his lot as Billie's husband. He even acknowledged his public identity whenever he scribbled his autograph: Mr. Billie Jean King. "Why do you do that?" she would ask. "That's what I'm known for," he would reply, always with that coy smile.

"I was just trying to fulfill the fans' interest," Larry explains. "They didn't really want my signature. They wanted the signature of Billie Jean's husband."

Larry didn't need the adoration or the public approval that Billie craved; he was content to play his scenes in the background. "Men tend to be process-oriented," Larry says. "We tend to be into projects and solutions, and we're totally happy if we have something to build. For women,

I think—and this is where somehow women get confused a little bit— their needs are totally different than men's needs. They take this as thinking that somehow they're different; well, they are different. But that doesn't mean they have to have all their needs fulfilled by women."

The reference, of course, was to Billie. Not that Larry was ever upset with her. He was patient. He loved her too much to feel neglected.

"I was lonely a lot," Larry recalls, "but I was actualized a lot, too, by all the things I got to do and make."

He was a man who had ideas about ideas. Larry would tell Billie all about his deals, but usually on the phone. The couple did occasionally meet at their San Mateo apartment, a nondescript pad with the furnishings of a truck stop: a bed, a fold-out couch, a small desk, and an airbrushed painting that took up a good chunk of wall space. On days when the fog lifted its veil from the city, their modest residence offered a panoramic view of the Sausalito lights and the Golden Gate Bridge.

The apartment provided the perfect perch for a transient couple. They were wonderful friends, if little more. At their hideaway, Billie and Larry sometimes guarded against interruption by disconnecting the telephone. Then they would stuff it under a pillow and shove it into a closet for good measure. With their solitude assured, they could finally relax and catch up. It was a slumber party for two. Larry and Billie would talk for hours about everything from politics to dreams.

Then the best pals went their separate ways again, scheduled to meet soon, real soon, in a call-me-later kind of way. It was an unconventional marriage, even by seventies standards, one that raised suspicions in some members of the press that there was trouble inside the fairytale Kingdom.

Billie reacted with amusement when rumors of a split with Larry began circulating in 1974. We're better than ever, she told everyone. Despite her reputation for candor, she found it relatively easy to lie about her personal life. The truth was, she had first asked Larry for a divorce in 1969.

"I would tell him I wanted a divorce, and he would say, 'We should stay together; we're great for each other. I love you and you love me,'"

Billie remembers today. "I think he played into my fears very well; and I also didn't want the public to know what was going on."

She understood. A handsome husband supplied a handy cover for her parallel life.

In May of 1972, Billie was locked in a battle with her fussy hair. She didn't know what to do with it. It was enviably thick, but difficult to manage. Several players on the women's tour patronized Gene Shacove's salon in Beverly Hills. Billie decided to give the place a try.

She walked in and met Marilyn Barnett, a flower-child stylist. Wispy blond hair spilled off her head, ease flowed from her thin frame. She had a live-in boyfriend, a vast collection of halter-top dresses, and not two thoughts about tennis.

Billie left the salon pleased with her haircut, and refreshed by her conversation with this tennis outsider. Marilyn was different, interesting, an escape from the ordinary. For one afternoon, she gave Billie a respite from the pressures of tennis life.

A few months later, after Billie had swept through the French, Wimbledon, and U.S. Open championships to become the dominant force in women's tennis, she met Marilyn again. They were at a party at a mutual friend's house.

"So, when are you coming by for a haircut?" Marilyn asked her.

That's how it started — casual, relaxed. Innocent. A few days later, Billie visited Marilyn at the house the hair stylist rented on Doheny Drive. It was a getaway for Billie, far from her husband, the tennis courts, the media glare, and the questions. She felt free, released.

Something was happening. Billie gradually became entranced by Marilyn's femininity and soothed by the tenderness of their relationship. The intensity of the attraction left Billie, rather uncharacteristically, dancing on a ledge. This was not the first time she had been drawn to a woman, but there were dangerously different variables to this liaison.

Marilyn lived outside the safety of the tennis community. Most of the sport's insiders knew Billie was searching for her sexual identity, but neither her peers nor a protective media would ever dish on a player's private life to the public. Lesbianism on tour was a contentious issue for players, even if the door didn't open to reveal it.

"It was just starting to happen, and my heart went out to the younger players because, you know, young people can be very influenced," Margaret Court says. "Some of them were very, very young on the tour and, you know, you saw the decline come."

Court's beliefs reflected societal prejudices: Lesbianism was immoral and depraved. Billie knew the hard truth about that stigma. So, for family snapshots, she stood happily hooked to Larry's elbow. Everywhere else in public, Marilyn clung boldly to Billie's side. Their relationship defied logic.

"I couldn't think," Billie says. "Everything was so tumultuous. Everything was up in the air: 'Was the tour going to make it; am I going to get a divorce or stay in this? I don't know my sexual preference. I'm just trying to figure things out.' I think there were a lot of questions and therefore I think I felt very vulnerable.

"I'd say to myself, 'What if this doesn't work? What if that doesn't work?' The future was so uncertain in every aspect of my life, I think."

Whenever she competed, Billie embraced pressure, even thrived on it. But off the court, she had always been a textbook pleaser, desperate to fulfill everyone's expectations with a wholesome smile and an every-gal attitude. Marilyn tapped into a different part of Billie, and it was oddly thrilling. The situation didn't compute. It wasn't rational.

Billie woke up next to Marilyn one morning, and an affair had begun.

Billie made a thin attempt to hide the relationship. Some tennis insiders realized an affair had developed after Billie started paying Marilyn $600 a month to be her traveling secretary, personal assistant, and all-around Girl Friday. Marilyn shadowed her on the tour from 1973 to 1974. She often provided quotes to reporters, and even supplied injury updates to the press. As writer Grace Lichtenstein noted at the time, many in tennis were amazed to see Marilyn sitting next to the umpire — a place normally reserved for a trainer — when Billie defaulted to Julie Heldman at Forest Hills.

It was Marilyn who took a sideline seat next to Billie during the Battle of the Sexes. The audience in the Astrodome and at home had watched the young woman massage Billie's tired legs near the end of the contest. On some trips, the two booked suites together while Larry stayed in a separate room. Larry was always on the phone — that's what they put out — yammering on about business deals, receiving calls at all hours of the night. How was Billie supposed to get her rest? Through all this, Larry's devotion to his wife remained unaltered. He had needs of his own; his piety didn't mean he was perfect.

"Far from perfect," Larry admits. "One time, Billie Jean surprised me and one of the tennis players downstairs when she was upstairs with Marilyn. But, like I said, nobody's perfect."

Billie and Larry were not the only couple trying to reconcile their unconventional relationship within an American culture newly emerged from Vietnam and Watergate and the civil rights movement. JFK, Malcolm X, Martin Luther King, and Bobby Kennedy had all died at the hands of assassins. The country had been stripped of political naïveté. Americans seemed to be engaged in a mass search for clarity. Disillusionment and anger permeated the country. One of the unexpected TV hits of 1973 was a PBS show called *An American Family*, a reality series that documented a family's emotional dissolution. And Carly Simon's "You're So Vain" was a top single. Everyone seemed to be anti-something. Boycotts were in vogue, and the heat of the women's movement intensified to the point where lesbians became unwanted.

In 1973, Betty Friedan, author of *The Feminine Mystique* and president of NOW, expressed her political homophobia, telling the *New York Times* that lesbians were CIA infiltrators sent to discredit feminism. This was the atmosphere Billie breathed in every day.

She knew her livelihood depended on secrecy. There was no way she could come out without suffering repercussions. But not coming out had consequences, as well. The double life exhausted Billie; the fear of exposure consumed her. This has to end, she thought. At first, Marilyn seemed like someone who could smooth Billie's frayed edges. Marilyn's Zen-like qualities appealed to Billie's frenetic disposition. "Marilyn seemed laid back, very passive," Larry King recalls. "I was very mistaken." Billie couldn't see that she was flirting with self-destruction; she couldn't immediately separate herself from a woman who grew more controlling by the day.

"She was very possessive," Billie says today. "She tried to control every day, each one more possessive and controlling. I started to realize what was happening. I had a feeling . . . I just didn't trust her. That was my sense, to not trust her as a person."

As the match with Bobby approached, Marilyn gradually tugged Billie away from her tour friends. Billie's acting weird, some players whispered. But most wrote off her aloof behavior as a reaction to the pressure from her upcoming date at the Astrodome. Part of it was indeed that, but the affair with Marilyn exacerbated the stress.

"She was a bad choice for me, but I was very vulnerable at the time we met," Billie says. "She was dangerous. I was screwed up."

Just two months into the relationship, Billie discovered Marilyn was a liar and a manipulator — toxic, but at the same time intoxicating. Unable to break the attachment, Billie continued to hide her personal life. Larry was her husband and Marilyn was her secretary and that was that. As long as she could maintain those two roles, the contradictions in her life could go on unresolved. But the pretense taxed her. Her emotions fluctuated with the deception, the confusion, and the hypocrisy. Her mind stayed in constant motion.

Almost daily, Billie dreaded falling over the tripwire that would blow the cover off the subterfuge. She spent her energy fretting. What if her parents found out? Their disapproval would crush her, and she knew it would come. Bill and Betty might have been supportive of their daughter's unconventional career choice, but Billie was aware of how inflexible they were on the issue of homosexuality.

One conversation provided all the proof she needed. When Billie was ten, she and her father had discussed prejudice in its various forms.

The subject of homosexuality popped up, and Bill made it clear that he had no tolerance for it, none at all. End of dialogue. To him, it was against the Bible, against the norm. Billie still needed to remain special in her father's eyes; she couldn't bear his thinking of her as a deviant. So, until the confusion over her sexual identity overtook her, she painted her Norman Rockwell life by the numbers.

She was the good girl, the virgin who strolled down the aisle with the boy she loved in a photo-album wedding. Her gown flowed in an ivory cascade, her husband came straight from the Troy Donahue collection, and her parents could proudly dance the night away. Billie played along with tradition at first; she fell in line with mainstream ideas about femininity, choosing a tennis dress as if it were a ball gown for her date with Bobby, carefully selecting the perfect shoes for the event, fussing over the right hairdo for prime time.

Wholesome and spirited, fun and fit, Billie was the ideal face for a tour trying to establish its identity. Mother Freedom as a lesbian? The idea was incomprehensible. Until 1973, the American Psychiatric Association had categorized homosexuality as a mental disorder; gays were perverted, depraved. For Billie to identify herself as one of *them* would have been a PR debacle.

"It was my sexuality; it was everything," Billie explains. "It was a huge burden to know that I couldn't really talk about who I truly was, and that if I did, the tour was going to go away and Title IX had just passed and well . . ."

She knew the progress women had made was too fragile to upset it with a whopping truth. Gloria Steinem was among the brilliant minds behind the women's movement, but Billie was its face, body, and spirit.

Billie was part of American pop culture — and even climbed its pop charts. Her best friend made sure of it. In the summer of 1974, Elton John tracked down Billie at a World Team Tennis event in Denver.

Dressed inconspicuously — as he always was when trying to go incognito — he looked everywhere for her. Finally, Elton found her in the locker room on the tennis grounds, sitting with Larry. He couldn't wait until later. Elton just had to show her something.

"He brought it in a tape recorder," Larry King recalls. "It was a rough-cut version of a song. He came all the way to Denver to bring us a rough cut. We sat there in the locker room and listened to it."

The song he played for Billie wasn't "Your Song," but it was her song. He called it "Philadelphia Freedom," named for the tennis team Billie owned in the city of brotherly love, and written in the spirit of his best friend.

"Billie was surprised and touched," Larry says. "She loved it. Perfect. It was written for Mother Freedom."

The song would become number one on the charts — just another indication of how deeply Billie had penetrated the American consciousness.

"Everyone knew what Billie Jean did," Larry King says. "She had a lot of power after she beat Riggs. People listened to her, and followed her every move."

So she kept quiet about her sexuality, and kept fighting against bias. If anything, the women's movement needed Billie as a symbol of strength — rather than as an exemplar of depravity — to face the first of many threats from the macho politics of Big Texas.

CHAPTER 8

Towering Threat

It was the summer of 1975, well before Donna Lopiano would plunge, cannonball-style, from a three-story diving tower just to draw attention to Lady Longhorn athletics, well before she vowed to start a kazoo quartet after the University of Texas pep band refused to play at the women's basketball games.

As UT's new women's athletic director, this twenty-nine-year-old from Brooklyn demonstrated her chutzpah from day one. She had barely unpacked the boxes in her patch-sized office — a space just big enough for the coffee table that doubled as a desk — when her phone rang. University president Lorene Lane Rogers was on the line.

"I hear you're going to Washington, D.C.," Rogers said.

"Yeah, I'm really excited," Lopiano replied. "My parents are coming up. I'm going to testify before Congress."

"I heard about that. I'm calling to try to save your job."

All at once, Lopiano's heart tumbled to her shoes. She was about to discover that it wasn't wise to mess with Texas.

A NECESSARY SPECTACLE

───────

In 1972, President Richard Nixon had signed the Education Amendments Act. The bill contained a nebulous piece of legislation called Title IX. In noble but undefined wording, Title IX stated that no person could be excluded on the basis of gender from participating in any education program or activity receiving federal dollars.

Bravo, activists cried. But did anyone know what those words meant? At first blush, Title IX was a piece of feel-good legislation designed to open graduate school doors to women who wanted careers outside of nursing and teaching.

Within two years, however, the Office for Civil Rights started sniffing around the nooks and crannies of the legislation. Armed with precedents that allowed them to apply broad language to specifics from earlier statutes, a group of government lawyers in the understaffed OCR office were charged with interpreting Title IX. One of them was twenty-eight-year-old Jeffrey Orleans.

"What isn't generally known is that this was not the first time we had to write a regulation like this," Orleans points out. "There was a little-known provision, maybe a year or two earlier, that basically said that institutions that had gotten money under the Public Health Service Act couldn't discriminate on the basis of sex. That happened to include every medical and nursing school in the country."

Poring over Title IX, attorneys like Orleans began to ask, does the sweeping language of equality in federally funded education apply to extracurricular activities — like football, for one? Yes, the lawyers said.

"That's when all hell broke loose," Lopiano recalls.

In the summer of 1974, the Department of Health, Education and Welfare, under Caspar Weinberger, proposed regulations that would end sex discrimination and require institutions to offer women athletic programs that were comparable to men's programs. Comparable. As in funding. As in taking from Peter to pay Paulette. As in the end of the world. At least that's what men like Texas football coach Darrell Royal thought.

"Title IX will bring an end to major-college football," Royal declared.

A group of chest-puffing college football lords decided to fight as soon as they discovered that the womenfolk — among others — were trying to crash the barriers protecting their exclusively male domain. Republican senator John Tower of Texas became their political leader. A preacher's son with an affinity for British cigarettes and local speakeasies, Tower was the ten-gallon politician of Lone Star State lore, a man who worshiped God, but would dance with the devil for the sake of Longhorn football. The senator would vote heaven out of El Paso if it meant stopping Title IX.

As far as the gridiron protectionists and tailgating boosters were concerned, President Nixon had put his signature on a ticking device that would obliterate men's college sports once the law was implemented. Did the president know the impact the legislation would have?

"No. In fact, I think everybody was surprised," Orleans says. "I mean, if you go through the legislative history of Title IX, there's maybe one, at most two, references to anything resembling athletics. But I don't think that ever occurred to people."

Once it did, though, fear washed over the mighty.

"You know what happened up at Kansas State, don't you?" Lon Farrell, an athletic official from Arkansas, asked a reporter from the *New York Times*. "Women up there have secured some equal rights and poor Jack Hartman can't even get his basketball team on to practice now."

The women hadn't taken over; they had merely demanded a reasonable split of the sandbox. Billie Jean King, a woman who was never offered a college scholarship to play tennis despite her prodigious skills, looked on with growing interest as college football's representatives attempted to distort a simple concept of fairness.

"The question was, 'Do you think tax money should be given to boys and girls equally?'" Billie says. "It sounded easy. This was not private money, but federal money, and it should be applied across the board. Simple."

A NECESSARY SPECTACLE

Donna de Varona had grown hoarse from saying so, too. America had first become smitten with de Varona when she captured two gold medals for swimming during the 1964 Summer Olympic Games. She had been the doe-eyed, wholesome face of those Olympics, the sweet sixteen-year-old with the glittering Pepsodent smile.

Out of the pool, Donna proved just as dazzling and daring. While Billie was preparing to wrap up Bobby Riggs in a nice pink bow, Donna had been canvassing Europe to drum up support for more Olympic events for women. People listened to her. This intense activist had a way of melting skeptics with her beauty before converting them with her gospel of inclusion.

Donna was fortunate; she could deliver her message from a powerful platform. In 1965, ABC had hired her as the network's first female sportscaster. She became a regular guest in American living rooms long before Billie came knocking. She and Billie were of like mind and spirit. But they didn't discover just how much they had in common until months after the Riggs match, when the two sat down in a restaurant near New York's Gramercy Park. They didn't move for hours.

Billie had ushered in the Open tennis era with her demands for above-board pay. Donna had made compensation for Olympic athletes a cause of her own. The two women discovered they agreed on other issues, as well, and became instant allies on Title IX. As the leaders of the Women's Sports Foundation, Billie and Donna lobbied Capitol Hill throughout 1974 and 1975. They popped up like door-to-door salesmen in front of senators from both parties, always pitching, pitching, pitching. The politicians were enamored with Billie's celebrity. They loved talking to one of the most famous women on the planet.

"I just kept telling those senators I was working two jobs while the guys got scholarships or grants in college," Billie says. "Larry had a grant in biochemistry and a tennis scholarship. I had zip."

Billie told the politicians how her talents had been largely ignored in high school while the boys received all the glory and the benefits, how the guys had the plum facilities in college, and how the playing field remained uneven for girls. To Billie, it was simple logic: Everyone in

America was equal, therefore everyone should receive the same shot at athletic success.

Billie and Donna fought their crusade with minimal support. There were no marchers or protesters to cheer them on. Initially, many women did not consider the debate over Title IX an important feminist issue. To this day, it amuses many Title IX advocates when opponents complain that feminists hijacked the legislation during the 1970s. It just wasn't so.

"The women's movement never embraced Title IX as an athletics position," Donna Lopiano says. "They thought that athletics was a male construct that taught violence against somebody else, inordinate levels of competition — that it was an unhealthy activity for women — and that we were going to follow in the footsteps of men's values, and not the best men's values at all."

This indifference on the part of feminists marginalized the cause, making it imperative for women like King, de Varona, and Lopiano to rattle Capitol Hill. Other female athletes understood the importance of Title IX. However, they were reluctant to ask out loud for equality on college campuses, particularly in the face of opposition from college presidents, NCAA chiefs, and athletic directors.

The bully factor felt real. Men had power suits and power ties. The male establishment could be intimidating on those looks alone, as Gloria Steinem encountered when she glanced around the newsroom of the *Washington Post* one day: "Guys in tweed jackets," she recalls, "unlit pipes clenched between their teeth and elbow patches over no holes."

Although many politicians and journalists were progressive supporters of women's equality in all reaches of education — like Indiana senator Birch Bayh and neophyte politician Bill Bradley — it was not easy for women to speak up when confronted by systemic male glowering.

"The inequities have been so great, women have gotten so little in the past, that many women fear a backlash from the men if they push too hard," Margaret Dunkle, a women's education scholar for the Association of American Colleges, noted at the time. "Once they get crumbs, they'll feel like they're gorging themselves."

The NCAA's male core had been spitting doom for months, claiming

Title IX would bring about the downfall of men's sports. John Tower appointed himself the savior for college football; he aggressively campaigned to put the game beyond the law's reach. The senator, and the men who thought like him, could not have been more condescending or confounding. They equated women sports with quilting bees and knitting circles. Had Tower and company been watching *Bonnie and Clyde* the night Billie beat Bobby, or counting football scholarships when swimmer de Varona overtook the sports headlines at the 1964 Summer Games?

As a member of the President's Council on Physical Fitness, Donna had been a familiar figure on Capitol Hill since the late sixties. She had enormous clout when she testified before Congress in support of Title IX. Her visibility as a television celebrity gave her voice undeniable credibility, but it also left her vulnerable. Football coaches from around the country started pressuring ABC executives to silence de Varona. "Get her off Capitol Hill," the coaches growled. Donna knew all about the campaign opponents had mounted against her. She didn't flinch.

"I had the perfect example," she recalls. "I said, 'Howard Cosell is on the Hill. He's talking about boxing. And I've been asked to speak and testify.'"

By refusing to retreat, Donna, Billie, and the women who fought alongside them had clearly slithered under the pigskin of the football coaches' political alliance. Several coaches—led by Darrell Royal, Arizona State's Frank Kush, Nebraska's Tom Osborne, and Michigan's Bo Schembechler—took their case for Title IX exemption to Congress in June 1975. They appeared in support of the Tower Amendment, the legislation the Texas senator had hatched to protect the good ol' boys of college football, namely his coaching pal Royal.

In their way stood de Varona, Billie, and the football lords' new nemesis, Donna Lopiano. All three women offered testimonials on Title IX, but Lopiano was the only one whose job was on the line.

Donna Lopiano sat in her tiny office with her ear to the phone. She listened intently as University of Texas president Lorene Rogers played the role of a supportive big sister, offering a primer on how to take a stand without stepping on the boots of Big Texas.

"Here's what you need to do," Rogers began. "Number one, you have to make a courtesy call on John Tower. Did you know he was best friends with Ed Clark, the chair of the Board of Regents of the University of Texas?

"You have to say to John Tower that you are representing yourself as an expert witness and not representing the views of the University of Texas at Austin. And then you must say the same thing when you submit your written testimony and your oral testimony, and then nobody can go after you."

Rogers made it clear that she didn't want the woman she had just hired to fail. Before leaving for D.C., Lopiano arranged an appointment with Tower. She walked into his Senate office on June 10, 1975, expecting to see a roomful of white guys in cowboy hats and string ties, with spurs on their dress boots. Instead, she found women, lots of them, gorgeous big-haired gals flapping their eyelashes.

"It seemed like every employee was a former Miss Texas," Lopiano says.

It would be years before the general public found out that Tower's favorite mixed drink was scotch and skirts. At the time, Lopiano had no clue.

"I get there," Donna says, "and I'm saying to myself, 'This guy is not a sexist, he has all women on his staff.' That's how naïve I was, because I didn't even think about what this might be at that point."

A few minutes after her arrival, one of Tower's lovely aides led Lopiano through the underground tunnel system that connects the Senate office building to the Capitol. The journey enthralled Donna; she felt as if she had just taken a peek into the political netherworld.

She exited the tunnel and strolled into a place of Gothic columns sprouting from a glossy marble floor. The click-clack of ladies' heels reminded her of busy typewriters. Cigarette smoke slithered through the air to put a gauzy finish on the Senate waiting room. Donna Lopiano stood waiting in the midst of it until a voice called out to her.

"Doctor Lopiano."

She glanced around the room, but saw no one. Then she heard the voice again.

"Doctor Lopiano."

In Texas, Tower lived large on the campaign billboards that lined every long stretch of highway. Donna knew John Tower's face, but she had never met him in person. She soon discovered that the senator's physical stature did not quite measure up to his lofty surname.

"John Tower, if he's five feet one, he is five foot tall," the six-foot-one Lopiano recalls. "He was right in front of me, down near my waist. And I was taken aback; I was so taken aback that I almost bent over to shake his hand."

Gathering herself with a respectful "Hello," she recited the purpose of her visit, keeping to the script Lorene Rogers had dictated: "Senator Tower, I'm here not as a representative of the University of Texas, but as an expert witness to testify against your bill. This is a law I studied as a Ph.D."

Lopiano went on, much to Tower's dismay. He didn't toss her out, though he might have reached up and wrung her neck right there, if not for all the witnesses. Later that afternoon — after lawyers had prepped her — Donna overcame a few jitters and testified as an advocate for Title IX.

These were the hard numbers of discrimination: At public universities like Arkansas, the operating budget for athletics was $2.5 million, none of it earmarked for women. All across the country, puny allocations forced female athletes to change into their uniforms in bathrooms rather than locker rooms. On some women's basketball teams, players practiced with only one worn ball, instead of a rack full of them. Women on golf teams at places like the University of Georgia often had to share six balls among them, while the men had bucketfuls on the range.

Football resisted sharing the most. Coaches did not want women stealing precious reps from their male athletes by scheduling time in the weight rooms. The coaches did not want to cut back on recruiting trips, scholarships, or stadium expansions in order to fund women's field hockey, volleyball, and swimming.

Donna Lopiano talked at length about facilities and access, but attitudes were an issue, as well. Many athletes and coaches dismissed women as unequal because they physically couldn't keep up with the men. In March of 1975, runner Francie Larrieu set a women's world record in the 1,500-meter race, but not everyone was impressed. When asked about the feat, Steve Prefontaine, one of the great distance runners of all time, sniffed, "I wish I could match her dedication, but the fact is her 4:29 was a world record for women. I can run six 4:29s in a row."

The debate over Title IX and its applications would continue through June and into July of 1975.

The commotion had Republicans in a bind. In the wake of Vietnam and Watergate, with the public distrustful of those who had ties to the vanquished Nixon, with the mood of the country charged by civil rights advocates, Weinberger was in a difficult position.

In fact, his first response to the football coaches and the Tower Amendment supporters was simple: He sent a memo to the legal team at the Office of Civil Rights. In the most basic terms, he asked them to fix this problem over the regulations.

"I am confident that the advice Weinberger was getting, at least the technical advice, was, there's not really a grounds for avoiding this," Jeffrey Orleans recalls. "So unless you want to pick a fight that's probably going to get lost either politically or judicially, just go ahead and do it."

In other words, what Nixon had signed in 1972 could not be reversed, diluted, or tweaked to exclude football. Weinberger had to capitulate. Appearing before a House education subcommittee on June 26, 1975, he defended the Title IX regulations and made it clear that they did indeed require schools to grant equal opportunity to women in athletics. He declared that the law required colleges to grant women equal access to training facilities and playing fields. The coaching and traveling allowances they received must also be on a par with those given to men. He didn't claim, however, that Title IX required equal funding for women's sports — which meant the dire warnings of the football lugs and NCAA fearmongers were unfounded. Implementing Title IX posed no threat to male sports.

"The NCAA position on this is wrong," Weinberger testified. "I again repeat, the new regulation does not mean equal funding, but the opportunities need to be made available."

With a nod to the contentious nature of the hearings, a smiling Weinberger then added this note of levity: "I had not realized until the comment period that athletics is the single most important thing in the United States. This does not mean the National Collegiate Athletic Association will be dissolved and will have to fire all of its highly vocal staff."

Weinberger's rebuke sent the coaches crawling back to their athletic programs, where they continued to boil. Big Texas, in particular, had never imagined it would lose this political football game.

"You know, with a Republican administration, a Republican senator in Tower, I think there was a sense that this would just be a cakewalk, that they'd get football exempt," Jeffrey Orleans says. "They were surprised when the establishment, including Weinberger and others, who actually had to make these decisions — however grudgingly — did the right thing and said, 'No, we really can't do this.'"

On July 21, 1975, President Gerald Ford signed Title IX into law. The statute included provisions that prohibited sex discrimination in athletics and established a three-year window for educational institutes to comply. The advocates of Title IX had won. The bold vibe was contagious. At Yale, in the spring of 1976, the women's crew team stripped naked in the office of their physical education director to protest the lack of shower facilities. Across their chests and backs, in Yale blue paint, they had emblazoned the words *Title IX*.

"It was an exciting time because I think when something's so right, nobody worries about who gets the credit; you're just together making it happen," Donna de Varona says. "You know, somebody suggesting a torch relay from Seneca Falls to Houston for the first women's conference. Somebody saying, 'Well, I can get this guy to help us and give us money.' You know, Colgate president David Foster saying, 'My gosh, this is going to be great for Colgate.'

"You're kind of all meeting together, whether it's a legislative initiative or a fund-raiser or a foundation or an event to bring awareness and money, you're bringing in every aspect of the culture. I mean, you had Charles Schulz, who *loved* Billie Jean, doing *Peanuts* cartoons."

Billie maintained her high profile on and off the court even after losing her number-one ranking to Chris Evert in 1975. She took a hiatus in 1976 to rest her surgically repaired knees, but returned to form the following year. She climbed all the way back to number two just behind Chrissie, and continued to mix tennis with politics. She threw the weight of her name behind yet another cause, this time one that was well beyond the mainstream.

Richard Raskind was a Yale graduate and a naval officer, a father and a husband with an ophthalmology practice in New York. He had enjoyed a modest tennis career on the amateur circuit. He also had a secret. Despite his personal and professional successes, Raskind had lived in agony for years. He had endured a dual consciousness that left him, as he would later write, "vacillating between masculinity and femininity."

Raskind believed that sex-reassignment surgery would end his torment. In the late 1960s, he divorced his wife and started hormone therapy. But when he traveled to Casablanca for his sex-change operation, Raskind stopped at the surgical facility "not fifty feet from the remedy." It would take a few more years and many hours of psychoanalysis before he finally found the courage to go through with the procedure. At age forty-one, the former Richard Raskind emerged from the operating room as Renée Richards.

Renée started her life in Newport Beach, California, and continued to play tennis with great success, but in women's events only. Her six-foot height, deep voice, and other masculine characteristics stoked the curiosity of reporters, who soon discovered the truth. The United States Tennis Association reacted by barring Renée from the 1976 U.S. Open. The organization claimed she could not pass the chromosome test required by the Olympic code. Actually, the USTA feared that Renée's participation would set off a stampede of transsexuals capable of muscling the petite Chris Evert right out of the game.

Richards was in the middle of a legal action against the USTA when she appeared in a small-scale tournament promoted by Gladys Heldman. Her presence at the event angered many of the other women in the draw. Billie was using the tournament to work her way back from knee surgery. She had no problem being on the same court with Renée.

"Look, Gladys," she told Heldman. "If the doctors say she's a woman, that's good enough for me. No, I'll go even further. If Renée thinks she's a woman in her heart and mind, then she is a woman."

Within an hour of sharing her feelings with Gladys, Billie met with Renée in New York. They quickly got to know each other. They chatted about tennis and, of course, Billie's terrible eyesight. Billie walked away with a prescription for an eye infection and an appreciation for Renée's fight to play on the tour.

Not long afterward, Richards entered the New York State Supreme Court where her case against the USTA was being heard. She and her lawyers stepped before Judge Alfred Ascione armed with a secret weapon.

"We told the judge we had an affidavit," Richards recalls. "The judge was falling asleep, literally. He said, 'Uh, huh,' and then we told him it was from Billie Jean King. All of a sudden, the judge was awake."

Billie's stamp of approval meant everything. Judge Ascione ruled in favor of Richards, writing, "When an individual such as the plaintiff, a successful physician, a husband and father, finds it necessary for his own mental sanity to undergo a sex reassignment, the unfounded fears and misconceptions of defendants must give way to the overwhelming medical evidence that this person is now a female."

Billie could empathize with Renée Richards. She knew the torture of sexual confusion. She understood misconceptions and fear. But although she had the power to help Renée, Billie still could not solve her own identity crisis. She stayed married to Larry and kept her sexuality private, all the while hoping Marilyn would keep quiet, too.

CHAPTER 9

End of an Image

It was the summer of 1978, and milky air hung over nearby Central Park. The quick click of a deadbolt echoed inside the apartment as Billie's assistant closed the door behind her.

Marilyn Barnett and Billie were alone. For several years, Billie had gently tried to separate from Marilyn, a weaning process that only made their complicated relationship that much more ambiguous.

"I didn't see her very much, but she acted like I did," Billie says. "She was around for one year, and traveled with me during 1973. Otherwise, you know, I really didn't see her that much. I knew this woman was not the person I would want to spend time with."

Here was Billie, a woman who had won fame as a gender liberator, yet she couldn't free herself from a woman. Forget her assertive veneer. When it came to confronting conflict in her personal life, Billie was a natural-born pacifist. She knew she had to be strong. She knew she had to be forceful. Choosing every word carefully, she started to explain why the couple had to split, but before the words tumbled out, the two women were in a full-blown argument.

Marilyn screamed. She rattled a pill bottle. She rained her fists on Billie's shoulders.

"Can't you see?" Billie cried as she defended herself. "It's over."

It was far from over, and Billie knew it. Marilyn's relationship-or-else attitude had unnerved her. Billie wondered what lengths this young woman might go to. In the weeks following their fight, Billie kept thinking Marilyn would show up at a match, stand to the side of the court, and end it all for the both of them.

"I always thought she might kill me. She wanted me to be with her."

In the middle of 1973, Marilyn started isolating Billie from her friends. She refused to deliver messages for Billie, and arranged their dinners strictly for two. Marilyn plotted their getaways; off-time was spent outside of the tour circle. She also acted as Billie's gatekeeper; access to the media for interviews was limited. As Billie's traveling companion, she was free to order room service — even cigarettes from the gift shop — and charge them on Billie's bill.

The claustrophobic relationship gradually gnawed at Billie; she tried ending the relationship in 1974. But Billie just couldn't toss out Marilyn. True to her nature, Billie felt compelled to appease Marilyn rather than confront her. She had to give her something.

That scent of salt air was a major selling point for Billie Jean and Larry when they plopped down $132,000 for a scenic Malibu home in 1973. "I think I set foot in that house once," Larry King recalls. "I was working in San Francisco. The Malibu place was Billie's house, her Southern California house, to use as she wanted to." A year later, Billie offered the dream house to Marilyn as part of a deal to end their relationship. All Marilyn had to do was pay $120 a month in rent and maintain the house and grounds. The offer did not represent a major sacrifice. Billie barely used the place because of her frenetic schedule. She spent more time on the East Coast than out West.

"I should have changed the locks on the doors when she left one day," Billie says. "Instead I was being nice. I let her stay at the place Larry and I bought, and she kept saying it's 'our house.' It's 'our house'? I was like, what?"

As a perpetual houseguest, Marilyn became even more territorial. Whenever Billie visited the Malibu getaway, Marilyn played the doting housewife by cooking all the meals. Sometimes they watched TV; sometimes they made love. However, throughout most of their time together, Billie could not escape her self-loathing.

"I hated myself during that time," Billie says. "To me, I wasn't living by my principles."

In utter confusion, Billie retreated from Marilyn to spend more time with her husband. Larry was safe. Larry was predictable. Larry was her calm center.

"We had a great year in 1975," Billie recalls. "We kind of got back together. He was running World Team Tennis, and he was responsible, and we were having a great time, laughing, intimate. I really liked it."

The euphoria didn't last. Larry was a comforting, unconditional lover, but that wasn't enough for Billie. She didn't want to be married to anyone anymore. She wanted the freedom to explore her sexuality openly and honestly.

"I had other people wanting to be with me. There were a couple of women who wanted to be with me. I was just trying to figure out who I was."

Whenever Billie gathered the courage to come out, panic immediately set in. By 1976, with Chrissie mesmerizing America, the tour could have survived Billie's disclosure. But her parents would have been crushed, the public would have felt betrayed, and her endorsements would have vanished. Friends warned her not to do it.

"That's probably what put me into even deeper shame, when people tell you things like that," Billie recalls, laughing now at the absurdity of the situation. "It's like, 'Oh my God! It's worse than I thought!'"

Despite her fears, Billie could not resolve her ambivalence over her relationship with Marilyn. As late as 1977, Marilyn still accompanied

Billie to the occasional tour event. Billie couldn't—or wouldn't—completely cut her off. Then that day arrived in 1980 when the situation finally combusted.

"I'm selling the Malibu house," Billie announced.

Marilyn responded by threatening to go public with evidence of their affair: a stack of the couple's love letters. Billie believed that the release of those letters would ruin her. Those same demons that had dogged her in the weeks before her match with Bobby visited once again. She was convinced that a single image-tainting moment could snuff out all the good she had accomplished during her career. She was petrified, so she turned to the one person she knew she could rely on.

"I didn't contribute anything other than I did not want to cause Billie Jean more grief," Larry King remembers. "And, you know, I just wanted to support her and what she wanted to do and make sure, to the best of my ability, that I could do that. We did as much as we could to protect Billie Jean and ourselves."

Larry advised Billie to offer Marilyn a compromise: the letters in exchange for house money. Hush money.

"How does fifty percent of the net profits sound to you if you have no further claims on my life, and if you will get out of the house when the house is sold . . . and if you will not be bothersome to me?" Billie asked Marilyn. "Please give me the letters back and have no further claims, lawsuits, or publicity."

Marilyn agreed to accept $125,000, half of the house's projected value. In April of 1981, after Marilyn had already received part of that money, she abruptly called off the deal, an act Billie now looks back on as "a function of money and revenge."

Through her lawyer, Marilyn told Billie she no longer wanted $125,000 for the hundreds of letters in her possession. She thought the cache was worth a good deal more than that. Marilyn wanted the whole house, plus a lifetime of benefits.

"They're going to hurt us," Billie told Larry. "They're really going to hurt us badly before this is over."

Billie was fading on the tour, and she thought constantly about retiring. In May 1981 she walked off the court after a loss at a tournament near Orlando, Florida. Another nobody had beaten the great Billie Jean King. After tossing her bag on the hotel bed, she picked up a piece of pink phone message paper. There was a check in the box next to "Please Call." A reporter from the *Los Angeles Times* wanted to question her about "the suit."

That's how Billie discovered Marilyn had filed a palimony suit against her in a Los Angeles court. Marilyn and her attorney were seeking half of Billie's career earnings as well as the Malibu home. In the suit, Marilyn depicted herself as the heartbroken devotee who had abandoned her career as a hair stylist to do everything "necessary so that Mrs. King's energy could be totally directed toward playing tennis."

The news stunned Billie. She had no idea Marilyn could stretch her scorn quite so far. She wanted to bolt the universe, to disappear. That was her inclination whenever stress piled up. In the past, Billie would have retreated to Stinson Beach or to South Carolina. This time she jumped on a night flight and returned to her New York apartment near Columbus Circle on Manhattan's West Side.

Once home, Billie prowled from one room to the next while bouncing a tennis ball off her racket strings. She had to think. Before reaching New York, Billie had issued a blanket dismissal of her relationship with Marilyn. In the press release, Billie admitted that Marilyn had been her secretary, but that she had eliminated the position when she decided to focus more on tennis than on her other business activities. That lie nagged at Billie. She had to make it right, and her media savvy told her that television was the proper venue for any act of contrition. She decided to hold a press conference in Los Angeles.

"Whatever you want," Larry replied when Billie told him over the phone.

"It's going to hurt you. It's going to hurt my parents. It's going to hurt women's tennis, women's sports."

"Look, don't worry about other people," Larry said. "For once in your life, do exactly what you want to do for yourself. No matter what happens, I'll take care of you, Billie Jean. The two of us can always get by."

"Wait a minute. Get by? I don't want to get by. I'm too old. I still need my comforts."

The laughter provided a brief respite from the anxiety. Against the advice of her own attorneys, Billie prepared for the press conference. She took off her glasses as she waited for her flight to L.A. She did not want anyone to recognize her; she needed time by herself. Billie knew there wouldn't be much of that left. She was about to become the subject of the most sensational story in the country.

On May 3, she arrived for a press conference that would be aired by local news outlets and replayed throughout the CNN news cycle. With Larry's hand on the small of her back, Billie walked into a conference room wearing a beige and pink argyle sweater with a white collar. Staring through her famous wire-rimmed aviator-style glasses, she maintained eye contact with the reporters seated in front of her.

Larry spoke first. In a coat and tie, his body and face appeared more rounded, his blond hair thinner than the last time he'd spoken up for Billie—the night he'd defended her against Jack Kramer before the match with Bobby Riggs. He was just as calm for this event, just as cool. His voice was even, unwavering. Typical Larry.

"I was the dumb one," Larry recalls. "I wasn't smart enough to be scared."

Larry opened by introducing his wife as the woman he had loved dearly for nineteen years. "This is a difficult time for our family and friends," Larry began, "but I don't think that anything that transpired will hurt our relationship."

As he sat to Billie's left, Larry's hand remained on the back of her chair. He was steadying her, as always. Billie's lawyers sat close by. Betty and Bill Moffitt had taken seats just off to the side. Billie's lawyer had requested their presence. "It was orchestrated to some degree," Larry recalls. "The attorneys wanted a show of solidarity. And Betty and Bill always wanted to be by their daughter's side. It was difficult for them — absolutely. They are Middle America in so many ways. I'm not sure they knew exactly what they were in for that day. I don't think it was until much later that they understood what it all meant." In a measured but soft voice, with words that were clear and a heart that was beating like a ragtime band, Billie confessed: "I did have an affair with Marilyn Barnett. It's been over for quite some time."

For the next twenty minutes she discussed her "mistake" and the ramifications of it.

"It's very important for a person to have privacy. Unfortunately, someone in my life didn't feel that way. I have no idea what the effect will be on my fans. I'm more concerned with the people around me."

Marilyn couldn't have expected the depth of Billie's revelations. Billie didn't bother to delve into the lawsuit; instead, she provided a character analysis of her former friend. "I've known for some time that Marilyn was unstable. What do you do with someone that unstable?"

Billie looked toward her parents. Though heartbroken, they remained right by her side in the moment of truth. In the elevator after the press conference, Billie would wrap her arms around her father to keep him from shaking. She could accept the inevitable scrutiny and scorn, and she knew Larry had the temperament to endure, as well. But her parents didn't deserve this anguish.

In front of the press, she thanked them for their love and support, and admitted that the exposure of her private life was the unfair part of celebrity. "Anyone who's in the limelight accepts it," she conceded. "Yes, I have accepted it."

She wasn't sure who among the tour accepted her, though. Billie was not only a founder of the WTA, but its president. The disclosure of her affair had turned the unspoken issue of lesbianism in women's tennis into the pressing issue of the day.

The scandal would chip the manicured image of the sport, but it proved healthy enough to withstand the lurid headlines. If anything,

Marilyn's lawsuit opened a dialogue. Some players even found the subject galvanizing; they had always bristled against the unspoken assumption that most female athletes were homosexual, when in truth the proportions reflected society's demographics: some were gay, many were not.

Other players, though, saw it differently. The constant chatter about the suit—everyone on the tour was talking about it—brought up their frustrations, their insecurities. They feared being lumped together in a group of man-haters feverish with girl crushes.

Billie offered to resign as WTA president if the members wished her to step aside. She did not want to inflict her turmoil on any of them. Billie understood the strain they were under, answering for her situation. For weeks, players had to cope with inquisitive reporters, worried sponsors, and parents of young players who were suddenly convinced the tour was ridden with lesbian recruiters.

Billie and Andrea Jaeger had been penciled in as doubles partners for the upcoming Bridgestone event in Tokyo. Andrea was only fifteen, and Billie let her parents know that she would understand if their daughter wanted to pull out. Andrea and her folks were adamant. They were sticking by Billie, who, as usual, was standing tall.

"Let the publications, parents, and officials deal with me," Billie told the *New York Times*. "I'm the one. Leave the players alone."

But they wouldn't. Some tabloids were offering up to $20,000 to any woman who would dish on Billie. One player who accepted the rag money paid for it when she walked into the locker room. "Come on, girls," JoAnne Russell announced as soon as she saw her. "Let's all of us pair up with our regulars and take our baths together." The embarrassed traitor ran into the bathroom and hid in a toilet stall.

Billie continued to handle everything head-on, right down to disclosing the intimate details of her sexual identity. Suddenly she became the voice of gay politics, and she emphasized the importance of equality for every race, gender, and sexual orientation.

"I feel that basically Marilyn was a mistake," Billie explained in the *Times*. "For me, it's an odd situation. I don't feel homosexual. That's not my feelings, and I don't understand why people feel that I'm any less of a person.

"What they're saying is that it equals bad if someone happens to be homosexual. It's a fear, an unknown fear, and people don't understand it."

She proclaimed as much on television, in an interview with Barbara Walters. Larry was in his usual position at his wife's side.

"She interviewed us at our PR person's house," Larry recalls. "After the interview she turned around to me and said, 'Do you have a brother?' It was a goofy time. I wasn't special in any way, that's why I kind of chuckled to Barbara Walters."

Barnett's suit came to trial in the winter of 1981. "The Marilyn problem," as Larry still calls it, was aggressively engaged from the beginning. Larry put the focus on offense by assembling the legal team best suited to attack Marilyn's credibility.

"The first time I met with the attorney that had been hired to represent Billie Jean, he was a family law attorney and he was totally lawyerlike," Larry explains. "I said, 'Billie Jean, forget this; I'm not going with this guy representing you. This isn't a family-law issue; there's no family involved. It's an issue of somebody extorting money from a supposed lover. That's all it is. And we're going to go get Henry Holmes. I want a bulldog. I don't want that nice guy to go to court representing us and keep the cuffs on. I want to go out and win and go for the jugular.'"

They hired Holmes, and steeled for a fight. Holmes was a budding Hollywood attorney to the stars, known for his aggressiveness. Years later he would go on to represent George Foreman and Chuck Norris, but Larry knew him first. They'd gone to Berkeley Law School together.

"He was exactly who we needed," Larry recalls. "He was tough."

Larry's unqualified support for his wife invited the juvenile instincts of some members of the press to rev into overdrive. Larry, they speculated, must be gay, too.

"I think we got some interesting raps," Larry says. "A lot of people thought Billie Jean was just in it for the money, or I must be gay or something to put up with the lifestyle. People have their own little views, and they have to distinguish themselves from everybody else on some basis. Where they view it as a putdown, it's more really kind of a stamp of approval: You must be doing something right if they don't like what you're doing."

Larry wore a sharp suit, and sat at the lawyers' table in the courtroom throughout the trial. After Marilyn had filed the palimony suit, Larry took it upon himself to explain the complex nature of his relationship with Billie, launching into one particularly passionate soliloquy. It was the voice of a man defending his marriage to the public.

"You have to look at it from the personalities involved," Larry explained. "Most people have some glimpse of Billie Jean as a high-charged, emotional person, with a high level of personal contact.

"She's very compelling and draining. She has a need for total attention. I'm different. . . . We have very different capacities for needing personal attention from each other, which has created a certain amount of conflict. You resolve these in any relationship by either making certain tolerances or breaking up the relationship. . . . There's a high degree of loyalty. Other people may not see it as loyalty, but I love Billie Jean. I've never stopped loving her, and that translates not into possession, but into trying to do whatever makes her the happiest.

"Most people look at love as an ability to possess people. I look at it as sharing with them, loving them, and wanting the best for them. I love Billie Jean and I'll always love Billie Jean. That doesn't mean that she might not be happier, because of her capacity and needs for attention, with some other person."

Larry's layered philosophy on the nature of relationships did little to satisfy nervous corporate moneymakers. They did not want Billie's affair with Marilyn attached to their product lines. They saw no market for married sports idols turned cheats, particularly if they cheated on their husbands with other women.

Before the suit, Billie had signed to represent a Wimbledon clothing line for $500,000. If anyone knew what to wear for a center-court curtsy, it was Billie, the winner of twenty Wimbledon championships. That deal fell apart. Her $300,000 contract with Murjani jeans? Gone. The lost endorsements were adding up, but the support Billie was receiving from the players buoyed her. Chris Evert, for one, stepped to Billie's side early on. She remembered how the older star had been there for her on many occasions.

"I was angry when I read about what she was going through with the gossip and everything. It angered me that people were judging her. Trust me, I went onto the tour very sheltered," Evert recalls, "and came off it knowing everything about life. It taught me a lot of lessons. The first few years I saw a lot and I learned a lot about life and about feelings and about not being judgmental.

"My parents were really cool about it, too, because they were, like, staunch Catholics, yet they loved Rosie and they loved Billie and they never made any judgments on their lifestyle."

The support was a lifeline for Billie. She wasn't alone, after all. Gloria Steinem wrote her a comforting letter, saying, "It breaks my heart to see you suffering or penalized in any way for living in a still unenlightened time, but please know your troubles have probably hastened a better understanding for everyone."

In a way, Billie's fight against Marilyn was just another rite of passage. Women's rights, abortion rights, gay rights. It all happened on her watch. Advocacy had found its breadwinner in Billie.

She remained as president of the WTA. But some members of the Women's Sports Foundation, the advocacy organization Billie had founded to fight for equality in athletics, wondered out loud whether to invite its most controversial executive to the annual year-end dinner.

"Some thought it would be better if she wasn't there," recalls Donna de Varona, the WSF president at the time. "It was ridiculous. Of course she should be there."

Billie entered the room. Everyone turned their heads, scooted back their chairs, and put their napkins on their tables. They gave her a standing ovation.

On December 11, 1981, Judge Julius Title of the Superior Court in Los Angeles took his seat behind the bench of a paneled courtroom. Then he succinctly ordered Marilyn Barnett to go away; he had no patience for her personal vendetta.

Judge Title gave her thirty days to gather her belongings and move out of the Kings' Malibu home. "An attempt at extortion" was how Judge Title described Marilyn's lawsuit. He assailed her attempt to blackmail Billie by using a stack of love letters for leverage. Miss Barnett, he said, "did not have clean hands" when she arrived in court.

Judge Title's verdict repaired Billie's spirit, but Marilyn had left her in a financial flatline; the tear in the King bank account was easily seven figures deep. It wasn't just the Wimbledon clothing and Murjani deals; other manufacturing partners of Billie's had simply phased her out of their advertising plans, or had refused to renew her contracts.

"The money is the least important aspect of life," Larry says. "It's all nice to have enough money to have choices, but all the choices in the world don't make up for not having kids, not having a family and support. Billie Jean paid a big price, but the price wasn't the money."

The price was suppressing the truth — the real truth. Within weeks, Billie was offered a chance to explain everything — to detail her life with Marilyn, to discuss her relationship with Larry, to make sense of the scandal to her public. She had begun the reparation process in bits and pieces, through interviews with newspapers. This was a chance to let it all go, to unleash the trauma in writing.

She contracted to do a book with the celebrated sports writer Frank Deford. With his prompting, she burst off the pages in an emotionally charged catharsis for an autobiography simply titled *Billie Jean by Billie Jean*.

"My manager kept saying, 'You have to do it,'" Billie recalls, "but I didn't want to do it; I was in a bad way. 'It will be so extreme,' I thought. 'It will be so distorted when I do it,' and it was."

The book was a candid lie, if there can be such a thing. Page after page, she revealed her thoughts on Marilyn and testified to her complex devotion to Larry. But Billie was also careful to make what she believed then was a necessary omission.

Billie had portrayed the affair with Marilyn as a singular mistake. It wasn't. As everyone on tour knew, and as Larry first discovered in the early years of the marriage, Billie had been exploring relationships with women long before Marilyn came along.

The book was dedicated to Larry, but that didn't mean she was back in her husband's arms. In 1979, Billie had met Ilana Kloss, a tour player thirteen years her junior. She soon became Billie's doubles partner and lover. Ilana was everything Marilyn wasn't: secure, honest, and solid. For the third time, Billie asked Larry for a divorce. For the third time, he talked her out of it. Although they were living apart, Larry still held tight to his position as Billie's husband. He relished his place in her reflective aura, his role as the caretaker of her legend.

"I'd say, 'I want a divorce.' And he'd say, 'You don't want a divorce; you know that will hurt your image,'" Billie says. "You know how when you know your partner, you know how to trip the triggers? Looking back, he knew me; he knew how to make me fearful. He didn't make me fearful; I reacted in a fearful way. He didn't make me do anything. I didn't accept responsibility."

Billie had twisted the truth about the breadth of her lesbian experiences, in part to protect Ilana. When whispers circulated about their relationship, Billie often bristled, "Can't I have a friend who is a woman?" Ilana became known as Billie's business assistant. They made sure to request double beds whenever they checked into hotels. They only held hands in dark theaters.

They stood together in public, but only as professionals. If there hadn't been a business side to Billie, it might have been different. In the late seventies and early eighties, however, Billie wasn't about to sashay through the corporate world introducing Ilana as her companion. The balance between the public life with Larry, her private relationship with Ilana, and her position as an enduring symbol of so many things to so many people continued to leave her in agony.

"I was thirty-seven in 1981. I was old," Billie recalls. "It was about the pain I brought to my family, and to Larry and to Ilana. I was totally confused."

The sleight of hand she had been playing with the public exhausted her. From the moment she fell in love with Marilyn in 1972, Billie walked through life fearing trapdoors. One misstep and she could drop out of sight. She would always wonder what kind of player she might have been without the stress of clandestine relationships, without the fear of disclosure, without the pressure of bias.

As she stood outside the L.A. courthouse in December of 1981, she was happy that Judge Title had finally released her from Marilyn's manipulations. She was still in prison, though. She still couldn't be herself. After all she had sacrificed for equality and inclusion, had the loss of her own freedom been worth it?

CHAPTER 10

Equal Assets

Fifteen miles from the L.A. courthouse, on the streets of Compton, two sisters went from door to door, walking on sidewalks colored with chalk art and littered with broken bottles, past the organ-grinder tunes of the ice-cream truck and a car's rusting carcass on cinderblocks. Venus and Serena Williams were delivering the Yellow Pages.

This was fitness training for toddlers, the madcap Richard Williams method.

"When they were around two years old, I wanted them to work; and my wife said, 'That's not going to happen,'" Richard recalls. "How could they work? Well, they could deliver phone books.

"People look at Venus and Serena today and say, 'Heck, they must lift weights.' They don't lift weights. They just end up that way when you develop their muscles early."

Every tale is a believe-it-or-not proposition with Richard Williams, but he promises he drew up a daydreamer's blueprint for his daughters' futures even before they were conceived. He had been flipping the TV channels one afternoon in 1978 when he came across Bud Collins, decked out in his trademark test-pattern attire, standing on a red clay court. The renowned sportswriter was handing a check to tennis player Virginia Ruzici.

A check for $30,000.

Not a bad payday for a few days' work, Richard thought. Did that check really carry that many zeros? The next morning he studied the sports pages to make sure his deep-set eyes hadn't deceived him.

"We need to make two more kids," he soon told his girlfriend.

Richard Williams and Oracene Price had met at a bus stop in 1973. Both were exiting previous marriages, but the similarities between them ended there. Richard believed that no good story was complete until he stretched it into a grand illusion. He had grown up in Shreveport, Louisiana, crammed with five other family members in a thirty-by-forty-foot wood-frame house. His mother worked as a school custodian. That didn't have enough drama for Richard, so he told people she was a cotton picker who spent her days bent under the unforgiving sun, her fingers cut and bleeding. Though he possessed only middling athletic skills, Richard often portrayed himself as a scratch golfer who had honed his game on irons stolen from a caddy shack. Reality and fantasy were one and the same for Richard.

Naturally, it would take a realist to attract the dreamer. Oracene Price was as sensible and understated as a navy blue suit. She grew up the daughter of a General Motors plant worker, and beneath the deceptive cloak of her sleepy eyes, confidence and conviction circulated through her. She was an achiever. Oracene graduated from Eastern Michigan University with a degree in education. She had briefly considered becoming a soul singer, but her bedrock common sense won out. She instead settled into a nursing career in Los Angeles. Her father wasn't the CEO of GM; she didn't turn down music offers from Motown or perform surgery on Compton orphans. That would be a Richard-spun version.

He would also depict Compton as a hellish wasteland with stumbling druggies under the streetlamps and gang lords toting AK-47s. Oracene would describe it as a dangerous but manageable suburban ghetto. He romanticized it; she was embarrassed by it.

"I never considered it a badge of honor," Oracene says.

The differences between them didn't matter. Richard had picked her as the mother of his invention. He continually hid her birth-control pills until she became pregnant. Venus was born two months after the couple married in 1980. One year later, Serena arrived.

The Williams sisters grew up twelve miles from the public park that Billie Jean King played in as a child in Long Beach, but without anything close to the same middle-class advantages. It didn't matter. Venus and Serena remained oblivious to the bleakness of Compton. Give them a patch of grass for a cartwheel, and they giggled happily. Give them a tennis racket, and they waved it like a soap-bubble wand.

At four, Venus spun her father's ludicrous plan into motion when she jumped out of a VW van in front of East Compton Park, gripping a dime-store racket in her hand. Behind her came Richard, carrying a milk crate full of beat-up tennis balls.

Serena joined Venus for practice a year later. They both wore pleated skirts that swished around their reed-thin bodies. Braids popped up like spring bulbs from their heads. When they looked across the net, they saw their father—a slightly hunched figure with high cheekbones—waiting to start their education.

On mottled courts with duct-taped nets, Richard fed Venus and Serena 550 balls a day out of a rickety grocery cart that he discovered was much more mobile than the milk crate. "Richard would chain the grocery cart to the fence at night to keep people from stealing it," recalls Leland Hardy, a longtime family friend and business associate. "Richard knew what he was doing. He learned everything on the fly. Amazing." He felt his way through lessons from an instructional video he had bought secondhand.

The girls did not mind indulging him; they loved creative outlets of every kind. Serena was known to walk around the house singing Whitney Houston songs, using a wooden spoon in place of a microphone. When someone told her, "It's not the greatest *glove* of all, it's the greatest *love* of all," she wasn't discouraged in the slightest. Venus often zoomed deep into the outer space of her imagination as an astronaut. She thought the other planets would be pleased to get a visit from Venus.

Active minds, active bodies. Not even far-fetched notions seemed out of reach when the girls were so eager to expand themselves. After practice, Venus often pleaded with her father to swat another five hundred balls her way. She hit each shot with the quiet confidence she had inherited from her mother.

There wasn't the day-to-day gang warfare turning the courts into fox-holes, as Richard often claimed. But one afternoon, when Venus was eight, a man rose up in the distance beyond the chain-link fence and started firing a gun. Venus dove belly-down to the court. Stay low, cover your head, her father had told her.

The incident didn't fluster her. After the fireworks, she continued her practice routine as if nothing unusual had happened. She was out there again the next day, slapping balls as if she were beating dust from a rug. And then she started beating opponents. A gangly collection of lug-nut knees and knobby elbows, Venus dominated the Southern California Circuit and became its biggest draw.

"The Ghetto Cinderella," Richard proclaimed her, and he used the same pitch with sponsors that a Ginsu Knife salesman might employ: she slices, she dices, she stays sharp forever. Richard and Oracene would hand out brochures that highlighted their daughter's goals and virtues to anyone who stopped to watch her play.

"They were a big draw," Hardy recalls. "Gang members stopped, too."

No pamphlet could capture Venus's flesh-and-blood intensity, though. Seeing Venus in action, that was her greatest selling point. She'd bite down on her bottom lip before a big point, unveil a stare hard enough to bend spoons, and race cross-court on size-nine shoes to re-trieve impossible gets. At five foot three, she was growing at time-lapse speed, and her skills weren't far behind. By the summer of 1990, she had won her seventeenth straight singles title.

Mainstream America noticed. On July 2, 1990, the *New York Times* described the prodigy from the graffiti streets in a succinct headline: UN-DEFEATED. FUTURE ROSY. AGE: 10. Agents and corporations jockeyed to sign Venus to their client lists. They believed she had it all, the fresh face, the engaging personality, the exotic name, and, above all, the talent. And they all knew: there was a little sister coming right behind her. It was the ultimate daily double. Imagine, two black girls of modest means with the white-male establishment courting them—the Original Nine's dream come true.

"Sponsors are standing in line now," Richard crowed.

Tennis stars such as Pete Sampras and John McEnroe watched Venus with interest, and even hit a few balls with her for kicks. At circuit events, agents and corporate execs compiled copious notes on her. Ath-letic, tactical, quick, and relentless. Very Billie, the marketing wizards wrote. Different, dominant, bold, and black. Very Michael Jordan.

Even the great Jack Kramer was impressed. He had never been one to praise any woman effusively. But when he got his first glimpse of Venus, he mused, "For being fourteen, she's pretty good."

"She's not fourteen, Jack," someone said. "She's only ten."

"Oh my gosh," he gasped.

The boxing-world hype around Venus and Serena wasn't complete without grandiose promoter Don King. He had been watching the girls' rise from afar, scratching his cotton-candy head of hair, wondering how to weasel into the Williams phenomenon.

King intrigued Richard. The Williams family dined on soul food with King at an L.A. joint, and Richard promised to think over his offer to promote his daughters. A month later the sisters were wearing polo shirts with King's logo on their sleeves, but this meant nothing. Like everyone else, the promoter had to take a number. Like everyone else, he had to wait.

The Venus-and-Serena sensation needed refinement that could only develop through match experience. But in one of Richard's many unorthodox moves, he defied logic by yanking Venus and Serena off the junior circuit in 1991. No daughters of his would be burnout victims before their sixteenth birthdays, he declared. No daughters of his would be shark bait for corporate America. With marketing firms chasing his winged daughters like butterfly catchers, Richard took his girls underground.

In the fall of 1991, Richard called Rick Macci, the owner of a renowned tennis academy in Haines City, Florida, and asked him to coach Venus and Serena. Many parents would have offered to take their children to Macci's retreat for a tryout, but Richard had other ideas.

"Come to Compton," Richard pleaded. "Know anything about Compton?"

"It's near Watts, that's about all I know."

"I can only promise you one thing," Richard assured him. "I won't let you get shot."

Richard's usual hype would have been lost on Macci. Nearly every parent who approached the coach claimed to be bringing him the next big thing. But Macci had heard the stories about this prodigy named Venus and about the little sister who was only a hop and a skip behind her. He booked a flight to Los Angeles.

A day later, Richard picked up Macci in a dented Volkswagen van that wobbled like a stagecoach as it sputtered down the road. The car's interior was stained, and an errant spring had popped through one of its cloth seats. Venus sat inside amid a clutter of McDonald's wrappers, Coke cans, and discarded clothing.

"It looked like someone had been living in it for months," Macci recalls.

At 7:30 a.m., the three of them drove to East Rancho Dominguez Park, where dozens of guys played pickup basketball while drunks curled up in the grass. On a vacant court, Venus worked through her drills. She hit for an hour or so without providing even a glimpse of the spectacular. Macci was ready to book a flight back home, but then Venus did something on her way to a bathroom break that changed his mind. The kid walked ten yards.

On her hands.

And then she launched into a dazzling series of cartwheels and handsprings.

"I've got a female Michael Jordan," Macci said to himself.

Venus's speed, athleticism, and savvy intrigued the coach. And Serena, Richard promised, would be even better. Macci was sold. But before he could bring this already famous pair of sisters to his academy, he had to fulfill the Williams family's wish list. That was a switch. Usually, it was Macci who had his demands met whenever parents enlisted his help.

But, as Richard was quick to point out, Venus and Serena weren't everyone else. Agents and marketers were already waving rich contracts at them. Unlike any other prodigies who had come before them — male or female, black or white — the sisters had the kind of financial leverage the young Billie had only imagined.

Macci gave the Williamses everything they asked for: a $92,000 motor coach with a VCR, bar, bedroom, and plush interior; a salaried position for Richard at $50,000 a year; a new Aerostar van; a four-bedroom house in Florida at a discounted rent of $1,600 a month; $5,000 worth of new furniture; boxing lessons; Disney World tickets; Tae Kwon Do sessions; and free meals at the Greenleaf resort's famous seafood buffet.

"Every Friday night, they were at the buffet," Macci remembers. "For a whole family, that was $250 a pop. They lived like kings."

In return for the concessions, Williams handed Macci a back-loaded deal front-loaded with risk. The coach would receive 10 percent of each sister's total earnings — including endorsement monies — until they turned twenty-one. With all the companies courting Venus and Serena, that could amount to quite a bundle. But what if the sisters were busts? What if they suffered career-ending injuries? Macci had no fallbacks, no guarantees of any kind. He poured $1 million of his own money into the Williams family, then held his breath and coached the girls for the next four years.

Rick Macci's Greenleaf academy stretched across a slice of orange-grove country in central Florida called Haines City, a town that was only a little less humid than the inside of a steamed clamshell. The nearest beach breeze was an hour's drive away. Venus and Serena adjusted to the uncomfortable surroundings almost immediately. They usually kept to themselves and their family, but they weren't aloof. In group tennis drills, the sisters mingled on the sidelines with peers like Andy Roddick, and played tag with the rest of the kids during the agility skills tests.

There was, however, one notable difference between the Williams sisters and the other tennis campers: their rigid intensity. Even in a game as innocuous as tag, against children big and small, Serena played with a clenched fist. She didn't need a bodyguard, but Venus watched over her just the same. As the older sibling by fourteen months, Venus made sure that Serena's safety strap was snapped tight to the horse whenever they rode the carousel. She gave up her lunch when her little sister forgot hers, and she fixed Serena's bows when they cocked crooked on her pigtails.

Serena was the copycat. She ate tomatoes and mushrooms simply because Venus ate tomatoes and mushrooms. It would be years before Serena admitted she didn't even like tomatoes and mushrooms. If Venus went through a yellow phase, so did Serena, even though pink was by far her favorite color.

On their own, however, the sisters were opposites. Serena had grown up spoiled. She was more effusive than the serious Venus, more careless than her cautious older sister, more Hollywood than homebody.

In Venus's company, however, Serena demurred. She often looked to her big sister for approval, and usually agreed with everything Venus said. Venus, in turn, guarded her greatest admirer with every ounce of her sinewy frame — even against their moody father.

Richard was not seen as an abusive parent, but he had a quick-draw temper that often came out on the practice courts. If the girls weren't being aggressive enough to suit him, he would snatch the racket from Venus's hand and pull his daughters nose-to-nose across the net.

"Hit it at her," Richard would tell Venus.

She wouldn't move. That was her little sister standing across from her.

"Go on, V, hit it," Richard ordered. "Serena, you hit it at her, too."

Venus and Serena would reluctantly fire volleys at each other until a blast on the shoulder, face, or stomach evoked a shriek — or a tear. Only then would Richard once again turn into the doting father, full of kisses and praise.

Macci had seen tennis dads lose it before, men who exploded like piñatas at the slightest poke, fathers who berated and badgered their children at the first whiff of success. After all, he had coached Stefano Capriati's child, Jennifer.

"I've seen the craziest of the crazy," Macci says, "but Richard handled his daughters well when the fame started coming."

Richard kept the girls disciplined with lectures and punishments. One day he caught Serena in a lie. His dentures hadn't been lost, Serena confessed during a drive, she had thrown them away. Richard promptly pulled the car off the road and spanked her.

Whether Richard's methods were appropriate, his daughters developed impeccable manners. They never left practice without thanking Macci. They liked and respected their coach. When he moved his academy to Delray Beach in 1992, the sisters went with him. Once again, the Williamses were as pampered as high-maintenance rock stars.

Despite all the perks, Richard abruptly jerked his daughters out of Macci's academy in 1993 and brought them to Nick Bollettieri's assembly-line-of-the-stars in Bradenton, Florida. When Richard refused to offer Bollettieri the same back-loaded contract he had given Macci, the experiment ended.

Then it was off to a United States Tennis Association facility in Miami. Venus performed in front of a group of officials charged with developing raw tennis skills with little money. After his daughter finished her show-and-tell, Richard inexplicably took off on a rant against greedy tennis parents.

"I'm sick of looking around tennis and seeing these poor kids making a living for their parents, seeing these parents drive around in their Mercedes and Rolls-Royces," Williams rambled. "To me, that's like the parents turning against the kids and prostituting them. I took my girls out of the tennis academies because I thought they looked at them as a commodity, and you know what happens when one commodity gets used up—they throw it away and get a new one."

Only a few weeks later, Richard revved up the $92,000 motor coach Rick Macci had given him, and returned his daughters to the coach's academy. Richard acted as if he were above all those other gluttonous tennis parents, but his righteousness had a caveat: His daughters were making money—just not in prizes. Money and gifts were pouring in, as much as $125,000 a year from companies trying to suck up to the family. Such spoils are usually reserved for hot high school talents on the verge of turning pro—in the NBA.

Richard held off the corporate mercenaries; Venus and Serena's value appreciated with the anticipation. By accepting the freebies—the shoes, the clothes, the candy, and the cash that every maker sent to the family—he placed his daughter's riches on a lay-away plan. He teased the three marketing giants—International Management Group, ProServ, and Advantage International—that were competing to represent his girls, and kept right on gambling even after Venus turned pro at fourteen.

"We've been offered millions of dollars, from homes to cars to anything you can name," Richard declared. "I've talked to everybody, but I've signed with nobody."

No one had seen Venus play competitively in more than three years, so a great fanfare greeted her arrival at the 1994 Bank of the West Classic in Oakland, California. Venus walked confidently out on the court for the start of her match. Hardly the gangly kid from Compton anymore, she stood nearly six feet tall.

Her sharpened arsenal turned Shaun Stafford into a trivia question. Venus captured her first pro-match win in front of a contingent of panting marketers and national press. A day later, she had one of the top players in the world, Arantxa Sanchez-Vicario, down 3–1 in the second set. In a slippery veteran move, Arantxa took a bathroom break to let Venus mull over her lead. When Sanchez-Vicario returned, Venus turned four-teen again, losing her momentum on her way to blowing the match.

No one other than Venus much cared about the loss. Everyone agreed she had delivered a hell of an opening act under pressure. Reebok and Nike all but found themselves stuck in the doorframe to-gether as they raced to sign her. The salivating ended in May 1995, when Reebok signed Venus to an unprecedented five-year, $12-million deal. Based on one pro tournament—based on spec, really—this black teen who didn't have a driver's license owned a shoe contract that paid the kind of loot usually commanded by established pro male athletes.

This is what Billie and her coalition had envisioned so many years before—this kind of financial equality, this kind of inclusion, this kind of attention.

"I used to argue with people in the seventies about what we were try-ing to do," Billie recalls. "They used to ask, 'What's going to happen ten years from now?' I'd say, 'Women will be playing for millions of dollars.' Okay, so it was twenty years. It happened."

It happened twice in the same family. Unfathomably, Serena would ultimately deliver a Venus sequel, but it wasn't as easy for the more emo-tional of the two siblings. She wasn't ready, but Serena wanted to slip into the pros under the WTA's new age limits established in the after-math of Jennifer Capriati's jailhouse mug shot.

The tour viewed Capriati—a teen star who melted under the pres-sure of being a pro—as a cautionary tale. The age limit to turn profes-sional was lowered. The WTA didn't need another teen trauma from little girls gone pro.

Jenny's meltdown came in a limelight she had always abhorred. She hated fame. Capriati didn't want to be the next Chris Evert. She didn't want to carry the money load for everyone. She wanted to be able to slouch if she felt like it, to suffer through acne in private, to hang out at the local mall in peace. In other words, she wanted to be a teenager.

About the time she began painting her fingernails black, eighteen-year-old Jenny vanished from the tour and found cover among a group of dropouts on drugs. They didn't give a damn if she was the tour darling, as long as she could supply a buzz.

In May 1994, the cops busted Capriati in room 109 of the Gables Inn — a fifty-dollars-per-night roadside hotel on a tawdry strip of Miami. She stared sullenly into the jailer's lens for the mug shot that would jolt a nation of parents: dark eyes lined with black pencil, silver nose ring through her right nostril, a dirty strand of hair slicing across her blank face.

Suddenly, Jenny was no longer big-time tennis's poster child for financial equality. She stood as a warning sign for parents like Richard, who were wary of the dysfunction that too often accompanied fame. But Serena knew she wasn't Jenny. She insisted on leaving the amateur ranks. Richard resisted at first, but he was either afraid to lose his daughter or afraid to lose out on the money that would flow in once she turned pro. He allowed Serena to accept a wild card for the qualifying round of the Bell Challenge in Quebec, Canada.

Their flight plan took them through Philadelphia on October 31, 1995. While searching for souvenirs in a terminal gift shop, they lost track of the time; their plane departed without them. Serena was in danger of missing her professional debut. She and her father were able to catch another flight to Canada, but their luggage ended up in two different places, and several of Serena's rackets were misplaced in the confusion.

Richard and Serena arrived at their destination so late, there was no time for practice. Tournament organizers felt little sympathy for Serena's predicament. They had already given her a free pass to play. Serena's wild card was based solely on her cachet rather than on her career; she had barely made a cameo on the junior circuit during the prior four years. They were not about to lavish her with special perks.

Bleary-eyed but eager to compete in her qualifying match, Serena dropped her racket bag on a court situated below a smoke-filled lounge at a suburban tennis club. This was nothing like Venus's debut. There were no blaring trumpets, no screaming fans. Serena entered without so much as an introduction.

It was one humble venue for a phenom who had been ballyhooed as Venus's hip little sister, the muscle-bound slugger on her way up, the dimple-cheeked dream date for sponsors. Her discount-tagged peers had rolled their eyes over the hype. Then the unimpressed and unassuming Anne Miller rolled over Serena, 6–1, 6–1.

"I guess I played a celebrity," Miller remarked afterward. "There really is no substitute for the real thing. I felt like a complete veteran compared to her."

The anti-Williams backlash had begun. They had to find an escape.

The dusty road that passed through swaying, sinewy pine trees led to a two-story brick-and-clapboard Colonial with four columns guarding the front porch, green shutters on the windows, and a receding lake barely deep enough for the family Jet Ski. On the path to the estate's three clay courts, there was a round trampoline, a yellow backhoe, and a bus with Serena's and Venus's likenesses painted across a window. All of it sat on land spotted with tufts of grass on sandy soil.

Small dogs ran everywhere, leaving their paw prints on the courts after providing happy interruptions from Venus and Serena's private practice sessions. Rick Macci and his academy were no longer necessary. On the fringe of Palm Beach Gardens, Florida, Venus's Reebok deal had produced enough money to buy a compound with courts that had "Williams" emblazoned in white on the green windscreens.

To the family, the compound's seclusion represented a safe harbor from the curiosity seekers. But others saw the property as a symbol of the sisters' Garboesque aloofness. Inside the locker rooms, and in some backward corners of the public, there were racially tinged criticisms from people who were just not ready to accept two confident black girls. Venus and Serena weren't pigtailed wonders like Jenny Capriati, quietly graceful types like Steffi Graf, downloadable Lolitas like Anna Kournikova, or petite upstarts like Martina Hingis. There had been opinionated white stars on the tour before — Billie Jean King and Martina Navratilova to name two — but never assertive black supernovas. Why, this was almost a revolution.

On the tour, players wanted to know just who these girls thought they were. Venus and Serena didn't dot their *i*'s with hearts for their peers. They didn't exchange phone numbers with Lindsay Davenport, make small talk with Martina Hingis, or shower in the locker room like everyone else.

"I don't go to tournaments to make friends, to go to parties, to hold conversation," Venus later explained. "I come to be the best, and I'm not mean, cruel, or dirty."

Venus's look contributed to her audacious style. As angular as a runway model, with an exaggerated pout, she waltzed on the court wearing 1,800 beads that swung in her hair like office-desk clackers. The accessories — which Serena mimicked — took ten hours to apply.

"It was our style," Venus recalls. "We were individuals — still are."

Martina Hingis was the catty, cocksure diva of the tour, and the sisters' brazenness actually amused her. She found sport in debunking the Williams mystique. Upon hearing Richard inform the world that Serena "would kick her butt coming and going," Martina countered, "Sometimes he should watch his mouth."

Richard didn't have much to say to anyone after Martina thrashed Venus at the 1997 Lipton Championships in Key Biscayne, Florida. During the match, a bead slipped from Venus's braids and bounced onto the court like a BB. A tennis official handed the bauble to Hingis after her victory.

Martina stared at the bead for a moment as if it were an alien artifact. Then she rolled it in her fingers and flipped it into the crowd of her waiting fans. "I have a present for you," she cackled. "One of Venus's pearls."

The general resentment against the Williams sisters continued to thread throughout locker rooms that year. It culminated in the Irina Spirlea Incident. During their semifinal match at the U.S. Open, Spirlea bumped Venus as she passed by on a changeover. After shaking it off, Venus uncoiled her six-foot frame to dismiss the bitter Spirlea.

"She thinks she's *the* fucking Venus Williams," Spirlea fumed.

"She's a big white turkey," Richard countered.

Venus and Serena did not comment on their father's remark. They knew his inflammatory words could damage their well-marketed image. Oracene prodded Richard to apologize. He made his mea culpa, but the simmering dislike of Venus and Serena didn't end.

It was Venus's obvious sophistication that especially galled many of her peers. While the court-rat players loitered in the lounges or huddled with Spectravision in their hotel rooms, Venus would venture out to absorb the local culture. After Venus wrote in an online diary of her interest in Russia, players started strutting through the locker room with their heads tilted high and haughty. "Oh, Russia is replete with history," they would chirp in faux European accents. "Oh, how I love their art."

For the most part, the sisters ignored the petty potshots. So the players didn't like them. The public fascination with Venus and Serena continued to grow. That was all that mattered to the girls' carefully attended bottom line. Nothing could shake their confidence. In January 1998, Serena sat in on the negotiations for her new shoe deal with Puma. During the twelfth hour of discussions, after her father had agreed to gamble her future on an incentive-based package, the Puma reps asked him how he could be so sure his daughter would attain greatness. Serena jerked her head out of a deep sleep. She stared at the executives for a moment and said, "Do you have any doubt I'll be in the top five?" "I was there," Hardy recalls. "Serena was listening the whole time."

The next day, Serena signed a deal worth $12 million if she cracked the top ten. A year later, the money was hers.

But all the dollars couldn't buy off the denigration or the doubts. After falling behind 7–5, 4–1, to Virginia Ruano-Pascual at Wimbledon, Serena pulled up lame with a calf injury.

"I read later that she was so hurt," Lindsay Davenport quipped. "She was getting her ass kicked. I thought she was a complete wimp about it. I played her two days later in mixed doubles, and she was jumping for lobs."

Maintaining composure was an ongoing challenge for the sisters. At the 1998 Australian Open, Venus suffered a bead crisis when her tiny hair accessories sprung a leak, popping out of her locks like Pez onto the court. Chair umpire Denis Overberg assessed her a penalty point for the disruption.

"Why is this happening?" Venus exclaimed. "This has never happened to me before." Rattled for one of the few times in her career, Venus did not win another game. The press wondered openly if the pressure was getting to her.

"There's no such thing as pressure," Oracene Williams explained to *Sports Illustrated*. "As black Americans, that's all we've ever had. It's life. So where's the pressure? It's like squish them down, they can't have that confidence. I teach my kids to live in reality. You're black, you always have to work harder, but you don't have to prove yourself to anybody. I don't expect you to, and I don't expect you to apologize. Ever."

There was no reason to apologize for progress. The pioneers of women's tennis had owned secondhand Fords. Venus steered a Porsche before her twenty-first birthday. The women of the sixties were short on confidence; Venus and Serena had self-esteem to spare.

"I like everything that I am," Venus declared. "My mom always says, 'Can't you find something you don't like about yourself?' Actually, I can't. That's just the way I've always been."

At the 1999 Lipton, Venus and Serena became the first sisters to meet in the final of a pro-level event in 115 years. In the stands, Richard held up a sign that read, "I told you so." On a hubristic high after the match, he informed everyone who would listen that he might stop running his daughters' careers: "We're thinking now about buying Rockefeller Center for $3.9 billion, so I don't have time to think about tennis anymore."

The billions were a stretch — even by Richard's grandiose calculations — but the Williams sisters were cashing daily checks that would have amounted to a year's pay for the average worker in the seventies. They were more than just amazing players. Venus and Serena both had stage presence and the instincts of entertainers. Their flair for on-court drama evoked memories of Billie Jean King.

"Their approach to tennis, as far as being entertainment and all that, was absolutely right on," Billie says today. "It's exactly what we started when we began the tour, exactly what we were talking about, that this is entertainment."

As the new millennium rolled in, Venus and Serena each had a major title, and they quickly became the ideal window dressing for Madison Avenue. The Wrigley Company hired them to pitch Doublemint Gum, even though they weren't twins. For Avon, Venus radiated Audrey Hepburn style in a retro ad that ended with her twirling among flower petals. She also modeled coats for Wilson leather.

Meanwhile, the lens-loving Serena went Hollywood. On the court, she would prowl between the lines in curve-hugging black cat suits for Puma. She hammed it up with rappers in videos and popped up in guest shots on cable television. The sisters were everywhere. They certainly didn't need a challenge from John McEnroe to raise their profile.

This wasn't 1973. And at forty-one, McEnroe was not a younger version of Bobby Riggs, though it certainly sounded as though he was bucking for the role. In an article that appeared in *The New Yorker* in August 2000, McEnroe declared that any male college player or senior tour member could take the measure of Venus or Serena. He wanted to prove to the world that the sisters, though good, were no better than an aging, retired professional male tennis player.

McEnroe's sponsor for his latter-day Battle of the Sexes was not Jerry Perenchio, but Donald Trump—the slick real estate tycoon with dust-bunny hair and a blank check for gimmicks. At the 2000 U.S. Open, Trump floated around his luxury box above the baseline in Arthur Ashe Stadium. With shrimp cocktail served on ornate trays, with exotic beverages flowing all around him, with lovely models stuffed in the corners like tropical plants, Trump fairly glowed in the reflection of the box's gold accents.

Plotting does that to the man. As he explained to a reporter who had walked into his luminous lair, he was ready to bankroll a $1-million winner-take-all match between McEnroe and Venus or Serena at his Taj Mahal casino in Atlantic City.

"I wrote a letter to my dear friend John, making him the offer," Trump cooed from his perch.

McEnroe, of course, thought the idea was brilliant. Richard Williams thought it was a farce. "We're not interested," he said.

Richard was nutty, but not nuts. His daughters didn't need a match against a man to validate them. With all the prize money and endorsements they had already earned, with all the credibility their celebrity had brought them, Venus and Serena could do what Billie could not. They could politely decline.

"I don't know if I could fit him in my schedule right now," Venus remarked. "I don't think it's fair to put a twenty-year-old against a forty-something person. So I'll let that pass."

Venus was on her way to more important things, like a date in the 2000 U.S. Open final. She came to the match wearing an orange sherbet halter dress, a sparkling choker, and earrings that shimmered under the towering banks of lights. Her opponent, Lindsay Davenport, wore a pale pink ensemble that blended into the background.

It was audacity and confidence versus insecurity and passivity.

In the most precarious situations that evening, Venus flashed defiance. She overcame a 4–1 deficit in the first set and strutted through changeovers with her head tilted high. It was all in the attitude. At the 1999 U.S. Open, a dispirited Venus had sat slumped in the players' box with her face hidden beneath a hooded top as she watched Serena win the family's first major title.

Now it was her turn to burst into joy on match point, to stagger happily over to the players' box and celebrate after winning the match 6–4, 7–5. It was her second major championship in a row. As Venus embraced Serena and her mother, Richard Williams worked his way down from the seats and into the spotlight he craved. Only the day before, Richard had left his seat when Venus appeared on the verge of losing an intense semifinal match against Martina Hingis. Now he walked Venus back onto the court. Though the dispirited Lindsay Davenport was still sitting only a few yards away on the sideline, Richard broke into a honky-tonk two-step, spinning in circles and pointing to the sky.

"I always turn my head," Davenport said after the exhibition. "It's better not to see how they act."

In July, Richard had danced on the roof of a television booth after Venus tucked away Davenport at Wimbledon. But this latest perform-ance had a lot more oomph, a bit more passion. Richard was clearly sending a message.

"I think Lindsay and Martina better come to me for advice," he would say later, "because they're not winning."

Venus was the one lifting the 2000 U.S. Open trophy. A half hour later she was ushered down a cinderblock hallway inside Arthur Ashe Stadium and into a CBS TV booth. Under the heat of the studio lights, Venus chilled out, even though President Bill Clinton was on the line. Other players would have simply thanked Mr. Clinton for the congratu-latory phone call, then let him steer the rest of the conversation. Not Venus. She practically commandeered the nation's commander-in-chief throughout their dialogue.

She teased Mr. Clinton for slipping into the U.S. Open during the week, but missing her match. "Where'd you go?" she asked him. Then she gently chastised the president for the cross-borough gridlock he brought on by the Millennium Summit in midtown. "We suffered through traffic," Venus told him, "while you guys had a straight shot through."

Her candor amused Mr. Clinton, made him chuckle so hard you could hear his eyes crinkle. The call was drawing to a close, but Venus wasn't quite done with him. She had this special request for the president:

"Do you think you could lower my taxes? Mr. President, did you see me today? I was working real hard."

"What state do you live in?" Clinton asked gamely.

"I'm in Florida. I pay a high property tax. So what can you do about it?"

"We're working on it." Clinton laughed again. "I think there ought to be special rules for athletes."

"Can I read your lips?" Venus cracked.

Match point, Williams. What a night. Venus had not only won the U.S. Open, she had also bested the president of the United States in a nationally televised verbal joust. And Mr. Clinton, to his credit, didn't seem to mind losing to a woman whose mind was just as strong as her body.

Venus and her sister were fortunate. Unlike Billie and her peers, they were born into a world in which women athletes finally had a chance to reap the same financial rewards as men. This new equality meant that two black girls from Compton could become genuine power brokers in a marketplace males had dominated for so long. They were the beneficiaries of Billie's risky roadwork. They were what the sacrifice had been all about.

The proof wasn't only embodied in Venus and Serena, it was alive in a new generation.

CHAPTER 11

"There's No Pain"

On July 10, 1999, the Rose Bowl burst into color, a dish full of jellybeans filled with the faces of girls and boys—some of them toddlers—painted in bright reds, blues, and golds. The children sat among the 90,189 fans who had been swept up in an improbable joyride that led to Pasadena, California. They had traveled by car and bus, by minivan and limo, by plane and motorcade, to watch the U.S. women's soccer team compete in the World Cup championship finals. There was no other place to be.

In a luxury box, President Clinton munched on a sack full of popcorn, while Hollywood's new box-office wonder, Ben Affleck, slipped into a celebrity section to sit near movie superstar Jack Nicholson. Jack sat coolly with sunglasses over his famously arched eyebrows; someone asked him if he loved women's soccer.

"No, but I love women," Jack cooed.

Four F-18s buzzed the crowd, unleashing thunder against a Windex-blue sky. On the plush grass, the players from the U.S.A. and

China assembled for the American national anthem, sung by the hottest blond boy band of the month, Hanson.

While "the rockets' red glare" echoed above the crowd, Julie Foudy — or Loudy Foudy, as her teammates called her — was turning green. She was standing at the center of a moment in women's history, in a stadium that was usually a venue for macho football games. She was in position, depending on the outcome that afternoon, to help validate or eviscerate the reasons the women's soccer team had captivated the nation's imagination. But Foudy did not feel queasy because of any pressure.

"It was that lunch," she uttered to teammate Michelle Akers before the last notes of the anthem hit the air. Julie embodied the essence of America's attraction to the women's World Cup team. She was just a regular gal, yet she and her teammates had managed to intertwine femininity and ferocity while meshing sex appeal with wholesome values. They threatened no one. These athletes took an unconventional approach to marketing, adopting a strategy that was fundamentally similar to the one Billie Jean King and the Original Nine had devised in the early days of the women's pro tennis tour.

Julie Foudy first encountered the King philosophy in 1995 at a roundtable discussion on the state of women in sports. At the time, the U.S. national team was struggling for visibility and fair contracts; players were forced to make do with ten-dollar per diems and trial-sized freebies from a handful of sponsors.

"We were like, a free 'USA' windbreaker? Great," Julie says.

The soccer star took a seat across the table from Billie. "We need some support," Foudy told her.

"Hello? Stop looking," Billie replied. "You as players have to decide what you want, and what you want your legacy to be, and what you want to leave behind for future players. Don't wait for anyone. Get out there. Take control."

That was the spirit of the Original Nine talking. That was the same do-it-yourself attitude that had once inspired a group of tennis-playing rebels to get out of bed at 5:00 a.m. to chat it up on small-town radio shows, that had shoved them out the door day after day to pass out tickets on street corners and glad-hand business executives. Charm and disarm, that was the mission. The Original Nine had created a fan base and sponsor core one grassroots effort at a time. With a one-dollar contract as a start. Billie reminded Julie of those risky and inauspicious beginnings. The message resonated.

"I remember flying home after that meeting and thinking, 'Billie is right; we can't let anyone else control our destiny,'" Julie says. "It was amazing to get that history—about how they started with a one-dollar contract—and to get it firsthand. She was the catalyst. She was the one who said, 'Get off your asses.'"

Julie was empowered. The U.S. women's soccer team knew they had to invent themselves outside the box to gain attention, but they also needed a success story to attract an audience. The 1996 Atlanta Games gave them their stage. Although NBC virtually ignored the U.S. women's team, they won the gold medal in front of more than 80,000 fans at the Olympics.

"That was the beginning," Foudy said. "Then it snowballed."

Julie and her teammates didn't market themselves through the usual channels. They didn't try to crash the sports sections dominated by the men, those places where female athletes were relegated to soft features on the inside pages. Instead, they created a presence through local morning shows and magazines like *Seventeen*, *Glamour*, and *People*— and even on the racy pages of *Gear*. But it wasn't until the summer of 1999 that their images would permeate a nation, thanks to the help of one gap-toothed fan.

It was June 16, 1999. Inside the Ed Sullivan Theater on Broadway, a copy of *Gear* rested on David Letterman's walnut desk. On the stage, seated in a chair next to him, was Brandi Chastain of the U.S. soccer team. If the squad's cover girl was Mia Hamm, if its voice belonged to Julie Foudy, Brandi Chastain was just one of the background players until she was invited to meet late-night TV's master mischief-maker.

Brandi appeared on the show the week the World Cup opened; she was supposed to promote the sixteen-team, thirty-two-match event. She and Letterman engaged in some small talk about the team and the cup. Then Dave pulled out his dog-eared copy of *Gear* and turned a glossy page of the magazine toward his live audience and all those millions of Americans sitting at home. There was Brandi, wearing only cleats and a strategically placed soccer ball, with her California blond hair pulled to one side. She had dared to bare all. The playful letch in Letterman was quickly on the loose. After Chastain's segment ended, Letterman told his viewers, "The U.S. Team — and this may come out wrong, I'll just say it now and forget about it — is Babe City, ladies and gentlemen. Babe City!"

For some feminists, Letterman's comments were a form of blasphemy. They considered Chastain's undraped appearance in *Gear* a sign of regression. To them, Brandi was just another bright woman pandering to sexual stereotyping. "It set us back a million years," the prominent sociologist Mary Joe Kane later declared.

Others reacted ambivalently. As an Olympic swimmer in the late sixties, Donna de Varona had often worn loose-fitting clothes to camouflage her broad shoulders; she was that concerned about appearing too muscular. The discussion about Chastain left Donna, in one breath, expressing how women had once been "punished for our sexuality and accused of not having it." And yet de Varona also wondered aloud why "Michael Jordan didn't have to take off his clothes."

Brandi blended both ideas in her defense. True, she might have chosen a more tasteful magazine in which to reveal herself, but, as she explained, "I ran my ass off for this body." She didn't see herself as a woman selling out to male fantasies for attention; she was exhibiting self-esteem by taking pride in her own body. This wasn't a gaunt vestige of heroin-chic for young girls to emulate; Brandi was the sturdy, glowing product of confidence. She had uncovered her sinewy body in a celebration of the work ethic that had carved it. In an instant, Brandi became a modern hybrid of marketability for women; she represented strength as an element of sexuality.

Billie Jean King, for one, took Brandi's answer to the debate as a sign of the young woman's marketing savvy. Billie had pitched curling irons on television commercials during the Battle of the Sexes. She had seen the mainstream recoil at the perception of female athletes as butch lesbians. She believed feminine sex appeal was a valid promotional tool in an American celebrity sports culture that was all about packaging.

"Sex is part of it," Billie explains. "It's the same as God giving some people better reflexes or better minds. It's an attribute. And it works in promoting sports. It's not demeaning if it's done with taste. It's how attention works.

"Let's be real, ninety percent of the media coverage is run by men. If you're an editor, and you know sex sells, you put it out there. It doesn't have to be a sign of weakness. It can be an athlete saying, 'Look, I'm proud of the work I've put into my body.' That's a healthy message."

The message Letterman sent wasn't magnanimous, but it was effective. Throughout the rest of the summer, Letterman titillated more than 4 million Americans as the self-proclaimed "team owner" of the U.S. "soccer mommas." He posted nightly images of the players standing like pageant contestants dressed in *Late Show* T-shirts — and *only* those T-shirts.

"I never could imagine being given the opportunity to spread the message to as many millions of people who watch that show," Brandi declared.

A few members of the women's team were uncomfortable with the Letterman promotion, but most took it with humor. "We tell the new photographers Brandi is available for nude centerfolds after practice," Foudy told reporters after Brandi's first television appearance.

Julie and her teammates were too secure to take Letterman seriously. They played along because he could draw the masses — including members of that valuable male demographic — to women of power, grit, and skill who played their game with a pure passion. These women understood that it sometimes took a spectacle to produce enlightenment. In 1973, Billie had arrived for her match with Bobby Riggs dressed in sequins and riding an Egyptian litter. She knew that the moment — and, by extension, her cause — would never be forgotten.

A NECESSARY SPECTACLE

In 1999 the women on the U.S. World Cup team created their own "scene" with a purpose. Like Billie, they realized that a woman can't change perceptions in a vacuum or make a point without witnesses. These soccer players were the sleek, muscular beneficiaries of Title IX. They had grown up in public schools during the late seventies, when administrators were first forced to apply the extracurricular interpretations of that legislation. They received equal access to sports facilities and extra funding for team athletics. As their popularity soared in 1999, these women became well-paid endorsers for corporate America, though they still had to battle for compensation equal to the U.S. men's team.

"They moved America," Billie recalls. "Corporations wanted to sign them up. They represented a revolution."

The team also served as a transition point in the evolution of women's sports. Until the summer of 1999, women athletes had been represented largely as adorable pixies, vixens, or victims. It was either Mary Lou Retton or Tonya and Nancy. Letterman may have turned those soccer players into party girls leaping out of cakes, but he also made them palatable to a society that remained uncomfortable with militant females.

By the time they entered the Rose Bowl to the high-pitched soundtrack of children's squealing cheers, the women of the U.S. team had become pop-culture phenomena. They had whipped the nation into a feel-good frenzy. But the attention was not enough. To make the point, to further their cause, they had to win the World Cup championship. Just as Billie had had to win more than a quarter-century earlier.

The U.S. team faced China, the behemoth of women's soccer, on a field with perimeter fences lined with ads from such major companies as Coca-Cola, MasterCard, and JVC. A TV audience of 40 million viewers was watching at home; a loss would be disastrous.

Through ninety minutes of excruciating tension, the two teams played to a scoreless tie. All those near makes and misses had the pro-American crowd as dizzy and drained as the athletes. Michelle Akers, one of the sport's pioneers, reached a state of delirium as she staggered through the match, battling the Chinese team and chronic fatigue syndrome. At the end of regulation, her body finally folded like a lawn chair. Akers dropped to the field, her wild strawberry hair splayed against the green grass, her resources and resolve evaporated.

She watched overtime on her back from a trauma-room table under the stadium. An oxygen mask was strapped over her mouth, I.V. tubes disappeared into her wrists, and her weary blue eyes remained fixed on the television.

Not even overtime was enough. The game would be decided on penalty kicks.

The Rose Bowl turned into a panic room. The jangled crowd watched as China converted four of five opportunities, missing one when goalkeeper Briana Scurry inched forward just enough for an illegal edge, but not enough to get caught. She lunged gracefully, and snared a shot to give the U.S. a lead.

The U.S. made all four of its kicks, and needed only to convert its fifth for the win and the championship. It was up to Brandi Chastain. With her teammates linked like paper dolls as they stood in the backdrop, the right-footed Brandi calmly sized up China's goalkeeper and flicked the ball with her left foot, an unexpected move that caught the goalkeeper leaning the wrong way. The ball bounced perfectly into the net.

It was over. A roar erupted in the stadium as teammates charged toward Brandi. Wouldn't you know it? She was disrobing. She fell to her knees in unfettered happiness and tore off her white jersey, revealing a black sports bra and corrugated abs. She waved the shirt like a checkered flag while a rush of women washed over her.

They'd done it. They had endured the pressure and transformed the perceptions while underscoring the value of women's sports — just as Billie had done at the Astrodome in 1973.

"That night's drama, of course, required the services of a man," as *Sports Illustrated*'s Michael Bamberger wrote eloquently in December 1999, when the magazine named the U.S. women's soccer team Sportswomen of the Year. "The three-act play performed at the Rose Bowl — the game, the overtime, the shootout—required nothing but women, forty of them. In the final summer of the twentieth century, the era of the woman in sports finally arrived."

President Clinton zipped out of the skybox to embrace that new era. He knew what history looked like when it happened in front of him. Down the elevator and into the hallway, the president skipped into a locker room filled with players, coaches, and giddy officials. He thanked the women for, as he put it, "the gift you have given the United States."

In the first of several post-match celebrations, the women showed their appreciation for his remarks. They doused the president's graying hair in champagne. The adrenaline carried them through the night and into the early hours of the next morning. First stop, the Pasadena Ritz-Carlton. Last stop, a Santa Monica dance spot called Lush. In between, defender Joy Fawcett, mother of two, and Carla Overbeck, mother of one, called up their babysitters so they could continue to ride the euphoria.

There was a trip the next day to Disneyland, where the team clowned around on a float. In the Goofy parking lot afterward, the players assembled a wish-list of junk food. "Doughnuts," Julie Foudy yelled. "Chili-cheese fries," Joy Fawcett shouted. "Oh bee-have," chimed Mia Hamm in her best Austin Powers impersonation.

They put on their best dresses later that week to accept the president's invitation to the White House. Then, on July 20, nine days after Team USA had captured the World Cup, the green room down the hall from David Letterman's set was filled with players and Joy Fawcett's kids.

"They were running all over the place," Sue Rodin, the agent to several of the 1999 World Cup champs recalls. "It was chaos."

The bedlam continued until it was time to go see Dave. The studio audience came alive as soon as Brandi and Mia walked onstage wearing yellow T-shirts with "World Champs" inscribed across them. The crowd stood in tribute and chanted "U-S-A! U-S-A!" over and over. Mia and Brandi took seats next to Dave. They talked soccer for a moment, going over the technical details of the World Cup's penalty-kick showdown. They were like any other athletes describing the climax of a big win.

Letterman indulged them, but it wasn't long before he burst out, "I don't know if we can say this, but terrific legs, my God, great legs." That was pure Letterman. The frat boy at the kegger just couldn't resist turning the women's triumph into a punchline. He told the audience how the players had given President Clinton a jersey at the White House, and said, "Clinton got all excited because it's the first time in a long time a woman has given him a piece of clothing that wasn't considered evidence."

Between gags, Letterman lavishly praised the women. They were role models, he said, bright, intelligent, and graceful. He went on and on, purposely saving the kicker, a concise explanation of why he found them so utterly attractive.

"They're just hot," Dave oozed. "Certifiably babes."

With that, the rest of the team appeared onstage. If Letterman's remarks had offended any of the players, none of them showed it. They appreciated the part he had played in their promotion. "He was talking tongue in cheek," Hamm later said in Dave's defense. "He's a comedian."

The women knew. Letterman's lowbrow humor had extended their reach to the masses. And the masses were ecstatic.

The USA team was part of a wonderful synergy that unfolded for women during the late nineties. In women's college basketball, Connecticut and Tennessee built a rivalry that hoisted TV ratings while debunking the myth that the sport was a clumsy, second-rate alternative to the men's game.

In the slumber-party atmosphere of the 1996 Olympics, the ladies did so well, so fast, everyone believed that the pro paychecks were already in the mail; Americans, it seemed, couldn't wait for ladies' night at the stadium. Five professional women's leagues formed in the Atlanta Games afterglow. In individual pro sports, Venus and Serena Williams continued to gain ground on male athletes. With annual earnings exceeding $10 million each, the sisters landed on *Forbes Magazine*'s Celebrity 100 List.

"Nowadays, in this market, you have to be an athlete who is super-special, and you have to win all the time," Venus recalls. "But the thing is, women are historically paid less than men."

The sisters had quickly closed that gap. All around them, differences were vanishing — and not just in the size of the paychecks. Women were making gains against the male thresholds of time and endurance in the marathon, swimming, track and field, and other sports.

"When you watch men and women compete separately, and you cannot discern the difference in their form, people don't think of gender differences," explains Bob Williams, a sports marketing executive at Burns Sports. "When anyone sees Venus and Serena perform, they see superb athletes, playing at a high level, changing perceptions of women as a less athletic version of men."

Throughout the nineties, the sports pages presented vivid evidence of the progress women athletes were making. In 1972, 32,000 women participated in varsity sports, according to NCAA statistics. By 2002 that number had soared to nearly 150,000. This was what Billie Jean King had fought for. This was why she had risked so much. She watched the evolution as an active leader with the Women's Sports Foundation she had helped found.

"There was a bandwagon atmosphere," Billie recalls. "Everyone was on board."

Title IX had given women opportunities they refused to cede. In 1995 a group of students sued Louisiana State University when it failed to upgrade the women's soccer facility. The testimony at the subsequent trial revealed much. It depicted athletic director Joe Dean as the kind of chauvinist that would have made Bobby Riggs blush. According to witnesses, he had referred to the plaintiffs as "honey" and "sweetie," and expressed the view that women softball players were symbols of lesbianism.

Witnesses described how Dean favored starting a varsity soccer program rather than a softball program because he considered soccer the more feminine game. He was also quoted as saying that women "looked cute in their shorts."

Dean's sexist behavior earned a stiff rebuke in January 2000, when the U.S. Court of Appeals for the Fifth Circuit overturned an earlier decision in favor of LSU and ruled that the school had violated Title IX. In the decision, Judge Carl Stewart wrote, "Our review of the record convinces us that an intent to discriminate, albeit one motivated by chauvinist notions as opposed to one fueled by enmity, drove LSU's decisions regarding athletic opportunities for its female students."

It was a profound win for Title IX supporters. Women were gaining solid ground, and male athletics continued to prosper. Yet some men still felt threatened. They believed any gain for the gals meant a little less turf for the guys. And no one claimed turf like college football. Big Texas was hootin' and hollerin' again in a startling rerun of the campaign it had waged against Title IX during the seventies. This time the football powers didn't look to Senator John Tower for assistance. This time they were counting on a newly elected star in Texas politics: a U.S. president who wore cowboy boots and blue jeans and walked like a gunslinger.

It was August 2000. Presidential hopeful Al Gore stood on the bow of a riverboat docked in Seneca, Wisconsin. The town was the proud home of the state's girls' high school volleyball champions, a fact one of Gore's writers made sure to reference in the candidate's campaign speech that day.

"How many of you here are for Title IX?" Gore asked.

The question framed, in part, a controversial election-year issue. The Republican candidate, George W. Bush, opposed quotas of any kind — and to many conservatives, that's exactly what Title IX represented. One conservative who opposed the legislation already had Bush's ear. Dennis Hastert was the burly Republican Speaker of the House, a political power broker and a former wrestling coach from the state of Illinois. Once George W. Bush took the oath of office, he began listening to the Speaker's ideas about women's athletics.

Hastert believed Title IX was crippling secondary sports for men. As an example, he pointed out how some schools were redirecting money from wrestling to women's teams. Hastert believed that the legislation that required schools to fund sports for women was a thinly disguised quota system.

Of course, Title IX wasn't about quotas — the law doesn't even mention the word — it was about proportions. To receive federal money, schools on all levels had to make an attempt to create as many athletic opportunities for women as men. And vice-versa.

Hastert made no secret of his contempt for the law. He demanded that Title IX be diluted — if not actually abolished — as a means of pulling the secondary male sports out of their decline. Hastert continually badmouthed Title IX. He overstated its impact on male sports and downplayed all the progress women athletes had made since its ratification. But when the Speaker requested a GAO survey on the subject, the results undermined his own arguments. The report concluded that, despite the strides women had made, they still lagged far behind men. It went on to say that male sports had not suffered from any competition, real or imagined, with women's athletics, but had instead suffered from lack of interest and economic autonomy.

"Some schools have helped justify their decisions to cut men's sports by blaming Title IX," NCAA president Cedric Dempsey explained. "That certainly is not the intent of the law, and it is almost never the only factor."

Nevertheless, Hastert's campaign to weaken Title IX swayed an already sympathetic President Bush. He decided the law needed reforming. The first sign of trouble came when Bush appointed Gerald Reynolds as chief of the Office of Civil Rights at the Education Department. Reynolds was a devout quota-buster who had publicly questioned the validity of Title IX numerous times in the past.

Women's groups immediately began to squirm. It was enough that the National Wrestling Coaches Association had filed a lawsuit against the Department of Education seeking to overturn proportionality. Now Bush was seeking to do the same. He was a swaggering sportsman, a ranch owner who fancied himself a big-time player in the macho world of athletics. He had owned baseball's Texas Rangers and had entertained ambitions of ascending to commissioner of Major League Baseball.

He was also a regular on the college sports scene, and had been a close ally of the Texas football elite while he was that state's governor. Bush saw sports in fifties black-and-white terms: girls in saddle oxfords cheering on the sidelines, boys in football cleats eating up yardage. The women watching, the men performing. As president, he was on a path to turn back the clock and subvert Title IX.

"He is the candidate of the male superior constituency," explains Gloria Steinem. "And that constituency tends to feel that anything women can do is devalued."

President Bush made women's groups bristle with his conservative politics and devout evangelicalism. He claimed his base was Americans with traditional values, but he was out of step with at least one mainstream group. While the nation was swept up in the soccer-dad and soccer-mom mania of '99, neither of Bush's twin daughters, Barbara and Jenna, had participated in high school or college sports.

"He comes from a misogynistic, old-model approach," explains Donna Lopiano. "The Bush administration operates on a locker-room mentality that is insidious, homophobic, and narrow."

The concerns of a setback morphed from concern to dismay in June of 2002 when the Bush administration, feeling Title IX had gone too far, assembled a blue-ribbon panel to assess the law and potentially reverse the dreams Billie Jean King had for the American girl.

"It was a nervous time," Billie says. "The threat was incredibly real. Everything was suddenly so fragile."

Bush's secretary of education, Rod Paige, called the panel the Commission on Opportunity in Athletics. Many women, though, called it a stacked deck, and with good reason: Of the fifteen panel members, ten were leaders from Division I football programs, including Stanford athletic director Ted Leland, Penn State president Graham Spanier, and Percy Bates, a University of Michigan professor and faculty rep for the Big Ten Conference. There was an irony in that lineup; if there was any threat to minor male sports, it was football.

"Go point by point and compare football to the cost of the teams that are getting eliminated," says Andrew Zimbalist, a professor of eco-

nomics at Smith College and a recognized authority on sports econom-
ics. "You can see there is more than enough money out there for everyone if they would just get rid of the waste."

Waste meant head coaching salaries that exceeded $1 million for
more than twenty top football programs in 2002. Waste meant housing
home teams in luxury hotels the night before a game to prevent players
from mixing, among other things, tequila shots with coeds. Waste meant
carrying more players on your team than necessary.

According to Zimbalist, the cost difference between a bloated 117-
player roster versus a 90-man roster was about $800,000 — or enough
money to field two wrestling teams. Clearly, it wasn't Title IX that was
threatening men's sports, but the entitlement of football programs. It
wasn't the outlay for women's uniforms and equipment, but the $250,000
a school like Oregon spent on a billboard in Manhattan for a Heisman
Trophy candidate in 2000.

And yet the panel was full of football protectionists, with college
administrators and athletic directors who fretted over how wealthy football boosters would perceive any actions the commission recommended.
They feared that anything they said for the record might upset those
"friends of the program" who often established their pride and identity
through the success of the football team. So, few of them said anything,
at least in public.

"I felt like the athletic directors had their hands tied," Julie Foudy
recalls. "It was similar to politics, where they have to deal with their own
interest groups. They didn't want to say anything to disenfranchise their
biggest donors."

There was also one anti-feminist woman on the panel, Rita Simon,
as well as an ex-WNBA player, Cynthia Cooper, who seemed oddly content to go along with the commission despite the role Title IX had played
in her own basketball career.

"I was just stunned at the ineptitude of the commission," says
Donna Lopiano. "It was loaded with extremists who had not done their
homework."

On a panel that seemed primed to weaken Title IX radically, there were two heroically stubborn holdouts: Donna de Varona, co-founder of the Women's Sports Foundation, and Julie Foudy, its 2002 president and the only active athlete on the commission. For six months the panel conducted town-hall meetings that appeared to be loaded with Title IX opponents. Noticeably absent were the civil rights experts and high school leaders who had made the law work.

"It was frustrating," Julie recalls. "We kept saying bring this person in, that person in. Our voice wasn't being heard. We weren't getting a fair representation in the town-hall meetings."

As the panel traveled the country, disillusionment and tension provoked an outcry among women's activists and parents. The tour landed in San Diego in November 2002. Dozens of colorful protesters marched outside the hotel before the Title IX commission held its final public forum.

There were six women in pink bowling jackets, yelling their support for Title IX. There were two dozen women dressed in lavender, holding placards that read TITLE IX CAN NEVER DIE. There were two fathers holding the hands of their soccer-cleated daughters. There were numerous moms with signs that spelled out, DON'T DROP THE BALL ON GIRLS, and school-aged girls wearing GIRLS, INC. T-shirts.

A willowy celebrity stood out in the middle of the rally. Actress Geena Davis, an amateur archer and former prep sports junkie, had a message for Education Secretary Rod Paige. Her words recalled a movie she had starred in, about two rebel women who were not afraid to take their lives into their own hands, who refused to surrender to society's antiquated roles.

"I am here," Davis proclaimed, "to take you for a short ride in Thelma and Louise's car if you think it's fair and just to limit a girl's opportunity to play sports based on an interest survey."

The rhetoric of the town-hall meeting inside the hotel was just as biting. Things grew heated when Donna Lopiano excoriated the panel members as puppets of Bush administration politics. She told the commission, "You have a vested interest, a conflict of interest in weakening the law, to make it less necessary for you to do the tough budget decision that has to be done to comply with Title IX. I think the composition of the commission therefore puts in question its integrity.

"I don't think what's happened so far has had the kind of integrity you should be proud of. I'm not saying it's your fault. I'm saying the appointment process is flawed, and you're trying to do the right thing and the DOE staff is obstructing you."

Tom Griffith, a panelist from Brigham Young, sat up stiffly in his chair and chastised Lopiano: "Your comments on our integrity are not helpful to the process."

The voices supporting Title IX were getting waxed. At times, Julie Foudy wasn't sure anyone was hearing either her or Donna de Varona. Billie had been there. She knew what Julie was going through as a young athlete faced with a political firestorm.

"I was on conference calls with Julie and Donna," Billie recalled. "It was a matter of being true to yourself. Julie had a great belief in what was right."

Many on the panel considered Julie an obstructionist, disrupting what should have been an orderly process. So that's why her soccer teammates called her Loudy Foudy, they mused. But this petite California-born child of conservative parents — a beloved rebel in her own household — had felt the impact of Title IX.

She had also seen worlds without it. Julie had been there when members of the women's Brazilian soccer team were mocked and heckled by their own countrymen for playing a man's sport. She knew just how much damage stereotypes could inflict.

"As a female athlete, you're living life as a caricature in some places," Julie recalls. "My in-laws are English, and when my husband told them he was marrying a soccer player, they had an image of me as six feet tall and Rugby-ish.

"When I went abroad to study in Spain, when we'd play soccer, the men would stop me and say, 'You're not from here.' They were thinking, 'What's wrong with you?'"

It was the attitudes that were wrong, not Julie. Just like men, women needed sports to boost their self-esteem, to maintain good health, to develop traits they would apply in relationships and in the workplace. That's why Title IX was so important. Julie had felt its transformative powers in the Atlanta Games of '96 and in the summer of '99. She knew the work of Title IX was not done. So she refused to stop fighting.

But, outside of Donna de Verona, the rest of the presidential commission pretty much ignored Foudy. In January 2003 the panel met in a Washington, D.C., meeting room to formulate its final report on Title IX. The tone of the first draft was all wrong, Foudy thought. It didn't reflect the support or passion for Title IX the commission members had seen at town halls and rallies across the country. The report focused more on men's lost opportunities than on the institutional bias that still remained against women. The panel wrote more about changing proportionality rules than about compliance with the rules already in place.

"We're giving one side and not the other," Julie told the other panelists. "If you want me to sign on to this, I need substantial changes, not just a comma here and a word there."

"Give us a chance to work on it," Ted Leland told her. "We'll get back to you." They had nothing more to offer, though.

"You're not going to be happy with us," Leland warned.

Leland was Stanford's athletic director; he had been Foudy's athletic director during her own college days. Now he was her antagonist.

On January 29, just as the panel was about to vote on the specifics of the report, Julie asked for a break to go to the bathroom. She was gone only a moment.

"When you vote on everything, you want to be present," Julie says. "It's going to be documented. But when I had to run to the restroom, a vote was taken while I was gone."

When she returned, she asked for a re-vote. The commission denied her motion.

"Can I ask that a Porta Potty be brought out here," she said in words that were officially recorded in the minutes of the meeting. "And I'll knock once for yes, and twice for no."

She couldn't bear being part of a report she didn't believe in. Only Donna de Varona, a woman who had jeopardized her career to campaign for Title IX in the seventies, stood by her side. On February 25, the two women officially protested the finding on the final report. The next day, Foudy was on a plane bound for Washington, D.C. She and Donna were going to issue a minority report from the Capitol steps. But when Foudy reached her destination, she discovered she wasn't quite prepared to face the nation.

"I lost my luggage," Julie recalls. "Can you believe it? I had nothing, no clothes, nothing."

It was after midnight. Julie tried phoning the only people she could turn to in D.C. — her soccer teammates Mia Hamm and goalkeeper Siri Mullinix. Both of them played for the Washington Freedom of WUSA, the newly formed pro league for women. Mia didn't answer. Just after 1:00 a.m., Siri picked up her phone.

"I have this press conference at 8:00 a.m., before any stores open, and I have no clothes," Julie told her. By 2:00 a.m., Siri had dumped all the clothes she had to offer on Julie's hotel-room bed.

"It was a mess," Julie says. "I grabbed a lipstick at the drugstore the next morning, and that was my makeup. I used it as blush, dual purpose."

In an oversized suit and ill-fitting shoes, Julie stood on the Capitol steps with de Varona, Geena Davis, and three senators — Ted Kennedy, Tom Daschle, and Olympia Snow. They presented a minority report that underscored the dangerous language that threatened Title IX. Julie and de Varona made it clear that they believed the law should remain intact and unaltered.

"I was sad that I had to do that," Julie says. "I felt if the process had worked, we could have had both voices in the one report. I got a lot of criticism from other members who said my agenda all along was to produce a minority report. I told them that was not fair, and it was not true."

Cynthia Cooper, for one, ridiculed Julie and de Varona. "They accuse the final report as being slanted and biased," Cooper told the press, "but it seems to me they were biased." Ted Leland added his ditto to Cooper's comments.

"It was the hardest thing I've ever done, going through that, but I had to speak my mind," Julie says. "There was too much at stake."

For months, everyone waited anxiously for the Education Department to release its recommendations. The mood was unsettled, with Title IX hanging in the balance. Then serendipity lightened the rancorous atmosphere. In May of 2003, a Swedish golfer with a ducklike walk ambled into America's hearts. Annika Sorenstam, a high-profile star of the LPGA, had agreed to play against the men at the PGA's Colonial tour event in Fort Worth, Texas. Bush Country. The announcement conjured images of Billie facing down Bobby, the press, and all those doubters in the Houston Astrodome.

Annika, too, faced cynicism from her own peers and skeptical male colleagues. Golfer Vijay Singh, for one, said he hoped she would miss the cut and that in the unlikely event of her being drawn to play with him he would withdraw from the event. "She does not belong here," he said. Echoing Singh, Nick Price said Annika's effort "reeked of publicity."

"I only wanted to play against the very best," Annika recalls. "It was nothing more than that as I approached it in my mind."

She wasn't playing for feminism as Billie once did. Annika was playing for herself. And yet her journey to the Colonial was covered as a spectacle just the same. She didn't need a Bobby Riggs to be her carnival barker—the media stood in for him quite nicely. She was constantly bathed in camera light during the weeks before the event, with her every word in the lead-up parsed. The hype evoked visions of the Battle of the Sexes, but with an important twist: Sorenstam was competing against men on the PGA Tour without an age handicap.

Though Annika had her detractors, something amazing also happened. One by one, men on the PGA Tour came to her defense. Tiger Woods phoned her constantly to urge her on. Her first-round playing partner, Aaron Barber, acted thrilled to be part of Annika history. "She was awesome," Barber exclaimed. And there was that gallery of ten thousand—men and women—wearing GO ANNIKA buttons, following her around the course.

The responses offered more evidence of progress. Players like Woods were the boys of Title IX. They had grown up next to women on the courses, courts, and playground. They saw them not as gate-crashers but as equals. Despite their support, the pressure on Annika was crushing. Billie had privately prepared her for everything she would face at the Colonial.

"I'm not telling the press that we talked," Billie told Annika. "This is about you, what you're about to do. You deserve all the glory here."

"Tell me how it felt for you," Annika said. "How should I handle all this?"

"Annika, if you handle yourself well, if you tell the press your truth — and I mean really talk to them as a human being, everyone will love you," Billie said. "This is your moment. Let people know who you really are."

Annika did just that. After firing a glorious one-over-par 71 on the first day, the fatigue of the scrutiny caught up to her on the second. She failed to make the cut at the Colonial, but she had placed higher than some of the best male golfers in the world. And for two days she had held a nation engrossed with her play — and with her demeanor.

She had been famously stoic, almost mechanical, while winning forty-three LPGA titles, but Annika let her guard down at Colonial. She playfully clutched her fluttering heart when she was nervous, and let her emotions roll down her cheeks when it was over. She was all at once athletic and vulnerable, a likeable groundbreaker.

"I'm living a dream that I want to live," she said through tears after her final-round 74. This was the full circle from '73, a woman playing against men again, but on equal terms.

Annika's incandescent moment dovetailed nicely with the Title IX decision when it was finally rendered in mid-July. The Education Department released a three-page letter that ended the debate by preserving Title IX without alteration. Women had won. Donna de Varona and Julie Foudy had made sure of it.

Responses across the nation ranged from celebration to disbelief. Jamie Moffatt, a former wrestler and executive director of the College

Sports Council, summed up the feelings of many when he accused the Bush administration of selling out to "the gender equity advocates."

"I don't think the Bush administration wanted to feel the wrath of the feminists," Moffatt went on to say. "They made the political decision that they didn't want to antagonize those people who want to keep the quota system there because they've been so vocal."

The conservative *Washington Post* columnist George Will wrote off the Bush administration's retreat on Title IX as political cowardice: "The administration reaffirmed the irrational and unfair implementation standards of the Title IX ban on sex discrimination in college athletics. Those standards are now immortal, having received a conservative administration's approval."

Some of the president's traditional critics expressed amusement over the Title IX decision. Ann Richards, whom Bush had once unseated as Texas governor, told reporters, "After a year of hearings and staff work that cost millions of dollars, what did the administration have to say? 'Forget we brought it up.' They caught so much flak that the findings were not much more than a tweak here and there and came to the conclusion that, 'Gee, Title IX is working better than we thought.'"

The feminists had reason to preen. They had handed the neoconservative forces of the Bush administration a rare loss.

"Bush had been able to keep his troops in lockstep," Donna Lopiano says. "Nobody had won on an issue against this administration until the exception of Title IX. Bush underestimated the public support for Title IX. He just missed it. Finally, there were enough people telling Bush — or rather, Karl Rove — 'Are you out of your mind?'"

Reality soon tempered the celebratory mood, though. The passion that had gripped the children-turned-women of Title IX was not enough to save the pro leagues that had sprouted during the nineties. In September of 2003, WUSA ceased operations as a professional soccer league for women after only three years. Corporate sponsors had stopped answering the organization's calls. A pro softball league, a beach volleyball league, and one of two basketball leagues would also fold before 2003 ended. Not one female athlete — not even Venus or Serena Williams — hit the *Forbes Magazine* list of the fifty best-paid athletes that year. The ponytailed mojo of 1996 had fizzled due to poor planning and a poor economy.

WUSA was too ambitious, too fast, for its financial structure. The American Basketball League, a pro women's league, overpaid its marquee stars in a futile attempt to compete with the WNBA, a struggling league bankrolled by the NBA. There had also been another, less evident element to affect pro women's sports: a lack of unique appeal in the fallout of cultural acceptance.

"Women in sports is not a novelty anymore," explains Peter Roby, the director of Northeastern University's Center for Sport in Society. "Title IX was thirty years ago. You've seen great women athletes perform in the years since, so the idea of a woman in sports is part of the culture now."

Which meant women had to work harder to distinguish themselves from the rest of the jam-packed sports landscape.

"We have to make our game reputable," the WNBA's Dawn Staley says. "We have to woo them every time out. That's hard to do in any upstart league, but if we hang around long enough, people will come and stay."

Persistence is for the hearty. Too much has been taken for granted by some women who enter fledgling pro leagues demanding budget-busting salaries. Too much has been taken for granted by some of the most successful women in sports. Many don't even know the suffering and sacrifice that made the benefits they enjoy today possible. For example, Jennifer Capriati represented everything Billie Jean King had fought for when Billie led a boycott demanding bigger purses for women in 1970. But young players like Capriati are into the here and now. So, when she was asked what she thought about President Bush's attempt to change Title IX, Capriati said this:

"I have no idea what Title IX is, sorry."

When the subject returned to the United States Open rather than some slice of the past, Capriati replied, "Oh, good, a tennis question."

Capriati's ignorance would unsettle anyone who cared about women's sports. Only a month earlier, the Tour had sent players a leaflet titled "Title IX: Its Importance and Impact." But Capriati was not alone. Many women have succeeded in crossing over from sports into the pop-culture mainstream—from track star Marion Jones to Venus Williams, from Anna Kournikova to Mia Hamm—but today's female athletes seldom cross over into advocacy roles.

Few will say anything that sounds even remotely controversial. They don't want to risk endorsement dollars or their celebrity status. They simply take the money and run from the issues.

"There's no pain," Billie says. "The girls make so much money; the boys make so much money. There's not enough pain. You've got to have some pain to change things, and, I think, to grow. They always want things so much better, which is good, but you know what? There's only a few people who drive it."

Title IX is still fragile. It will be challenged again. But will pioneers like de Varona and Billie be around for the next fight? They spent hundreds of hours pressing the flesh and shooting the breeze with the politicians who eventually advanced their cause. Will the younger stars ever be interested enough to perform the political maintenance needed to keep Title IX alive? Perhaps the future will need its own version of the Original Nine so that the World Cup Summer of '99 remains a turning point rather than a peak in women's history.

Any caretakers of the future will have to be throwbacks. Someone like a certain soccer player who's not afraid to speak her mind. Someone whose voice and actions inspire Donna Lopiano to declare, "I've never met anyone who reminds me more of Billie Jean King than Julie Foudy."

In October of 2003, Foudy would reveal just how closely she could resemble Billie as she carried an old Ted Tinling dress to a New York City hotel.

CHAPTER 12

Last Call

B ut for the red glow of an exit sign, the vast ballroom in the Waldorf-Astoria was completely dark as Billie Jean King approached the doorway. On the night of October 19, 2003, she walked through the opulent lobby off Park Avenue, past the circular mosaic tile and nine-foot gold clock. She expected to see members of the Women's Sports Foundation assembling for a thank-you dinner for its sponsors. But there was no one milling about, no one running up to greet her.

That was strange. Billie always attracted a crowd.

Suddenly the ballroom door swung open, and the chandeliers splashed on with a halo of light flooding a stage. In the middle of that stage stood a red velvet throne that burgeoned with white, pink, and purple feathers tacked around the velour headrest. It was a glitter-and-glue replica of the Egyptian litter Billie had ridden into the Astrodome thirty years earlier. But on this night—without any buffed college boys or Howard Cosell's commentary to escort her—it served not as transportation, but as a seat of honor for Billie on her birthday.

As she walked in, 125 friends, fellow athletes, and associates burst into an old-fashioned "Happy Birthday" serenade. The event was a month early, adding to the element of surprise. Billie stood riveted, her mouth open, a captivated child once again. Almost sixty years old, and she was still dazzled by spectacle. It had been Queen Elizabeth's turn in 1953. This time the coronation was for Billie.

Laughing wildly, greeting everyone in sight, Billie was ushered to her throne. Once she'd been a five-year-old who'd shared her dreams of greatness with her mother at the kitchen sink. Now she was a woman whose accomplishments had exceeded the boundaries of her own expansive imagination.

"I don't know if I'll ever grasp it," Billie says. "It's been an amazing life."

They celebrated that life at the Waldorf, this roomful of people who expressed their awe at this remarkable woman. She had ridden the leading edge of social transition with courage. She had used her celebrity to focus attention on the cause of women's rights and other social issues. She had done it all despite the great cost to her privacy.

"Here we were, looking back at a remarkable life that is still in progress," says Dorothy Blaney, a longtime friend of Billie's and a foundation board member. "Now we all know her. But in the dark days of the seventies, what she did, I can say, took great courage and vision."

Billie had seen what no one else had even contemplated. She believed women had the right to demand the same prize money that men received. She believed that women had the appeal to attract endorsement deals on a scale with men. She believed little girls could grow up with the same sports dreams as little boys, and that electronic images could dispel perceptions of women as weak. She understood the power of those images in shaping history. Which is why she agreed to play Bobby Riggs in blue shoes, in living color, in front of 90 million TV viewers.

Billie was, as she often admitted, a first-generation TV junkie. How appropriate for her friends and associates to show how much they appreciated her with a "This Is Your Life" birthday party. From her feathery litter, she had a front-row seat as the people who loved her told her story. One after another, friends traced Billie's journey, touching all of its milestones, transforming the ballroom into a time machine. Wearing tennis dresses with wide lapels and glasses the size of Mason jars, they offered up their own impersonations of Billie. "I had the mullet haircut going and everything," Foudy says. "I was wearing one of her sparkling tennis dresses, a Ted Tinling. I was like, how amazing is this?" Rosie Casals played Billie as a child; Julie Foudy was Billie after her match with Bobby.

"I challenged this oink of a chauvinist pig in a match that everyone thought was about tennis," Foudy proclaimed. "I knew it wasn't. You know, it wasn't and everyone eventually knew it, too. It was all about women's rights and women getting respect."

So many faces in the room transported Billie back in time, through a maze that began with fear and ended in triumph. Susan Catherwood, of Long Beach, California, sat at one of the tables with her eyes fixed on her childhood friend. She was formerly Susan Williams, the pal who introduced Billie to tennis so many years before by simply asking, "Wanna play?"

At another table sat Joseph Cullman, in his late eighties, but still in Billie's corner. He was the Philip Morris executive who had first believed in the drawing power of women athletes, the man who had loosened his company's purse strings to give the Original Nine the big stage they craved: the Virginia Slims circuit.

"The women needed money," Larry King would say. "And Joe gave and gave."

Joe invested heavily in those women, but as much as anything he placed Philip Morris's money on Billie Jean King. She was the star of the tour, the one charged with carrying the marquee. Billie's birthday wasn't about the passing of years. It embodied her spirit of resilience through every crusade, and her work for the Slims tour was a big part of that. She was the one who delivered, whether sick or stressed, burdened or weary.

"I think the whole night was about what Billie represents, and that's the best in human character," Dorothy Blaney says.

The evening would mark the first — but not the last — lavish celebration of Billie's sixtieth. On November 9, guests pulled up to the pink stucco façade of the Beverly Hills Hotel, with its swaying palms and Hollywood history, to pay tribute to Billie's personal evolution. In many ways the hotel was the perfect site for Billie's party. During the 1940s, the "No slacks for ladies" rule in the Polo Lounge bar was changed nearly the moment that starlet Marlene Dietrich slipped onto a barstool in pants. More than anyone, Billie could appreciate that kind of daring.

They held the party inside the Crystal Room, a splendid art deco ballroom with a cozy stage framed by champagne-colored drapes and topped with a chandelier of golden bulbs arranged like a fistful of poppies. "Everything was very lavish, just gorgeous," Bud Collins recalls. "It had to be a million-dollar affair." Two hundred guests settled into their seats, from tennis star Pete Sampras and his movie-star wife, Bridgette Wilson, to former USLTA president Bob Kelleher and swimmer Diana Nyad. Betty and Bill Moffitt were also on hand.

Years earlier, the Moffitts had sold their Long Beach home and gone to Prescott, Arizona, in search of dry heat. Billie had ensured their attendance by ordering a chartered jet to whisk them out of their retirement oasis. They deserved the best, Billie thought. A driver and a car awaited their arrival, ready to ferry them through the traffic of Los Angeles's jammed freeways. The Moffitts checked in, with time to rest before changing into their party clothes.

The bash began with Billie standing at the head table to thank everyone for coming. Visibly overwhelmed by the gathering, speaking quickly before her emotions closed her throat, Billie was uncharacteristically short-winded.

"Shortest speech in history," Kelleher recalls. "She wasn't up there for two seconds."

Well, what birthday girl wouldn't want the party to begin? A grand piano was onstage, tuned and ready for the evening's exquisite host. In a black suit, Elton John alighted on the bench and poured his soul into the keyboard for nearly two hours. In an intimate concert, he rocked his way through Billie's wish list of hit songs that included "Philadelphia Freedom"—the number-one chart topper in 1975, and the song Elton had written especially for Billie.

The song lyrics were a testimony to Billie's spirit: "Shine a light through the eyes of the ones left behind." He understood the essence of Billie. He got her from the day they listened to those eight-tracks inside his Rolls-Royce in 1974. They'd been through so much together, experiencing the light and dark of celebrity, coming to terms with personal demons. Arm in arm, they had outlasted the madness of fame.

"They could turn to each other," Larry King recalls. "With all they had in common—big personalities, big lives—they could talk about everything and exist with a certain empathy for one another that I'm sure comforted both of them when things were great and not so great."

The songs of survival filled the Crystal Room. It was defiance and triumph set to a beat, a revolution you could dance to. Bill and Betty glided across the floor as if it were their living room on 36th Street, with Glenn Miller playing while Billie and her little brother, Randy, watched from the couch. The octogenarians hadn't lost a step.

"It took us three or four days to recover," Betty admits. They were too thrilled for fatigue, waltzing through the evening on a natural high of pride in their daughter.

"All of us in our family are more or less teetotalers," Betty says. "People would have thought we'd had a lot to drink that night—which we didn't, we didn't have anything to drink—but we danced and danced. You know, I still do physical fitness classes three days a week. And Bill, he played racquetball until he was eighty."

Billie watched her parents and marveled. What energy, what endurance. They had been by her side through the good and bad. They'd sat courtside in the Astrodome to cheer on their daughter when Billie risked so much to play Bobby Riggs. They'd stood next to her during the Marilyn Barnett press conference. They'd responded to each moment, sometimes with deep breaths and sometimes with tears, but always with unconditional love.

"They were so happy," Billie says. "That's all I wanted."

That and one other gift that she would not receive until her actual birthday—November 22, 2003. Billie was in Moscow on that date, serving as the tireless Federation Cup captain for the U.S. women's tennis team. She hadn't abandoned tennis. Billie was still giving back to the sport, whether as an adviser to the tour she had once founded, as a mentor to young players, or as an Olympic coach and Fed Cup captain.

Tennis had been her spiritual healer since she was eleven. When she felt compelled to lash out against bias, tennis gave her a voice. When she felt confused about where she fit in, tennis cemented her identity. The game always centered her. On the morning of her birthday, with the distinctive Kremlin onion gleaming outside her window, Billie pulled on her warm-ups, laced up her tennis shoes, and grabbed her racket.

There was hardly a soul in the stands surrounding the court when her final birthday wish was granted. She didn't need the Wimbledon crowds of her youth anymore, or a press corps or photographers, to experience the priceless sensation of a ball connecting firmly on the sweet spot of her racket strings.

"I got on the court," Billie says, "and I killed myself for forty minutes. And that made my day."

On the other side of the net, Ilana Kloss dutifully returned each shot as she had for the past twenty-four years. Ilana was Billie's linchpin, the one she always turned to, the confidante who calmed her, the woman she had fallen in love with in 1979. Their relationship was no longer a guarded secret. At the Beverly Hills Hotel on Billie's birthday, Ilana had been introduced as her partner, one of the first open acknowledgments of their romantic relationship. No one murmured. No one raised an eyebrow.

"It was no big deal," Billie says.

No big deal at all. Just validation for the life and love Billie had chosen.

"I think sixty has been my best birthday yet," Billie says. "I'm happier, more at peace. Life is great, and I'm lucky to be alive. I just feel serenity. And it feels good. I feel at peace more often than I used to."

Attaining peace had been a laborious process for Billie. There were no instant revelations along the way. Her sixtieth-birthday parties — both of them — illuminated her long journey to simplicity after so many complex and painful years. Her anguish hadn't crested with the Marilyn Barnett lawsuit in 1981; it had simply begun a new phase. Her life didn't begin anew; it remained painfully repressed throughout the eighties—a decade of survival for Billie. The palimony suit had left her facing a very different financial future from the one she had planned.

"The Marilyn thing was tough," Billie acknowledges. "I don't think I'll ever recover from that in many ways."

Instead of retiring, Billie kept playing competitively to replenish the income and corporate endorsement money she had lost after the salacious details of her personal life became headlines. At first she wasn't sure she could play through the scandal. On the night of February 4, 1982, Billie did the unthinkable: She walked out in the middle of a match against Ann Kiyomura in Detroit.

"I was fighting myself the whole time," she confessed that evening. "I apologize. It was very unprofessional. But I couldn't stand out there and go through the motions."

She regrouped, gave her heart a pep talk, and found a second wind for her sport at age thirty-eight. With her knees laced together by surgical thread, she was able to maintain a top-twenty ranking in 1982 and 1983, during an era when Chris Evert, Martina Navratilova, Hana Mandlikova, Pam Shriver, and Zina Garrison were younger, stronger, and better.

"You are sad for anyone who feels, for financial reasons, they have to keep going," Shriver says. "But when you watched Billie Jean play, her spirit never deteriorated and her volleys never deteriorated. To this day, you see her volleys and shake your head. What she did in '82 and '83 was remarkable."

She attracted criticism, though. It came from journalists who believed she was hanging on too long, and from people who didn't know how much she needed to complete her career without the taint of the Barnett affair. Billie turned defensive whenever anyone suggested it was time for her to retire. Just days before Wimbledon in 1983, she explained, "It's like asking Nureyev to stop dancing and Sinatra to stop singing. Why don't they stop?"

She needed a sign to let her know when she was done; the young sensation Andrea Jaeger supplied it. In Billie's fourteenth Wimbledon semifinal, on grass that had always been her own backyard, Jaeger ushered her off Centre Court in fifty-six minutes, losing 6–1, 6–1. It was Billie's worst defeat in 110 Wimbledon singles matches. She shook hands with her eighteen-year-old opponent, and, with her gear in hand, scanned the court carefully as she exited, absorbing each detail.

"I took a last look," Billie explained later. "I've never done that when I've walked off. I've never looked back over my shoulder."

With twelve major singles titles behind her — including six at Wimbledon — Billie departed competitive tennis ten years after her match with Bobby Riggs. For a long time she had felt ambivalent about the legacy of the Astrodome spectacle. She bristled when fans approached her to say how the match had changed women's tennis. Don't you get it, she would think to herself, it was about transforming society, not just women's tennis. And yet, that fans still stopped her in restaurants and on the street proved the importance of her victory over Bobby. The match had defined her celebrity and provided cachet for her business career and advocacy efforts.

After retiring from competitive play, Billie dedicated herself to the Women's Sports Foundation and worked with Larry to revive World Team Tennis. This was the immersion strategy all over again. By staying busy, she could put off any soul-searching. Billie remained married to Larry. If anyone asked, Ilana was just her business partner. The deception grew more stressful by the year. Ilana eventually refused to participate in the subterfuge. She wanted Billie as her partner without a husband attached. Billie wanted that, too.

"Ilana is just like a rock," Billie explains. "She's loyal and smart. She's just very bright. She gets it. She gets me."

Billie didn't want to lose Ilana, but it was difficult for her to shed her safety net. She knew Larry still loved her. Over the years, he had convinced Billie that he was an important ingredient in her success, and that maintaining their marriage, at least in the eyes of the public, had a quantifiable material value.

"Larry liked it, and Larry promoted it," Billie says of their relationship. "I think Larry had some great qualities, but people close to me knew what was going on. I wanted a divorce, and I wanted to be with Ilana. She was the love of my life. It was real simple."

Eight years after she and Ilana had started their relationship—and after a half-dozen failed attempts to separate from Larry—Billie finally gathered enough courage to end the marriage for good.

"I was nervous," Billie says. "Ilana felt like leaving. And that probably got my butt in gear. It was in '84, '85, and '86, and I started saying, 'I don't need this marriage.' Ilana was like, 'I don't need it, either.' And she was right."

In 1987, Billie divorced her dear friend and caretaker, putting an end to years of using her marriage as a front. Larry had lived a fulfilling life with Billie. He was the man behind her greatness, the one who had nurtured her passions, the cute college student in the red socks who had taught her to be a feminist.

"Larry hated it when we legally got divorced," Billie says. "He still tried not to let go."

There was nothing Larry could do. For once, he had met a problem he could not solve. Billie had chosen Ilana over him. The thought of living without Billie as his wife crushed Larry. Who would actualize him now? Who would indulge his idealism? Who would challenge him?

"I was trying to help her figure out who she was, but ultimately, you know, I lost her because of who she was and who I was," Larry says. "The reality is I would still be married to Billie Jean if it were up to me. Even though I think Billie Jean, in some ways, felt she was setting me free by divorcing me, I'm old-school. I have a worldview, but the worldview is when you marry—whether it's good, bad, or indifferent—that's it. It was her choice that we got divorced, even though I am immensely better off that we were divorced. But I would have never divorced Billie Jean, never."

Larry would go on to remarry and chase more big ideas. He would start and promote a roller-hockey league, only to see it fail before going off to the next venture.

Billie did not change her last name. She understood the power of brands. Billie Jean King was the moniker America had grown to know.

But the divorce provided a clear-cut ending to one of the most intricate relationships that has ever unfolded before the public. The split did not, however, provide serenity for Billie. She continued to cloak her homosexuality.

When she and Ilana checked into hotels, they still requested two beds instead of one. They maintained a professional front at parties and events. "We would hide," Billie admits.

The broader acceptance of homosexuality in the early nineties changed nothing. Billie remained convinced that a more public relationship would repel corporate sponsors for her World Team Tennis organization. The child of the McCarthy era fretted over being blackballed because of her lifestyle.

"I think if Ilana and I hadn't been in business, it might have been different," Billie says. "But when you are, you don't go around acting like a straight couple, introducing your wife, et cetera. I think the people who are out, really out, and are truly comfortable, just go for it. But there are consequences in business."

She resisted disclosing her homosexuality for other reasons, as well. Despite the Barnett palimony suit, her parents didn't know the whole truth yet. They knew nothing of the other women Billie had been involved with. They didn't know the depth of Billie's relationship with Ilana. Throughout Billie's life, she had respected her parents' conservative ideals. She didn't want to disappoint or hurt them by telling them that her affair with Marilyn wasn't a one-time experiment, as Billie had indicated to the press.

"I had a lot of fear," Billie admits. "My sexuality has been the most difficult challenge."

The Marilyn Barnett scandal was well behind her, but Billie did not want to complicate her feminist image. She didn't want anything to detract from what she had accomplished for the women's movement. She knew women had a hard enough time gaining acceptance for their achievements. The more she lived, the more Billie discovered even legends had their glass ceilings.

In 1990, *Life* magazine named Billie one of their "100 Most Important Americans of the 20th Century," but — as happened too often — she was still relegated to playing bystander on the banquet circle of famous figures.

"What Billie has accomplished is huge," Larry King says. "That's the fate of most pioneers. The tip of the arrow is what gets worn off, not all that follows."

The vision of Muhammad Ali shaking from Parkinson's disease as he lit the flame to open the 1996 Atlanta Summer Olympics is one of the Games' most enduring images. His familiar face would be seen in commercials for years to come. His life story would be celebrated in a major motion picture. Ali continues to be revered as a social symbol wherever he travels.

"He and I have been to every single awards dinner together, but he is the big cheese. I'm not," Billie says with a hint of frustration. "No one would ever think that I had the impact that he has had."

She doesn't say this out of ego, but to highlight how some elements of society's gender bias remain unchanged.

"It makes me sad," Billie continues. "What it does is it represents our gender. Over fifty percent of the world has the same trouble. It's not right."

The fight in her voice hasn't changed. At sixty, she sounded forceful and spirited, invigorated by debate. Issues still engaged this fierce advocate, but Billie had discovered an inner peace in reconciling her fears about an open relationship with Ilana.

"A lot of therapy," Billie explains with a smile.

She doesn't put her partnership on display, but she no longer hides it.

"Now when we go to the desk clerk," Billie says, "and they ask, 'Two beds?' I say no."

There is freedom in living without the burden of shame. Given the doors she has opened for others, Billie's path to personal liberation has made for a deserving celebration — no birthday candles required.

"We have been through so much, Ilana and I," Billie says. "We've held together this long. Think of all we've overcome. We made it."

There is so much to endure when you're the woman who beat Bobby Riggs. He was one of the three people who had combined with Billie to create her defining moment. Bobby had provided the hype behind the showdown in the Astrodome; Larry King had honed Billie's feminist instincts for the moment; and Margaret Court had set the scene by losing the Mother's Day Massacre.

Each searched for contentment after playing his or her part in Billie's journey.

The lanky Aussie, nicknamed "the Arm" by Billie, retired from tennis in 1975 with a phenomenal twenty-four majors in her pocket. Margaret Court had no time for tour life anymore; she had a family to rear in Australia. Court retreated to her homeland, but there was something different about this Margaret. She'd lost her desire for invisibility. She no longer wished, as she had in the late sixties, to fade into obscurity.

She became Pastor Margaret in 1991. Religion had long given her life a purpose; now it supplied her with a cause and a pulpit, a place to drop the shrinking-violet reputation that had marked her during the women's movement of the 1970s.

"I guess I was very shy in many ways," Margaret admits. "And I think probably from studying the Scriptures and looking into the mirror of the Word today, I can see how much I've changed, because I never liked public speaking; I used to hate it."

She was a misfit when the Original Nine separated from the tennis establishment. But eventually, if begrudgingly, Margaret grew to understand Billie's fight for gender equality, even though she never felt comfortable as a member of a tour that had its share of militants and lesbians.

"You saw some things which you just didn't think were really healthy," Pastor Margaret says.

With hindsight, Margaret could appreciate the gift Billie had for stirring up a cause, for making things happen, for being the ringleader in starting up a tour separate from the men. Billie had a calling.

"She loved doing that, and I think in some way probably she had a vision and a goal in that area," Margaret says. "I wasn't looking for it. I was quite comfortable really, I guess, with the way tennis was. Even though I can look back and think, well, you know, the financial side did come into it, things did come in that helped women's tennis a lot. I can say that.

"It had its good points, and then to me it didn't have such good points. You know, I could see the good things about it; I could see the great things, you know, with the men and women coming back in the Grand Slam tournaments. I think, well, why couldn't we have had it all together instead of ever separating?"

That was pure Margaret. Her conservative views had shaped her future. Today, Pastor Margaret stands tall and thin at the preacher's pulpit, her hair neatly cropped as always, with a presence just as dominating as it had been on court thirty years earlier.

She often towers onstage while a band plays to the side and the faithful swoon in the aisles. As they give praise to their God, the congregation of nearly one thousand absorbs her sermon's message. Their eyes trace her every move, like tennis fans following the ball. This is her new court, this house of worship. Margaret's only opponent is the evil she challenges in a temple of her own making.

In 1996, Margaret founded the nondenominational Victory Life Center as a spiritual warehouse of sorts, an answer to a jolting call from God. She had been taken to a hospital in 1990 with heart trouble after prolonged bouts of insomnia. During her stay, she steeped herself in the Bible; its words became medicine for her soul.

"I could have gone to hell," she confessed at the time. "Now I'm going to heaven."

The woman who had shied away from political causes began embracing them in her ministry. In 2002, Pastor Margaret caused a stir in Western Australia when she took on the government in a personal crusade against gay rights. "If we change this legislation, it means that we are saying this sort of thing is right," she told reporters. "In the Scriptures it is a sin of the flesh."

She roamed the countryside, spreading the word. A tennis ball dangling from her keychain was the only relic from her previous life.

Though she condemned homosexuality as morally wrong, she did so in words that were often compassionate, if somewhat confused. She would say, "I love homosexuals, and I am here to help them because they don't have to be like that. There is a way to change."

Margaret continued preaching her message through three Sunday services. She extolled the value of morals and denounced the deterioration of society. She would often lay her hands on those who needed comfort. She opened one sermon with a line that Billie might have appreciated. "The Bible," Pastor Margaret declared, "is the *TV Guide* to life. My heart goes out to a lot of young people because they get so mixed up in society today, they don't know what is right and wrong. There's no respect anymore. There's no honor anymore. We used to honor each other more on the tennis court."

She was not alluding to Bobby Riggs. Margaret considered him an underhanded character. She believed he had made a mockery of the game — and made a fool of her — when they met on that court ringed by makeshift bleachers in the California desert.

But Pastor Margaret would, one day, pray for Bobby's soul.

On Valentine's Day, 1991, Bobby Riggs fiddled with the rose in his lapel as he stood at the altar for his third marriage, but only his second wife. Next to him, in a white lace dress, stood Priscilla Wheelan — the woman Bobby had divorced nineteen years earlier.

The mother to four of his six children, Wheelan had remained close to Bobby over the years despite his numerous relationships and her own struggle with alcohol. The minister for the service was their son Reverend John W. Riggs.

John was a Yale graduate and professor at Eden Theology Seminary. He was also one of the first to realize that his parents were falling in love all over again.

"One day my wife and I noticed them snuggling up in the back of the car," John recalls. "I was very happy and honored to perform the service. You could say I married my own parents."

The wedding ceremony was purely Bobby. Who else would choose a charcoal-colored standard poodle as his best man?

"My mom and dad had a full-sized poodle named Jasper," John says. "He was the best dog. I think my dad held the leash during the ceremony."

The reunion of Bobby and Priscilla started over a real-estate transaction. After her second husband died, Priscilla decided to move back to California. She took a tour of Bobby's barren bachelor pad in Encinitas. Bobby's home had the décor of a loading dock, with stuffed boxes everywhere. The place was unkempt, but the location was unbeatable. On the third level of the house, Priscilla caught a glimpse of the ocean view. Above the sand and waves, with nothing but the glitter of sun on water in front of her, Priscilla was mesmerized and sold.

"She went hunting for a place to rent," Bobby would later say, "and came to see me. She went into every room and said, 'Hey, I like this place.' I said, 'All right. I'll sell it to you.'"

The house was too large for one person, though. Priscilla didn't want to live there alone. Months later, Bobby moved into the guesthouse, and, as he would slyly reveal, "I moved back into her life."

She knew him as well as anyone could. Priscilla accepted all of Bobby's faults and quirks. On the golf course one day, when Bobby couldn't scare up a bet from anyone else, Priscilla knew exactly what to do.

"I'll keep you company," she told him. "I'll go around the golf course with you, but I don't want to play."

"That's okay," Bobby replied. "I'll play two balls, yours and mine. His and hers."

They agreed on fifty dollars a hole. Priscilla didn't hit a ball, but by Bobby's book of rules, he beat her out of $750. When they returned home, she wrote a check for the amount to humor him. Money still motivated Bobby, though he no longer needed it. His grand gig with Billie had left him with plenty of earning opportunities. Whatever undermining his manhood had suffered, whatever depression he had slipped into, he emerged from the defeat as the darling Bobby Riggs.

He pitched Sugar Daddy all around the country. And kept his name out front with his attention-getting wagers against the crusty Evel Knievel. Bobby became the TV cameo king. He appeared with Billie on, appropriately enough, *The Odd Couple*, goofed around with Rosie Casals on *Love, American Style*, and turned up on *What's My Line?*

He showed up in exhibition halls for tennis gear, in gambling casinos for action, and on television as an analyst. In 1992, in the biggest bet he ever made, he wagered $30,000 to $10,000 that Jimmy Connors wouldn't lose a set to Martina Navratilova in a retread version of a Battle of the Sexes match with a twist in the rules: Martina was given use of the doubles alley.

Instead of providing the running commentary his audience expected, Bobby barely squeaked. He couldn't breathe, couldn't swallow. He couldn't say a word. The match was too close. The bet was in jeopardy.

"I was a little tongue-tied," he later admitted.

Luckily for Bobby, Connors won the match.

The adrenaline from gambling acted as a preservative for Bobby's youth. He felt alive whenever something was on the line. While Billie reveled in the wisdom of age, Bobby loathed growing old. He kept his hair as shaggy as that of a groovy hipster, and worked dye into his roots to stave off the gray. He fancied himself a Peter Pan, constantly indulging in schoolboy pranks, forever looking for mischief. Bobby craved immortality, but his body wouldn't cooperate. He was seventy in 1988 when doctors diagnosed him with prostate cancer. After the disease went into remission, Bobby proclaimed himself cured, even though he knew he was living year to year.

In 1995 the cancer returned. That same year, Priscilla died of emphysema, leaving Bobby distraught and angry. Life was cheating him, he thought. He had hoodwinked so many rubes, but he couldn't outwit death.

"It wasn't in Bobby's nature to plan on dying, but I think he went through what a lot of people do when they get cancer — denial, bitterness," Lornie Kuhle recalls. "Bobby tried to stay upbeat, though. He really tried."

Publicly, he remained the affable Bobby Riggs, gamely facing up to the inevitable whenever the press came by to write what amounted to a living obit. In April of 1995, he joked with a reporter from the *Los Angeles Times*, telling him that he had finally settled on his epitaph: "He put women on the map."

Privately, Bobby was often morose. All the men in his family had lived well past their eightieth birthdays; he had expected to be just as long-lived. But, at other times, he acted as if the joyride through life would never end. He still kept an eye out for suckers on the golf course, even though he often had to labor through rounds wearing a colostomy bag.

"I watched him die," Lornie Kuhle says. "I was with him. He was fighting hard. He was so weak, he could hardly putt, but, if it meant a dollar, he gritted and made it. That was Bobby."

Bobby had a certain vision of what his life should be: a rollicking adventure to be explored and enjoyed with vigor and laughter. Cancer had taken a toll on that ideal.

"I don't think he was shocked by the possibility of death but by the slow erosion of who he was," his son John recalls. "He liked living life. He was so vital, and yet slowly but surely he couldn't do what he loved to do anymore. At the end, he had a colostomy bag and urinostomy bag. By that point, he didn't recognize his life."

The death of his beloved Priscilla helped Bobby come to terms with his own mortality. At her funeral, Bobby talked about letting go. "Looking back, he was telling me that he was reconciled to letting his own life go," John says. "He had made peace with that."

Bobby could have likely lived more years in a deteriorating state, but soon after Priscilla's death, he told doctors to take him off of a cocktail of antibiotics. He knew the consequences of infection. He knew his death would be hastened. The final weeks of his life left him more melancholy than angry. His wistful state did not, however, soften his desire for mischief.

"The Sunday before he died, he finally couldn't even watch TV, he just kind of slept half the time off and on," Lornie says. "So I came in with a newspaper on a Monday morning."

Lornie began reading from the scoreboard page of the sports section.

"Here are the football results from Sunday, Bobby. You wanna hear them?"

"Yeah, read 'em to me."

"You guess on who won: Green Bay and Chicago."

"Chicago, Chicago by seven points," Bobby said.

"Yeah, you're right. Chicago beat them by ten. What about Kansas City and San Diego?"

"San Diego by fourteen," Bobby replied.

"Yeah, you're right, only they won by seventeen."

Lornie went through every football game on the schedule. Bobby called every one of the outcomes right until Lornie ticked off the last one.

"Miami and New York," Kuhle said.

"New York by twelve."

"No, Bobby, you're wrong. Miami won. You missed one."

Bobby smiled weakly. He was amused that even with life draining from him, he could still hide a secret up his sleeve even from someone who knew all of his moves.

"I found out that my friend was around and had read him all the results earlier that morning," Kuhle says. "He didn't even tell me that. He was just bullshitting me, and here he was, on his deathbed. He loved to do that kind of stuff. He put people on. He put the whole United States on. He put the whole world on with the match in the Astrodome."

The match was more than a tennis exhibition gone wild, and in the end, Bobby realized how deep into society his loss to Billie Jean King had penetrated. He came to understand that it mattered beyond women's tennis. And it was Billie who had taught him that. In numerous conversations, she did her best to make Bobby see the importance of the event. She wanted him to appreciate the match's far-reaching consequences.

"I'd keep bringing him back to it, saying, 'Bobby! It's not about the money. It's not about hustling. It's about the big picture,'" Billie says. "I'd tell him, 'You have an addiction, and I have an eating disorder;

you're a gambler. You need to go to Gamblers Anonymous. Man, we both need to go get help. We'll go together. Wherever.' We both had our little addictions going here. Our little problems, you know, our issues.

"But I'll say this, Bobby never got himself in debt. He was very smart with the way he bet. Very smart. Very calculated in the way he thought, too. He was much more of a percentage kind."

Their discussions over the years brought them closer. They discovered they were more alike than anyone could imagine. He was the scrubby outcast from one set of public courts in L.A.; she was the pudgy talent without a pedigree from another. He was hooked on fame. So was she. He craved spectacles; she was entranced by the stage. They had both wished for outsized lives.

In the fall of 1995, Billie learned that Bobby was dying. The king hustler's merry journey was coming to an end, and the thought of that devastated Billie. She longed to see him one more time to share a laugh. She wanted to tell him she adored him.

"I'm coming down to see you," Billie told him on the phone. She had a car revved up and ready to bolt for his bedside at his home outside Encinitas.

"I'm not feeling good today," Bobby told her.

"I'll stay over."

"No, I don't want you to see me."

"Bobby, it's no effort. I'll come right down."

"No, I don't want you to."

Bobby preferred Billie's last memory of him to be of the healthy huckster, not of a sickly, wasting man in the last stages of life. The plan for a visit was scuttled, but a few days before his death on October 25, 1995, Billie called once more. Bobby talked to her from his bed, trying to keep his voice steady.

"I love you," she told him.

"I love you," he said.

She let Bobby know how much she appreciated him, how much his friendship had meant to her, how important he was to women, of all people. To Billie, he wasn't a sexist runt in horn-rimmed frames anymore. To Billie, Bobby was her perfect partner in making history.

Billie Jean King couldn't have changed the world without him.

"Well, we did it," Bobby ended, with a brief lift in his thin voice. "We really made a difference, didn't we?"

BIBLIOGRAPHY

Amdur, Neil. "Riggs, Mrs. Court Meet in Battle of Sexes Today." *New York Times*, 13 September 1973.

——. "Mrs. King Defeats Bobby Riggs, 6–4, 6–3, 6–3, Amid a Circus Atmosphere." *New York Times*, 21 September 1973.

——. "She Played Too Well, Says Riggs of Mrs. King." *New York Times*, 22 September 1973.

Barnes, Bart. "Tennis Star Bobby Riggs Dies." *Washington Post*, 27 October 1995.

Brady, Erik. "Commission Co-Chair Stands Behind Disputed Title IX Report." *USA Today*, 26 February 2003.

Chabria, Anita. "Ms. Understood." *Los Angeles Times*, 31 August 2003.

Bibliography

Collins, Bud. "The Intrasexual Saga of Tennis." *Rod Laver's Tennis Digest*, 1975.

———. *Total Tennis: The Ultimate Tennis Encyclopedia.* Toronto: Sport Classic Books, 2003.

Court, Margaret. *Court on Court: A Life in Tennis.* New York: Dodd, Mead & Co., 1975.

Dobie, Michael. "Emotions Run High as Title IX Meetings Close." *Newsday*, 21 November 2002.

Eskenazi, Gerald. "Title IX Rules Issued for Equality in Sports." *New York Times*, 5 June 1975.

Faderman, Lillian. *Odd Girls and Twilight Lovers.* New York: Columbia University Press, 1991.

Fiske, Edward B. "Congress Moves to Modify Law Restricting Sex Bias by Schools." *New York Times*, 25 November 1974.

Flamini, Roland. "How Bobby Runs and Talks, Talks, Talks." *Time*, 10 September 1973.

Friedan, Betty. *The Feminine Mystique.* New York: Norton, 1963. Reprint, 2001.

Gavora, Jessica. *Tilting the Playing Field: Schools, Sex, and Title IX.* San Francisco: Encounter Books, 2002.

Gold, Herbert. "Portrait of a Beautiful Hustler." *New York Times Sunday Magazine*, 5 August 1973.

Goodridge, Francie Kraker. "Women Athletes and the Comparison Game: What Are the Rules?" *New York Times*, 30 March 1975.

Guilbeau, Glenn. "Women Win Ruling on LSU." *The Baton Rouge Advocate*, 29 January 2002.

Howard, Johnette. "Donna Lopiano and the Art of Reform." In *A Kind of Grace*, edited by Ron Rapoport. Berkeley, CA: Zenobia Press, 1994. Originally published in *The National*, 1994.

Isaacson, Melissa. "Gussie Moran Clothes Misery in Stoic Calm." *Orlando Sentinel*, 27 June 1988.

Kilpatrick, Carroll. "President Refuses to Turn Over Tapes." *Washington Post*, 24 July 1973.

King, Billie Jean, with Kim Chapin. *Billie Jean*. New York: Harper & Row, 1974.

King, Billie Jean, with Frank Deford. *Billie Jean*. New York: Viking Press, 1982.

Kirkpatrick, Curry. "Mother's Day Ms. Match." *Sports Illustrated*, 21 May 1973.

Knaggs, John R. *Two-Party Texas: The John Tower Era*. Austin: Eakin Press, 1986.

LeCompte, Tom. *The Last Sure Thing: The Life and Times of Bobby Riggs*. Easthampton, MA: Skunkworks Publishing, 2003.

Lichtenstein, Grace. "King-Riggs Match Point Is Money." *New York Times*, 19 September 1973.

Bibliography

———. *A Long Way, Baby.* New York: William Morrow & Company, Inc., 1974.

Longman, Jere. *The Girls of Summer.* New York: HarperCollins, 2000.

Oakley, Vivian. "In God's Court." *Hobart Mercury,* 20 September 2003.

Oates, Bob. "His Last Match Can't Be Rigged." *Los Angeles Times,* 15 April 1995.

Pennington, Bill. "College: More Men's Teams Benched as Colleges Level the Field." *New York Times,* 9 May 2002.

Peterson, Iver. "U.S. Warns Single-Sex Colleges of Bias." *New York Times,* 14 May 1973.

Price, S. L. "Who's Your Daddy?" *Sports Illustrated,* 31 May 1999.

Prugh, Jeff. "Bobby Riggs, the Hustler." *Los Angeles Times,* 12 June 1972.

Raising Tennis Aces: The Williams Story. Produced by Terry Jervis. Xenon Pictures, Inc., 2002.

Reid, Scott M. "Foudy, de Varona Protesting Final Report." *Orange County Register,* 26 February 2003.

Richards, Renée. *Second Serve: The Renée Richards Story.* New York: Stein and Day, 1983.

Riggs, Bobby, with George McGann. *Court Hustler.* New York and Philadelphia: J.B. Lippincott Company, 1973.

Schaap, Dick. "Pancho Gonzalez: The Lone Wolf of Tennis." In *Total*

Tennis: The Ultimate Tennis Encyclopedia, by Bud Collins. Toronto: Sport Classic Books, 2003. Originally published in *Sport* magazine, September 1958.

Searcy, Jay. "Women Battle for Funds on College Sports Scene." *New York Times,* 19 May 1974.

———. "Foe of Men's Myth Braces for Battle." *New York Times,* 14 July 1974.

Smith, Marshall. "Larceny on the Links." *Life,* 26 March 1956.

Suggs, Welch. "Title IX at 30." *Chronicle of Higher Education,* 21 June 2002.

TSHA Online. "Tower, John Goodwin." Biography from www.TSHA.Utexas.edu.

Wertheim, L. Jon. *Venus Envy.* New York: HarperCollins, 2001.

Wharton, David. "Title IX: 25 Years Later." *Los Angeles Times,* 23 June 1997.

White, Gordon S. "College Heads Ponder Athletic Ethics, Costs, Title IX." *New York Times,* 6 January 1975.

———. "Women Are a Problem." *New York Times,* 7 January 1975.

———. "NCAA in New Bid to Women." *New York Times,* 9 January 1975.

White, Joseph. "Title IX Panel to Exclude Minority Views." Associated Press release, 29 January 2003.

Bibliography

www.Whirligig-tv.co.uk. "The Coronation of Queen Elizabeth II."
Video archive. June 2, 1953.

"Yale Women Strip to Protest a Lack of Crew's Showers." *Special to the
New York Times*, 4 March 1976.

ACKNOWLEDGMENTS

Waiting for a table at Gramercy Park Tavern with Billie Jean King one winter day, I noticed that even usually disengaged New Yorkers, never ones to make a fuss over a celebrity, couldn't help but whisper when they recognized Mother Freedom.

One patron ripped the matches out of a matchbook to create a surface large enough for an autograph. "I just think the world of you," the woman told Billie.

Others approached. Billie happily obliged the autograph seekers and engaged in conversation, making each of them feel important, special.

This is her gift. When Billie talks to you, she pours herself into the conversation, fluttering from one subject to another, never shortchanging you on her conviction or passion.

I am incredibly grateful to Billie for this generosity of openness. Her energy never waned throughout the hours we spent together discussing America's social evolution and her personal evolution, as well.

I am also indebted to Larry King for answering the phone each time I called for the smallest of details. His insight was invaluable. Ilana Kloss was infinitely helpful with her assistance, patience, and wisdom. And I was awestruck by Betty and Bill Moffitt, Billie's indefatigable parents.

Capturing the cultural climate around tennis in the seventies would not have been complete without the help of Margaret Court. Understanding the huckster genius and innate gentleness of Bobby Riggs would not have been possible without his longtime friend Lornie Kuhle and Bobby's sons Reverend John W. Riggs and Larry Riggs. And grasping the political balance of feminism surrounding Billie's match with Bobby would have been enormously more difficult without the memories of Gloria Steinem.

An important assist in piecing together the Battle of the Sexes scene came from Grace Lichtenstein and her insider's book from 1973, A Long Way, Baby, as well as two of my favorite mentors in the business: Bud Collins, of the Boston Globe, and Neil Amdur, of the New York Times.

Bud helped christen me as a tennis reporter the instant he sat beside me — and gently guided me — through the 1990 Davis Cup in St. Petersburg, Florida. I was a clueless cub. He was a legend. And yet he treated me as an equal.

Bud's eloquent tennis stories in the 1970s and his colorful input over the years was indispensable to this book. His tennis bible, Total Tennis: The Ultimate Tennis Encyclopedia, was a fixture on my desk through the process. Neil, who hired me at the Times and made tennis assignments part of my career rite of passage, shared his memories as a tennis reporter in the seventies and eighties. And at my every turn in the archives, there was an article by Neil Amdur to illuminate a passage in this book.

Other legends of tennis also provided anecdotes that made the storytelling possible, including Chris Evert, Rosie Casals, Nancy Richey, Pam Shriver, Renée Richards, Jack Kramer, Pancho Segura, Gardnar Mulloy, and Gene Mako.

To comprehend the roots of Title IX, I am indebted to Jeffrey Orleans, Donna Lopiano, Donna de Varona, and Dorothy Blaney for educating me on the past. To see the miracle of the law's reach today, I appreciate Julie Foudy for her insight and Sue Rodin for her help in connecting me with the 1999 Women's World Cup soccer team. A look back at that summer of 1999 was out of the question without rereading Jere Longman's *The Girls of Summer.*

For years, I have covered Title IX and the cultural influence of women in sports. In writing this book, I became more grateful for the expertise imparted by economist Andrew Zimbalist, Peter Roby from Northeastern University's Center for Sport in Society, and sports market- ing guru Bob Williams.

I can thank career serendipity for my knowledge of the Williams sis- ters. Few wrote more about Venus and Serena's early years than *Times* tennis writer Robin Finn. Her work was an important guide when I began covering Venus and Serena after they alighted at the U.S. Open in 1997 and 1998. Interviews over the years with Venus and Serena, as well as with their parents, Richard Williams and Oracene Price, provided a working background for Chapter 10.

Richard, as always, offered extra details when I pestered him for more, as did Oracene. Leland Hardy and Keven Davis, longtime friends and business associates of the Williams family, were also helpful. I'm grateful for the insight of Rick Macci and for L. Jon Wertheim's mar- velous book *Venus Envy*, which was required reading in assembling the history of the Williams sisters.

Jon is just one of many friends and colleagues who made research- ing and writing this book less arduous with their support, advice, and as- sistance. It has been a pleasure to have the tennis company of Lisa Dillman, Linda Pearce, Harvey Araton, Rachel Nichols, Peter Bodo, Joel Drucker, Chris Clarey, Sandra Harwitt, Matt Cronin, Scott Price, Cindy Shmerler, and Doug Smith. Susie Adams also holds a special place in my heart.

At Crown, I cannot imagine a more enthusiastic editor than Annik LaFarge, who inspired me through each stage of this book. Her assistant, Mario Rojas, was especially helpful. In making the writing transition from newspapers to books, I thank Richard Lally for his guidance and my agent, Mark Reiter, for his spot-on suggestions.

At the *New York Times*, sports editor Tom Jolly as well as Kristin

Acknowledgments

Huckshorn and Jill Agostino were especially generous in providing me with the time and flexible schedule to research and write this book. Fern Turkowitz was also invaluable in her assistance.

My family was incredibly supportive, and Tom Hill was, as usual, a patient friend through my mood swings during the writing process — and after, for that matter. I especially cherished the unconditional love and friendship of Laura Price. Without complaint, Laura undertook the tedious dirty work of transcribing hours of tape and organizing my research. She also tapped into her inner therapist when my spirits started spiraling into the abyss as another deadline approached. So thank you for being my norm.

INDEX

Index

Index

Index

Index

Index

About the Author

SELENA ROBERTS is a sports columnist for *The New York Times*. In 2003 and 2004 she was named one of the country's top ten columnists by the Associated Press sports editors. She lives in Brooklyn, New York.

A Note on the Type

The text of this book was set in Electra, the first original book face created by American type designer William Addison Dwiggins (1880–1956), in 1935; its italic, or cursive, was revised in 1944. Electra reflects the influence of both Venetian and Bauhaus and Art Deco letter forms.